CLINICAL FREUD
SEXUAL THERAPY
EXISTENTIAL AN
TRANSACTIONAL
SULLIVANIAN AN
GESTALT THERA
CHILD ANALYSIS
FAMILY THERAPY
BEHAVIOR THERAPY
RATIONAL-EMOTIVE THERAPY
COGNITIVE THERAPY

There is no better way of understanding these and the other major schools of psychotherapy than through the writings of their originators—writings that convey both the excitement of discovery and the insights of genius. In this volume, the reader will find twenty such essays— selected and arranged to provide a pathway of perception through what today often seems a labyrinth of conflict and confusion.

THE ESSENTIAL PSYCHOTHERAPIES

ABOUT THE AUTHORS

DANIEL GOLEMAN, Ph.D., is a Senior Editor of *Psychology Today*. A clinical psychologist by training, Goleman has written and edited several books on psychology, among them *What Psychology Knows That Everyone Should*. He has received awards for magazine writing from the American Psychological Association, and the National Association for Mental Health.

KATHLEEN RIORDAN SPEETH, Ph.D., is a psychologist in private practice in Easthampton, New York. Her Ph.D. is from Columbia University, and she is currently Professor-at-Large of the California Institute of Transpersonal Psychology. Dr. Speeth is the author of several articles in scholarly journals.

SIGNET Books of Special Interest

☐ **TEST YOUR OWN MENTAL HEALTH by William Gladstone.** An exciting new test for over 100 insightful questions that will, in less than an hour, give you a "pictograph" of the intricate goings-on in your mind. By checking off symptoms in seven categories, you can now determine whether you fit the norm, whether you're a neurotic coper, or whether you require professional help. (#J8757—$1.95)*

☐ **BIORHYTHMS: How to Live with Your Life Cycles by Barbara O'Neil and Richard Phillips.** Get in touch with your inner rhythms for maximum success and fulfillment in every area of life. This book shows you how to easily and exactly calculate your own personal biorhythm patterns and use them as invaluable allies rather than hidden enemies. (#W7181—$1.50)

☐ **BT—BEHAVIOR THERAPY: Strategies for Solving Problems in Living by Spencer A. Rathus, Ph.D., and Jeffrey S. Nevid, Ph.D.** Take charge of #1—with today's most effective method of self-help and self-improvement. (#E9949—$2.95)

☐ **HOW TO GET ANGRY WITHOUT FEELING GUILTY by Adelaide Bry.** Are you one of the many people whose anger comes out in ways that they do not suspect but most certainly suffer from? This book by a leading psychologist will show you how to face the anger within you without fear or guilt—and how you can make it the most creative force in your life. (#E8329—$1.75)

☐ **LOVE AND ADDICTION by Stanton Peele with Archie Brodsky.** This provocative book focuses on interpersonal relationships to explore what addiction really is—psychologically, socially, and culturally. "A rare book, like *Future Shock* and *The Pursuit of Loneliness*, that is destined to become a classic!"—*Psychology Today* (#E9389—$2.50)

*Price slightly higher in Canada

THE ESSENTIAL PSYCHOTHERAPIES

Theory and Practice by the Masters

Edited by
DANIEL GOLEMAN, Ph.D.

and

KATHLEEN RIORDAN SPEETH, Ph.D.

A MENTOR BOOK
NEW AMERICAN LIBRARY
TIMES MIRROR
New York and Scarborough, Ontario

Library of Congress Catalog Card Number: 81-85145

PERMISSIONS ACKNOWLEDGMENTS

Freud, Sigmund: "Recommendations to Physicians Practising Psycho-analysis." Reprinted with the permission of Basic Books, Inc., from THE COLLECTED PAPERS OF SIGMUND FREUD, Vol. 2, edited by Ernest Jones. Authorized translation under the supervision of Joan Riviere. Published by Basic Books, Inc., New York, by arrangement with Hogarth Press Ltd. and the Institute of Psychoanalysis, London.

Freud, Sigmund: "On Psychotherapy." Reprinted with the permission of Basic Books, Inc., from THE COLLECTED PAPERS OF SIGMUND FREUD, Vol. 1, edited by Ernest Jones. Authorized translation under the supervision of Joan Riviere. Published by Basic Books, Inc., New York, by arrangement with Hogarth Press Ltd. and the Institute of Psychoanalysis, London.

Reik, Theodor: "Free-floating Attention." From LISTENING WITH THE THIRD EAR by Theodor Reik. Copyright 1948 by Theodor Reik. Copyright renewed © 1975 by Arthur Reik. Reprinted by permission of Farrar, Straus and Giroux, Inc.

Adler, Alfred: "Understanding and Treating the Patient." From THE INDIVIDUAL PSYCHOLOGY OF ALFRED ADLER, edited by Heinz L. Ansbacher and Rowena R. Ansbacher, pp. 326–342. © 1956 by Basic Books, Inc., New York.

Freud, Anna: "The Role of Transference in the Analysis of Children." Reprinted from THE PSYCHO-ANALYTICAL TREATMENT OF CHILDREN by Anna Freud with the permission of Mark Paterson and Associates.

Reich, Wilhelm: Reprinted by permission of Farrar, Straus & Giroux, Inc. "The Technique of Character Analysis," from CHARACTER ANALYSIS by Wilhelm Reich, newly translated by Vincent R. Carfagno. Copyright © 1945, 1949, 1972 by Mary Boyd Higgins, as trustee of the Wilhelm Reich Infant Trust Fund.

The following pages constitute an extension of this copyright page.

MENTOR TRADEMARK REG. U.S. PAT. OFF. AND FOREIGN COUNTRIES
REGISTERED TRADEMARK—MARCA REGISTRADA
HECHO EN CHICAGO, U.S.A.

SIGNET, SIGNET CLASSICS, MENTOR, PLUME, MERIDIAN AND NAL
BOOKS are published *in the United States* by
The New American Library, Inc.,
1633 Broadway, New York, New York 10019,
in Canada by The New American Library of Canada Limited,
81 Mack Avenue, Scarborough, Ontario

First Printing, April, 1982

1   2   3   4   5   6   7   8   9

PRINTED IN THE UNITED STATES OF AMERICA

Contents

Introduction

The array of therapies offered on the contemporary scene is bewildering. There are, within easy reach of most Americans, therapists who offer classical psychoanalysis and those who offer variations of it; therapists who emphasize the present and those who delve into the past; therapists who treat psychological problems as errors in thinking and therapists who treat the same problems as though they were based in the body; therapists who offer insight, and therapists who see it as irrelevant; therapists who treat patients singly and those who treat entire families. A recent handbook* lists over 250 brand-name therapies.

Therapies have proliferated to the point where even therapists have trouble keeping them straight. There are innumerable strains, brands, and types of therapy offered today, each of which seems quite different in method and theory from the rest. Yet if one traces the history of how these numerous therapies evolved, it is possible to isolate less than two dozen or so main pathways of evolution. This collection of articles is designed to highlight the major avenues of innovation into new therapy types: to pinpoint the key formulations that have been the impetus for major new directions in therapy's growth.

As such, we hope the articles collected here will offer the student of therapy—as well as prospective and practicing therapists, patients and would-be patients, and any others with a keen interest in therapy—a strong sense of the true range of variation within the spectrum of therapies.

Many, if not most, therapists would probably say, if asked, that they were eclectic, borrowing from a range of approaches as the needs of their patients dictate. A second large group would claim to practice a personally evolved, highly unique form of therapy, the antecedents of which they have forgotten or consider irrelevant to their current practice. These attitudes each reflect a certain fuzziness about historicity—or a downright rejection of it. Such attitudes ignore the significance of the pioneering contributions that the therapists included in

---

*Herink, R. *The Psychotherapy Handbook*. New York: New American Library, 1980.

this volume have made, whose masterful insights most therapists casually borrow or take for granted as common knowledge.

What is standard practice today in therapy began as radical invention. The articles in this collection are the original statements of many of these key inventions. Each of the selections is a seminal statement by someone who has generated a therapy lineage. Each was chosen for the immediacy with which it renders the unique nature of its formulator's contribution to the therapeutic endeavor.

From the meetings of the first psychoanalytic circle in Vienna to the latest therapy fad, the history of therapy may be seen as a family tree. But it is not the sort of tree that proceeds regularly from generation to generation, growing in a predictable and orderly fashion. Instead, it is shaped by surprising changes in direction and strange liaisons. The evolution of therapy might best be visualized as a billibong or banyan, the exotic tree that sends off sturdy branches whose shoots extend down to form new roots, with their own auxiliary trunks and branches. In attempting to define the shape of this tree, we have pruned away much of the excess shrubbery, so that the points of added trunks and branchings off are apparent.

In a very real sense, Sigmund Freud represents the main trunk of modern therapies, the source from which even those in rival camps—such as the behavior therapists—have borrowed at least the shell of the format in which the therapist works. Many of the newer lineages in therapy, such as transactional analysis or cognitive therapy, were founded by therapists who had psychoanalytic backgrounds— or whose teachers did (or their teachers' teachers).

We have taken Freud's work as marking the beginning of modern therapy. But that starting point is arbitrary: Freud had immediate predecessors from whom he learned and borrowed. He was also another link in a long chain of those who have treated mental suffering, a chain that extends back in time to the healing temples of Aesculapius in ancient Greece —and beyond.

Therapy has evolved at a fantastic rate since Freud's first formulations at the turn of the century. The number 250 is certainly a low estimate for all those who claim to offer a unique brand of therapy. There is, of course, a great deal of redundancy in method and view among these numerous therapies. Many, for example, adopt Freud's technique of using "transference"—the feelings of the patient toward the therapist—as a microcosm in which to work out the patient's general problems in relationships. Others, though, partake of none of Freud's notions of how therapy should be conducted; most of these have taproots in traditions utterly separate from the Freudian. For example, the principles derived from the laboratory experiments of behaviorists were applied directly to mental disorder in the form of behavior therapy.

Some, like Freud himself, are the founding fathers for a vast lineage and innumerable spin-off schools of therapy. Some, like Harry Stack Sullivan, have a relatively small number of therapists who claim a direct descent, but have had a widespread—if more diffuse—influence on a wide range of therapists. Others, like Helen Singer Kaplan for sex therapy and Salvador Minuchin for family therapy, represent a typical formulation for their entire class of therapy; while they are not solitary founders, they are leaders who embody the essence of their therapeutic focus. Still others, like Wilhelm Reich, made innovations in one school of therapy (in his case, psychoanalysis) before moving out of the fold to formulate an entirely different type (for Reich, body-based therapy).

Each therapist included here is a master of the craft. Most have spawned key innovations that have in turn given rise to still other new therapy forms. The selections do not cover the entire range of therapies, but rather represent the main lines of its growth, the taproots from which have sprung new approaches to therapy.

If any of the innumerable techniques that are available in the therapeutic marketplace are delved into deeply, and their overlay of particulars put aside, one or another—or several—of the formulations included here will most certainly be found. These statements articulate therapy fundamentals: these are the essential formulations at the heart of therapy today.

Daniel Goleman, Ph.D.
Kathleen Riordan Speeth, Ph.D.

Sigmund Freud

Sigmund Freud (1865–1939) whose impact on the understanding of the human mind was perhaps the greatest in the history of the Western world, was an Austrian neurologist whose interest migrated from the physiological to the psychological. He studied in France under Charcot and then Bernheim, who used hypnotic methods on hysterics, but later rejected hypnosis in favor of catharsis, the "talking cure."

Freud's first significant contribution to psychological methodology was "Studies in Hysteria," published in 1895 in collaboration with a Viennese physician, Joseph Breuer, who had treated hysterics successfully using this approach. Breuer later repudiated Freud's additions to his methods, such as the interpretation of dreams and free association. Freud saw dreams as "the language of the unconscious," and searched them for clues to his patients' inner life. One source of clues to dreams was free association, wherein the patient said whatever thoughts came into his mind, without censoring them. Both dream interpretations and free association became hallmarks of Freud's technique.

In 1904 Freud addressed the Vienna College of Physicians, giving his first technical account of the new method of psychoanalysis—a method based in part on Freud's study of his own mind. He contrasted psychoanalysis with hypnosis and carefully limited the kind of patient who he felt could benefit from his new technique, ruling out, for example, those who were too disturbed. Freud described his method as rendering unconscious ideas conscious, in a series of uncomfortable discoveries that produce psychological resistance in the patient. But for Freud, there was no path to a successful psychoanalysis other than bringing unconscious material into awareness. The therapist's job, then, was to help the patient accept whatever lurked in his unconscious mind, a process Freud saw as

1

a kind of education. Because much of this repressed material deals with sexual matters, Freud emphasized the need for the therapist to have an impeccable character, as well as the necessity to have overcome "that mixture of lewdness and prudery" with which so many people regard sexual matters.

Freud elaborated on the necessary attitudes of the therapist, and the training required to achieve them in the following 1912 lecture to physicians who wished to employ psychoanalytic methods. Since Freud himself continually revised his theories and techniques on the basis of his ongoing clinical experience, he aptly noted at the outset that research and treatment went hand in hand. Even so, he admonished against note-taking, since it would interfere with the conduct of the sessions.

How Freud himself actually conducted psychoanalytic sessions is hinted at in the tips he offered other would-be analysts. Freud described a simple but revolutionary attitude: The analyst was to maintain an "evenly-suspended attention," not overly intrigued by any one point the patient brings up, but calmly noting it all. "He should simply listen," said Freud, "and not bother about whether he is keeping anything in mind." By taking this passive approach, the therapist would be able to use his *own* unconscious mind as an instrument in analysis, letting his own associations bubble up into the foreground of awareness, spontaneously capturing the themes in the patient's life that were most salient for treatment.

One of the main tasks of therapy was to analyze the patient's resistances to the uncovering of his unconscious conflicts. A major part of this would occur through pointing out to the patient his "transference," the strong feelings that the patient feels toward the analyst and that have their roots in the unresolved needs and conflicts of childhood.

But in order to undertake such an approach, the therapist's mind must be free of preconceptions, biases, and blind spots. For that reason Freud urged the therapist himself to go through a "psycho-analytic purification," a training analysis where he could become aware of his own conflicts. Every unresolved conflict within the therapist, Freud contended, could become a blind spot that would distort his perception of the patient. Freud's dictum that anyone who wishes to be an analyst should first himself be analyzed is today a main tenet of orthodox psychoanalytic circles.

The therapist, Freud advised, should reveal little of his

own life to the patient, even as a way to evoke confidences in return. Instead, he should be like a mirror, "opaque to his patients," accurately reflecting back "nothing but what is shown to him" by the patient. Another caveat is that the therapist should avoid intellectual discussions of psychoanalytic theory; such digressions into the abstract, said Freud, are only ways the patient hides from confronting his own problems.

Many of Freud's ideas—such as the attribution of mental suffering to fixation of sexual energy during childhood—raised Victorian eyebrows and led to derision. Yet a dedicated group of physicians began to form around Freud and in 1907 the Vienna Psychoanalytic Society was formed. Its original members included Otto Rank, Carl Jung, and Alfred Adler, all of whom went on to make important contributions to the theory and practice of psychotherapy.

Yet this circle was to be far from permanent. Within five years Jung had broken with Freud, in large part because Freud rejected his theory that psychological energy (libido) is not primarily sexual. Adler, too, rebelled against the Freudian primacy of sexuality in his substitution of aggression as primary. A decade or so later Otto Rank left the fold, rejecting Freud's theory of the Oedipus complex.

Most of the doctrines Freud proposed are still venerated by orthodox psychoanalysts, who by and large remain true to his dictates in how they practice therapy. Even so, over the course of the last three-quarters of a century virtually every one of Freud's views on the proper conduct of therapy has been disputed. Many such challenges have led to the spawning of new therapeutic schools, as we shall see in the course of this collection. Yet, even if only indirectly, every school of therapy traces its origins to Freud's pioneering efforts in deciphering the riddles of human behavior and the causes of psychological suffering.

RECOMMENDATIONS TO PHYSICIANS PRACTISING PSYCHO-ANALYSIS

by Sigmund Freud

The technical rules which I am putting forward here have been arrived at from my own experience in the course of many years, after unfortunate results had led me to abandon other methods. It will easily be seen that they (or at least many of them) may be summed up in a single precept. My hope is that observance of them will spare physicians practising analysis much unnecessary effort and guard them against some oversights. I must however make it clear that what I am asserting is that this technique is the only one suited to my individuality; I do not venture to deny that a physician quite differently constituted might find himself driven to adopt a different attitude to his patients and to the task before him.

(*a*) The first problem confronting an analyst who is treating more than one patient in the day will seem to him the hardest. It is the task of keeping in mind all the innumerable names, dates, detailed memories and pathological products which each patient communicates in the course of months and years of treatment, and of not confusing them with similar material produced by other patients under treatment simultaneously or previously. If one is required to analyse six, eight, or even more patients daily, the feat of memory involved in achieving this will provoke incredulity, astonishment or even commiseration in uninformed observers. Curiosity will in any case be felt about the technique which makes it possible to master such an abundance of material, and the expectation will be that some special expedients are required for the purpose.

The technique, however, is a very simple one. As we shall see, it rejects the use of any special expedient (even that of taking notes). It consists simply in not directing one's notice to anything in particular and in maintaining the same 'evenly-suspended attention' (as I have called it) in the face of all that one hears. In this way we spare ourselves a strain on our attention which could not in any case be kept up for several hours daily, and we avoid a danger which is inseparable from the exercise of deliberate attention. For as soon as anyone deliberately concentrates his attention to a certain degree, he begins to select from the material before him; one point will be fixed in his mind with particular clearness and some other will be correspondingly disregarded, and in making this selection he will be following his expectations or inclinations. This, however, is precisely what must not be done. In making the selection, if he follows his expectations he is in danger of never finding anything but what he already knows; and if he follows his inclinations he will certainly falsify what he may perceive. It must not be forgotten that the things one hears are for the most part things whose meaning is only recognized later on.

It will be seen that the rule of giving equal notice to everything is the necessary counterpart to the demand made on the patient that he should communicate everything that occurs to him without criticism or selection. If the doctor behaves otherwise, he is throwing away most of the advantage which results from the patient's obeying the 'fundamental rule of psycho-analysis'. The rule for the doctor may be expressed: 'He should withhold all conscious influences from his capacity to attend, and give himself over completely to his "unconscious memory".' Or, to put it purely in terms of technique: 'He should simply listen, and not bother about whether he is keeping anything in mind.'

What is achieved in this manner will be sufficient for all requirements during the treatment. Those elements of the material which already form a connected context will be at the doctor's conscious disposal; the rest, as yet unconnected and in chaotic disorder, seems at first to be submerged, but rises readily into recollection as soon as the patient brings up something new to which it can be related and by which it can be continued. The undeserved compliment of having 'a remarkably good memory' which the patient pays one when one reproduces some detail after a year and a day can then be accepted with a smile, whereas a conscious determination to recollect the point would probably have resulted in failure.

Mistakes in this process of remembering occur only at times and places at which one is disturbed by some personal consideration—that is, when one has fallen seriously below the standard of an ideal analyst. Confusion with material brought up by other patients occurs very rarely. Where there is a dispute with the patient as to whether or how he has said some particular thing, the doctor is usually in the right.*

(b) I cannot advise the taking of full notes, the keeping of a shorthand record, etc., during analytic sessions. Apart from the unfavourable impression which this makes on some patients, the same considerations as have been advanced with regard to attention apply here too. A detrimental selection from the material will necessarily be made as one writes the notes or shorthand, and part of one's own mental activity is tied up in this way, which would be better employed in interpreting what one has heard. No objection can be raised to making exceptions to this rule in the case of dates, the text of dreams, or particularly noteworthy events which can easily be detached from their context and are suitable for independent use as instances. But I am not in the habit of doing this either. As regards instances, I write them down from memory in the evening after work is over; as regards texts of dreams to which I attach importance, I get the patient to repeat them to me after he has related them so that I can fix them in my mind.

(c) Taking notes during the session with the patient might be justified by an intention of publishing a scientific study of the case. On general grounds this can scarcely be denied. Nevertheless it must be borne in mind that exact reports of analytic case histories are of less value than might be expected. Strictly speaking, they only possess the *ostensible* exactness of which 'modern' psychiatry affords us some striking examples. They are, as a rule, fatiguing to the reader and yet do not succeed in being a substitute for his actual presence at an analysis. Experience invariably shows that if readers are willing to believe an analyst they will have confidence in any slight revision to which he has submitted his material; if, on the other hand, they are unwilling to take analysis and the

---

*A patient will often assert that he has already told the doctor something on a previous occasion, while the doctor can assure him with a quiet feeling of superiority that it has come up now for the first time. It then turns out that the patient had previously had the intention of saying it, but had been prevented from performing his intention by a resistance which was still present. His recollection of his intention is indistinguishable to him from a recollection of its performance.

analyst seriously, they will pay no attention to accurate verbatim records of the treatment either. This is not the way, it seems, to remedy the lack of convincing evidence to be found in psycho-analytic reports.

(*d*) One of the claims of psycho-analysis to distinction is, no doubt, that in its execution research and treatment coincide; nevertheless, after a certain point, the technique required for the one opposes that required for the other. It is not a good thing to work on a case scientifically while treatment is still proceeding—to piece together its structure, to try to foretell its further progress, and to get a picture from time to time of the current state of affairs, as scientific interest would demand. Cases which are devoted from the first to scientific purposes and are treated accordingly suffer in their outcome; while the most successful cases are those in which one proceeds, as it were, without any purpose in view, allows oneself to be taken by surprise by any new turn in them, and always meets them with an open mind, free from any presuppositions. The correct behaviour for an analyst lies in swinging over according to need from the one mental attitude to the other, in avoiding speculation or brooding over cases while they are in analysis, and in submitting the material obtained to a synthetic process of thought only after the analysis is concluded. The distinction between the two attitudes would be meaningless if we already possessed all the knowledge (or at least the essential knowledge) about the psychology of the unconscious and about the structure of the neuroses that we can obtain from psycho-analytic work. At present we are still far from that goal and we ought not to cut ourselves off from the possibility of testing what we have already learnt and of extending our knowledge further.

(*e*) I cannot advise my colleagues too urgently to model themselves during psycho-analytic treatment on the surgeon, who puts aside all his feelings, even his human sympathy, and concentrates his mental forces on the single aim of performing the operation as skilfully as possible. Under present-day conditions the feeling that is most dangerous to a psycho-analyst is the therapeutic ambition to achieve by this novel and much disputed method something that will produce a convincing effect upon other people. This will not only put him into a state of mind which is unfavourable for his work, but will make him helpless against certain resistances of the patient, whose recovery, as we know, primarily depends on the interplay of forces in him. The justification for requiring this emotional coldness in the analyst is that it creates the most advantageous conditions for both parties: for the doctor a desirable protection for his own emotional life and for the patient the largest amount of help that we can give him to-day. A surgeon of earlier times took as his motto the words: 'Je le pansai. Dieu le guérit.'* The analyst should be content with something similar.

(*f*) It is easy to see upon what aim the different rules I have brought forward converge. They are all intended to create for the doctor a counterpart to the 'fundamental rule of psycho-analysis' which is laid down for the patient. Just as the patient must relate everything that his self-observation can detect, and keep back all the logical and affective objections that seek to induce him to make a selection from among them, so the doctor must put himself in a position to make use of everything he is told for the purposes of interpretation and of recognizing the concealed unconscious material without substituting a censorship of his own for the selection that the patient has forgone. To put it in a formula: he must turn his own unconscious like a receptive organ towards the transmitting unconscious of the patient. He must adjust himself to the patient as a telephone receiver is adjusted to the transmitting microphone. Just as the receiver converts back into sound-waves the electric oscillations in the telephone line which were set up by sound-waves, so the doctor's unconscious is able, from the derivatives of the unconscious which are communicated to him, to reconstruct that unconscious, which has determined the patient's free associations.

But if the doctor is to be in a position to use his unconscious in this way as an instrument in the analysis, he must himself fulfil one psychological condition to a high degree. He may not tolerate any resistances in himself which hold back from his consciousness what has been perceived by his unconscious; otherwise he would introduce into the analysis a new species of selection and distortion which would be far more detrimental than that resulting from concentration of conscious attention. It is not enough for this that he himself should be an approximately normal person. It may be insist-

---

*['I dressed his wounds, God cured him.' The saying is attributed to the French surgeon, Ambroise Paré (*c.* 1517–1590).]

ed, rather, that he should have undergone a psycho-analytic purification and have become aware of those complexes of his own which would be apt to interfere with his grasp of what the patient tells him. There can be no reasonable doubt about the disqualifying effect of such defects in the doctor; every unresolved repression in him constitutes what has been aptly described by Stekel as a 'blind spot' in his analytic perception.

Some years ago I gave as an answer to the question of how one can become an analyst: 'By analysing one's own dreams.' This preparation is no doubt enough for many people, but not for everyone who wishes to learn analysis. Nor can everyone succeed in interpreting his own dreams without outside help. I count it as one of the many merits of the Zurich school of analysis that they have laid increased emphasis on this requirement, and have embodied it in the demand that everyone who wishes to carry out analyses on other people shall first himself undergo an analysis by someone with expert knowledge. Anyone who takes up the work seriously should choose this course, which offers more than one advantage; the sacrifice involved in laying oneself open to another person without being driven to it by illness is amply rewarded. Not only is one's aim of learning to know what is hidden in one's own mind far more rapidly attained and with less expense of affect, but impressions and convictions will be gained in relation to oneself which will be sought in vain from studying books and attending lectures. And lastly, we must not underestimate the advantage to be derived from the lasting mental contact that is as a rule established between the student and his guide.

An analysis such as this of someone who is practically healthy will, as may be imagined, remain incomplete. Anyone who can appreciate the high value of the self-knowledge and increase in self-control thus acquired will, when it is over, continue the analytic examination of his personality in the form of a self-analysis, and be content to realize that, within himself as well as in the external world, he must always expect to find something new. But anyone who has scorned to take the precaution of being analysed himself will not merely be punished by being incapable of learning more than a certain amount from his patients, he will risk a more serious danger and one which may become a danger to others. He will easily fall into the temptation of projecting outwards some of the peculiarities of his own personality, which he has dimly perceived, into the field of science, as a theory having universal validity; he will bring the psycho-analytic method into discredit, and lead the inexperienced astray.

(g) I shall now add a few other rules, that will serve as a transition from the attitude of the doctor to the treatment of the patient.

Young and eager psycho-analysts will no doubt be tempted to bring their own individuality freely into the discussion, in order to carry the patient along with them and lift him over the barriers of his own narrow personality. It might be expected that it would be quite allowable and indeed useful, with a view to overcoming the patient's existing resistances, for the doctor to afford him a glimpse of his own mental defects and conflicts and, by giving him intimate information about his own life, enable him to put himself on an equal footing. One confidence deserves another, and anyone who demands intimacy from someone else must be prepared to give it in return.

But in psycho-analytic relations things often happen differently from what the psychology of consciousness might lead us to expect. Experience does not speak in favour of an affective technique of this kind. Nor is it hard to see that it involves a departure from psycho-analytic principles and verges upon treatment by suggestion. It may induce the patient to bring forward sooner and with less difficulty things he already knows but would otherwise have kept back for a time through conventional resistances. But this technique achieves nothing towards the uncovering of what is unconscious to the patient. It makes him even more incapable of overcoming his deeper resistances, and in severer cases it invariably fails by encouraging the patient to be insatiable: he would like to reverse the situation, and finds the analysis of the doctor more interesting than his own. The resolution of the transference, too—one of the main tasks of the treatment—is made more difficult by an intimate attitude on the doctor's part, so that any gain there may be at the beginning is more than outweighed at the end. I have no hesitation, therefore, in condemning this kind of technique as incorrect. The doctor should be opaque to his patients and, like a mirror, should show them nothing but what is shown to him. In practice, it is true, there is nothing to be said against a psychotherapist combining a certain amount of analysis with some suggestive influence in order to achieve a perceptible result in a shorter time—as is necessary, for instance, in institutions. But one has a right to insist that he himself should be in no doubt about what he is doing and should know that his method is not that of true psycho-analysis.

(*h*) Another temptation arises out of the educative activity which, in psycho-analytic treatment, devolves on the doctor without any deliberate intention on his part. When the developmental inhibitions are resolved, it happens of itself that the doctor finds himself in a position to indicate new aims for the trends that have been liberated. It is then no more than a natural ambition if he endeavours to make something specially excellent of a person whom he has been at such pains to free from his neurosis and if he prescribes high aims for his wishes. But here again the doctor should hold himself in check, and take the patient's capacities rather than his own desires as guide. Not every neurotic has a high talent for sublimation; one can assume of many of them that they would not have fallen ill at all if they had possessed the art of sublimating their instincts. If we press them unduly towards sublimation and cut them off from the most accessible and convenient instinctual satisfactions, we shall usually make life even harder for them than they feel it in any case. As a doctor, one must above all be tolerant to the weakness of a patient, and must be content if one has won back some degree of capacity for work and enjoyment for a person even of only moderate worth. Educative ambition is of as little use as therapeutic ambition. It must further be borne in mind that many people fall ill precisely from an attempt to sublimate their instincts beyond the degree permitted by their organization and that in those who have a capacity for sublimation the process usually takes place of itself as soon as their inhibitions have been overcome by analysis. In my opinion, therefore, efforts invariably to make use of the analytic treatment to bring about sublimation of instinct are, though no doubt always laudable, far from being in every case advisable.

(*i*) To what extent should the patient's intellectual co-operation be sought for in the treatment? It is difficult to say anything of general applicability on this point: the patient's personality is the determining factor. But in any case caution and self-restraint must be observed in this connection. It is wrong to set a patient tasks, such as collecting his memories or thinking over some particular period of his life. On the contrary, he has to learan above all—what never comes easily to anyone—that mental activities such as thinking something over or concentrating the attention solve none of the riddles of a neurosis; that can only be done by patiently obeying the psycho-analytic rule, which enjoins the exclusion of all criticism of the unconscious or of its derivatives. One must be especially unyielding about obedience to that rule with patients who practise the art of sheering off into intellectual discussion during their treatment, who speculate a great deal and often very wisely about their condition and in that way avoid doing anything to overcome it. For this reason I dislike making use of analytic writings as an assistance to my patients; I require them to learn by personal experience, and I assure them that they will acquire wider and more valuable knowledge than the whole literature of psycho-analysis could teach them. I recognize, however, that under institutional conditions it may be of great advantage to employ reading as a preparation for patients in analysis and as a means of creating an atmosphere of influence.

I must give a most earnest warning against any attempt to gain the confidence or support of parents or relatives by giving them psycho-analytic books to read, whether of an introductory or an advanced kind. This well-meant step usually has the effect of bringing on prematurely the natural opposition of the relatives to the treatment—an opposition which is bound to appear sooner or later—so that the treatment is never even begun.

Let me express a hope that the increasing experience of psycho-analysts will soon lead to agreement on questions of technique and on the most effective method of treating neurotic patients. As regards the treatment of their relatives I must confess myself utterly at a loss, and I have in general little faith in any individual treatment of them.

From "ON PSYCHOTHERAPY"

by Sigmund Freud

I must confess that it is hardly fair to take up your attention for so long on the subject of psychoanalytic therapy without telling you in what this treatment consists and on what it is based. Still, as I am forced to be brief, I can only hint at this. This therapy, then, is based on the recognition that unconscious ideas—or better, the unconsciousness of certain mental processes—constitute the direct cause of the morbid symptoms. We hold this opinion in common with the French school (Janet) which, by the way, owing to too crude a schematization, refers the cause of hysterical symptoms to an unconscious *idée fixe*. Now please do not be afraid that this is going to land us in the depths of philosophical obscurities. Our unconscious is not quite the same thing as that of philosophers and, moreover, the majority of philosophers decline all knowledge of "unconscious mentality." If, however, you will look at the matter from our point of view, you will understand that the transformation of this unconscious material in the mind of the patient into conscious material must have the result of correcting his deviation from normality and of lifting the compulsion to which his mind has been subjected. For conscious will-power governs only the conscious mental processes, and every mental compulsion is rooted in the unconscious. Nor need you ever fear that the patient will be harmed by the shock accompanying the introduction of the unconscious into consciousness, for you can convince yourselves theoretically that the somatic and emotional effect of an impulse that has become conscious can never be so powerful as that of an unconscious one. It is only by the application of our highest mental energies, which are bound up with consciousness, that we can command all our impulses.

There is, however, another point of view which you may take up in order to understand the psychoanalytic method.

The discovery of the unconscious and the introduction of it into consciousness is performed in the face of a continuous *resistance* on the part of the patient. The process of bringing this unconscious material to light is associated with "pain" (*Unlust*), and because of this pain the patient again and again rejects it. It is for you then to interpose in this conflict in the patient's mental life. If you succeed in persuading him to accept, by virtue of a better understanding, something that up to now, in consequence of this automatic regulation by pain, he has rejected (repressed), you will then have accomplished something towards his education. For it is an education even to induce a person who dislikes leaving his bed early in the morning to do so all the same. Psychoanalytic treatment may in general be conceived of as such a *re-education in overcoming internal resistances*. Re-education of this kind is, however, in no respect more necessary to nervous patients than in regard to the mental element in their sexual life. For nowhere else have civilization and education done so much harm as in this field, and this is the point, as experience will show you, at which to look for those aetiologies of the neuroses that are amenable to influence; since the other aetiological factor, the constitutional component, consists of something fixed and unalterable. And from this it comes that one important qualification is required of the physician in this work: not only must his own character be irreproachable—"As to morals, that goes without saying," as the hero of Vischer's novel *Auch Einer* was wont to say—but he must also have overcome in his own mind that mixture of lewdness and prudery with which, unfortunately, so many people habitually consider sexual problems. . . .

Theodor Reik

Reik (1888–1969) was a loyal apostle of Freud. A psychoanalyst in Vienna for ten years, Reik was secretary of the Vienna Psychoanalytic Society, the center of Freudian orthodoxy. Reik was for a brief time a patient of Freud's, and on emigrating to New York in 1938, remained a staunch spokesman for a strict interpretation of Freud's theories and methods.

Holder of a doctorate in psychology, Reik was one of the first to practice psychoanalysis without having medical training. In the early days of psychoanalysis, Reik's status as a psychologist among physicians was a sore point. He was one of the first "lay" analysts—psychoanalysts without an M.D.—and even though he had studied with Freud, he was denied membership in the New York Psychoanalytic Society. While still in Vienna, Reik faced a court charge for practicing therapy under a Viennese law against quackery. Freud himself rose to Reik's defense, writing a book on lay analysis on Reik's behalf.

Reik wrote prolifically, and his books were instrumental in making psychoanalysis familiar to the American public. The following excerpt, from *Listening with the Third Ear*, is an account of the inner work of the psychoanalyst. Reik describes how to maintain the "evenly-suspended attention" recommended by Freud, and does so in a more lucid and concise fashion than much of what the master himself wrote on the same topic. Reik elaborates on how the analyst is to remain sensitive to his inner reactions and associations on the one hand, and to the nuances of the client's gesture, posture, tone, and words on the other—and how to hold off premature conclusions in the process. Reik, in short, portrays the mechanics of the psychoanalyst's mental craft.

FREE-FLOATING ATTENTION

by Theodor Reik

Do you picture the psychoanalyst as a man leaning forward in his chair, watching with all five senses for minute psychological signs, anxious lest one should escape him? I've talked about tiny signals, the faint stimuli that flit and waver, slip past, and attain such suggestive significance for the conjecture of unconscious processes. In the face of such differentiated data, so hard to take hold of, you would think that the keenest attention is called for. Do you imagine the analyst not just attentive but tense?

The picture is false, and the analyst's attention is of a different kind. Freud defined this particular kind of attention as *"gleichschwebend."* The word is difficult to translate; simultaneously with its connotation of equal distribution, it also has the meaning of revolving or circling.* The closest I can come to the German word is "freely floating." Another possibility, which emphasizes the psychological balance rather than the motion, would be "poised attention." Two factors induced Freud to recommend such free-floating attention.

It saves tension, which, after all, is not possible to maintain for hours, and it avoids the dangers that threaten in the case of deliberate attention directed toward a particular aim. If we strain our attention to a certain point, if we begin to select from among the data offered and seize upon one fragment especially, then, Freud warns us, we follow our own expectations or inclinations. The danger naturally arises that we may never find anything but what we are prepared to find. If we

---

*A. A. Brill translates it "mobile attention." This is correct only in the sense that a lamp, which can be carried from one room to another, may be called mobile. It cannot be denied that the dancer Pavlova can be described as mobile, but it does not give one a good picture of her activity on the stage.

follow our inclinations, we are sure to falsify the possible perception. The rule that we must note everything equally is the necessary counterpart to the demand we make upon the patient to tell everything that occurs to him without criticism or selection.

When we hear free-floating attention recommended, we get the impression that it is a course easy to pursue. But in practice it is hardly less difficult than the course required of the patient, of which it is the counterpart.

Only ignorance of how the basic principle of analysis is carried out has prevented psychologists from beginning to criticize this point of psychoanalytic theory and practice. By way of experiment, I shall anticipate their criticism and begin with the last sentence of Freud's recommendations, in which he advises the particular kind of attention in which everything is noted equally. It is plain that two notions are here confused that, strictly speaking, have nothing to do with one another: poised attention and taking note. The first notion has to do with a particular attitude of mind or reaction to data presented, the other to a feat of memory. It is true that the word "note" can be used for both. But in fact it seems that Freud passed from the subject of attention to the far-removed theme of capacity for taking note, without being fully aware of it. Is attention inseparably associated with taking note, with memory? Assuredly not. When I stand at a crossing and direct my attention to the traffic, is there anything of which I need take note, that I need impress upon my memory?

And now, how can free-floating attention and taking note be brought into consonance? If from the wealth of a mass of passing data we want to take note of something, we must direct a keen gaze upon special points, turn our attention to them in particular, must we not? How can I take note of anything, if I do not direct my whole attention to it, if I treat insignificant detail in exactly the same way as that which is important? Perhaps it will be said that the notion of "poised" attention aims precisely at taking note of everything and remembering everything. But is not that notion self-contradictory? Attention is always directed only to particular objects. Attention, we have always been taught, implies selection. How can we avoid the danger of selection, if we want to be attentive?

Anyone who has studied the psychological literature on this question will immediately cite passages from a number of books by distinguished psychologists, in which particular stress is laid upon the statement that the notion of attention does imply selection, nay, that without that essential feature it is meaningless. Let me quote a representative passage from Hermann Ebbinghaus' *Outline of Psychology* (*Abriss der Psychologie*):

"Attention is a phenomenon of selection and limitation. The mind escapes from the excessive mass of demands that are perpetually being made upon it in favor of a few that bear a special relation to its own aims."

Indeed attention has been defined as "the preference consciously shown to certain mental contents." We might also point to the "narrowness of consciousness," fully investigated by science. It is a well-known fact that only a certain number of ideas can find a place in our field of consciousness, and that a kind of rivalry or struggle goes on at its threshold among the ideas pressing for admittance. A large number of experiments, prepared and carried out with remarkable precision and acumen, have led to the establishment of the exact number of perceptions and ideas for which our consciousness has room. All this argues against the possibility of "poised" attention. Let us consider, further, what academic psychology tells us of the origin of attention. I will take as a representative example the hypothesis of Karl Groos, a distinguished investigator who claimed, with the support of very intriguing arguments, the "instinct of spying" as the original form of attention. Out of this primary form, which, indeed, represents the "expectation of future events," out of what we may call motor attention, theoretical attention has evolved. Allowing for the distance traveled from this basic form, we should be compelled to recognize in every type of attention its derivation from an instinctive motor reaction. But surely the idea of a poised spying appears absurd.

I would beg my readers to note that my improvised criticism does not aim at investigating an analytic theory of attention, for no such theory exists, certainly none set up by Freud. We will, therefore, only treat the subject insofar as is necessary in connection with our problem, attention in analysis. And here we must first admit that in one direction the criticism is justified. It would have been more to the point, more advantageous, to treat the question of attention separately, and not to confuse it with that of memory. Still, the association of the two sets of problems may be accounted for by the peculiar nature of the technique of analysis. Freud himself points out that the analyst is usually told things whose significance he cannot recognize until afterward, sometimes long afterward. Perhaps Freud's frequent use of the term "taking note" (*sich merken*) is a peculiarity of Austrian speech. At the same time, it is not mere chance that we speak of attention and the capacity for paying attention. An important psychological association is here revealed. It generally remains at the back of our minds because we are accustomed to connect attention with a mental achievement corresponding to an instantaneous or immediate reaction. For instance, we test the attention of a subject in the laboratory by causing auditory stimuli to act upon him at definite intervals, and telling him to make some movement, give some signal, as soon as he hears them. A teacher tests his pupil's attention by calling upon him suddenly to continue a sentence that another has just begun to translate. It will be objected that these are very primitive examples. No doubt, but it is just such examples that I chiefly want to bring forward. Attention generally enables us to react immediately to an event or impression. This cannot be the kind of attention used in analysis because we often do not recognize the psychological significance of the things that we are told until afterward. Even when we recognize a certain meaning immediately, our reaction is restricted to the acknowledgment of the recognition; we have to wait until new insight leads to its full understanding.

I have already said that attention directed—for instance in a laboratory experiment—to an impression, serves to grasp it clearly, to appraise its significance at once, to master it, so to speak, by understanding as soon as possible. That, of course, presupposes that, simultaneously with the impression or soon afterward, its significance can be recognized. If I go for a walk in a field and something leaps up out of the grass and runs across the path, I recognize it at once: Oh-ho! a hare. If I have good eyesight and there is sufficient light, there can be no doubt. I need not wait until later, perhaps several hours afterward, for the conviction to come over me: That was a hare. My attention was, so to speak, rewarded at once by recognizing the object, and perhaps, if I had had a gun, there might have been a further reward.

There are, of course, other impressions whose recognition requires time and severe effort. Think, for instance, of the psychical process which we call observation. Such observation may be prolonged, our recognition of the significance of a process may not occur for a considerable time. And here we are really approaching the essential character of analytic attention. It is akin to that of an observer, but important differences remain to be considered. An observer generally selects a definite section of a process, and his attention helps him to recognize the meaning of one or the other feature. Undoubtedly the analyst does something of the same kind. He, too, selects a section, for instance, the utterances and expressive gestures of a person, and he wants to know what they mean. But we must reflect that he grasps this section in two different ways. We may say that he reaches two apprehensions: one in which he clearly recognizes what the words and movements of the person observed mean, just what they say; and a second that sets small value upon the conscious meaning in contrast with another, which he does not know and which is still to be discovered.

That is not very clear. Perhaps, then, I may have to resort to an analogy.

Let us suppose we are in a foreign country and that we hear a certain sentence in the native language, of which we already know many words. We come upon an unknown expression, retain the word, and resolve to look it up later in the dictionary. There we find it, and we immediately understand the sentence. Here, too, then, our attention is directed to preparation for subsequent understanding.

Let's vary the example a little. We do find the word in question in the dictionary. When we insert it in the sentence, it gives a definite meaning, but not one that would possibly have been intended by the speaker. The whole situation refutes it; the word must have another meaning not in the dictionary. Perhaps we have a case of an ordinary, everyday expression that is used in a special meaning in those circles, e.g., among students, or perhaps it is an allusion only understood in that particular social sphere. The dictionary has been of no use to us, and we decide to await future illumination, when, for instance, the same expression appears in a new connection. We save up the expression, so to speak, and on some future occasion we mean to guess the hidden secondary meaning. Now many impressions that we receive during the analytic observation are of a like nature.

We shall occupy ourselves a little with the most important distinctions drawn by psychology in respect to attention. It is one of the most disputed subjects of research. In fact everything about it is the subject of dispute; whether it is an activity or a state is as hotly debated as its premises and motives, its psychogenesis and its psychopathology. Nay, its every existence is open to question. Not long ago a Copenhagen professor seriously maintained at a psychological congress that it was only a pseudo conception, and spoke of the nonexistence of attention.

We shall not be surprised at the importance attributed to the problem of attention in psychology, if we bear in mind how inseparably it is connected with the phenomena of consciousness and the system of memory, how it accompanies the psychical process from sense-perceptions to ideas. It applies equally to our sensations and emotions, is placed in the service of our will, and runs like a thread through our whole inner life.

Psychology distinguishes voluntary and involuntary attention. The former is derived from selective interest, conscious of an aim, while the latter is sometimes described as a partially mechanized instinctive function. The former is mainly active in character, the latter mainly reactive. We may say that, in general, voluntary attention is directed toward a selected content; involuntary attention, toward an obtruding one. Since the days of Lotze and Wundt it has been a favorite illustration of psychological writers to compare the phenomenon of attention with a searchlight. Rightly so, when we realize that attention marks out a zone of light in the field of experience.

And now let us turn to another distinction, determined by the content. External and internal attention are distinguished by their object, that is, by the question whether we direct our interest to the external or the inner world. Let us revert to the comparison and imagine a searchlight turned upon the walls of a fort. It can be turned either upon the foreground of the fortification or upon the interior, the separate objects belonging to the fort, the courtyards, and storehouses.

It is, of course, possible to unite these two kinds of attention. The justification of associating active or passive attention with the external world is self-evident. The second connection, with the inner world, is much more difficult to grasp. As an example of voluntary attention directed inward, I need only cite self-observation as a psychological action. The second possibility, too, will be made clear to us if we think, for instance, of surprising ourselves in a sudden feeling of sadness under cheerful circumstances, or cheerfulness in a tragic situation.

But after all, what we want is to learn more of the nature

of attention in analysis. We are coming to that. We distinguish the result of attention directed inward toward our own psychical processes by the very name that we give it. When, perhaps in trying to solve a problem, we turn our attention inward and try to realize causal and other connections and to understand the phenomena genetically, the outcome is thought. But if we approach the problem differently, if we tackle it indirectly or allow it to act upon us, so to speak, without directly attacking it, if we only pay attention to what arises in our mind on the occasion, then the outcome is that ideas occur to us, or at least that they may occur. We now realize that the analyst's heuristic activities are especially dominated by inward, involuntary attention. There remains room enough for the other kind of attention as well, which is automatically called in when needed.

The quality of the attention in psychoanalysis may be well illustrated by the comparison with a searchlight. Voluntary attention, which is restricted to a narrow sector of our field of experience, may be compared in its effect to the turning of the searchlight upon a particular piece of ground. If we know beforehand that the enemy is coming from that direction, or that something is going to happen upon that field, then we have anticipated the event, as it were. It is advantageous to illuminate that particular sector brightly. Let us assume a different case, that something, for instance a noise, has turned our attention to a particular zone. Only then do we turn the searchlight upon it. Our attention did not rush on in advance of the perception, but followed it. This is the case of involuntary attention. If we drive at night along a road near New York, we may notice that a searchlight in the middle of the road is scouring the surrounding country uninterruptedly. It illuminates the road, is then directed to the fields, turns toward the town, and swings in a wide curve back to the road, and so repeats its circuit. This kind of activity, which is not confined to one point but is constantly scouring a wide radius, provides the best comparison with the function of free-floating attention.

From out of the wealth of psychological problems arising at this point, I will pick out one special question as being of interest to the technique of analysis: that of the relation between the various kinds of attention and surprise. It will be seen at once that the time factor plays a great part in this matter. If I know that the enemy is coming from one particular direction and turn the searchlight in that direction from the outset, I shall be able to determine the precise moment of his appearance and thus be in a position to recognize the nature of the danger and the steps to be taken for defense. He will not succeed in surprising me. The great advantage of voluntary attention, which knows its object from the outset and maintains a particular direction, is especially that it enables us to be mentally prepared. "Readiness is everything," might be its motto. Involuntary attention offers a much feebler protection against the danger of being taken by surprise. If it is an external stimulus, a sudden perception, that first calls my attention to the appearance of the enemy, he has the advantage over me in the matter of time. I have less time to prepare myself. "Poised" attention maintains the mean between the two extremes. I cannot escape the danger of surprise, but only attenuate it.

But voluntary attention, which offers such excellent protection against the dangers of surprise, also deprives us from its advantages. It involves an excellent protection against irritant stimuli; but it may, in a certain sense, almost amount to an exclusion of stimuli. And that brings us to its negative aspect, one which many psychoanalysts have failed to appraise at all adequately. Now attention consists of the fact that certain images present themselves vividly and become effective at the expense of others. The concentration of attention involves a setting up of inhibitions, so that keen observation of particular things corresponds to the ignoring of others. Withdrawal of certain contents from consciousness is no less a part of attention than the appearance of others at the center. It is open to question which part is the more significant to the essence and action of attention, the illumination of particular objects, the bestowal of intensive interest upon them, or its diversion away from others. Some investigators, for instance S. Ferenczi, regard the inhibition of all actions except the one contemplated as the prime feature of the act of attention. If all the paths leading to consciousness are blocked, with the one exception, then psychic energy flows in the one direction that is still free, spontaneously and without the need of any exertion on its part.

What I like to call the reconnoitering character of "poised" attention does not enable us to discern objects and their connection as sharply and clearly as does voluntary attention. Its aim cannot, therefore, be instantaneous understanding, immediate placing among things known. But that disadvantage is accompanied by a number of advantages that fully counterbalance the renunciation of sharply and narrowly outlined immediate clarity. Perhaps I ought to establish the nature of poised attention theoretically, but I choose to illustrate it by means of an example, the solution of a picture-riddle. We should certainly not despise an illustration of this kind when we remember that Freud compared dreams to such a riddle, and the interpretation of dreams to the intellectual labor of solving them.

The first picture is of a piece of cloth with a rent in it, and a needle and thread mending it. *Rent? Hole? Darn?* Then two *LL's. Rentells? Holells?* Both nonsense. *Darnells? Mendells?* Or should it be: *Mendels,* because the two *LL's* signify just *l's?* Let us go on. We next have an arrangement of letters: S, and beneath it GS. GS under S? No, that does not make sense. S over GS? That is no better. Or S above GS? Also nonsense. S on GS? *Songs*—that is it, of course. Then the first part must surely be *Mendelssohn.* But where is the last syllable on the name? *Mendelssohn? Mendels-sohn?* Why, it is *Mend-els-on-Songs.*

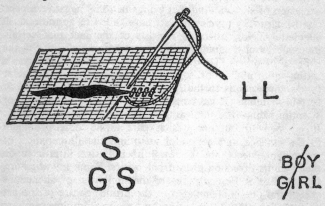

We must not let ourselves be put off by orthography, nor by the exact pronunciation. We must be satisfied with the sound represented under the conditions obtaining in a rebus. To proceed, the crossing out of a letter or syllable often means something negative in these puzzles. *Songs not? Songs deduct? Songs take away?* None of them promising beginnings, followed by *boy girl.* What can these mean? *Songs without?* Then of course it must be: *Songs without Words.*

We have it in a flash. On reflection we realize that it is the sense of the riddle. *Boy girl* means nothing. They are simply words, two words crossed out, which means: without words. The solution: *Mendelssohn Songs without Words*.

After all, the solution of a riddle like this can teach us something of the nature of poised attention. Let us recall the minor difficulties that we had with the initial word, and overcame. We were checked by picturing the exact spelling of the word to ourselves. Our attention was not exactly imprisoned, and yet it was a little hedged in, by an orthographically determined image of a word. Every dream-interpretation displays the same phenomenon, and every psychoanalyst can report cases of this kind in which his understanding of the hidden meaning of the dream was delayed by precisely this difficulty. I am in the fortunate situation where I can cite three instances that represent three languages.

A patient dreamed of a dress she had seen. In the dream she was in doubt as to whether she should buy the dress. What is more appropriate than that she should consider the waistline in a subsequent part of the dream? The meaning of the dream escaped us, however, until we paid no attention to the spelling and then it occurred to us that the *waistline* really meant *the line of waste*, namely, whether it would not be a waste to take a certain line of action in the situation of the patient.

A man had a long and complicated dream in which he went to the Sorbonne and walked about its rooms. His thought-associations led back to the time when he really visited the University of Paris. Who would think of a connection beween *Sorbonne* and *Soeur bonne?*

I can give another example directly, not taken from the dream world but from daylight, waking life, in which orthography played a certain part that I failed to recognize. It struck me that, during the early months of his analysis, a certain Viennese patient stopped short at certain points in his account of his experiences, as if there were an unknown obstacle just at these places. I could not account for it and thought he was concealing some part of his experience. It was the more striking because his statement was altogether honest and serious. Nor did I find any sign in the subject matter of his stories that could lead me to surmise the nature of the block. For instance, he told me of a little quarrel that he had had with his sweetheart the day before, and ended with the passionate words, "I hate her." I did not surmise that the thought that checked him, and which he himself afterwards explained, was that the sentence could be applied to me, the analyst, by a change in the way of writing a single initial letter. The German for both "her" and "you" is *"sie,"* but in the latter case it is written with a capital *S*. (The German *"Ich hasse sie"* and *"Ich hasse Sie"* thus differ only in the writing of the pronoun.) Even at a later stage the double meaning of the word, caused by similarity of sound, acted as a check on the patient's talk, and he often had to wage his "war on the capital *S*," as he prettily called it.

But let us return to our rebus. We have speedily cast off the slight burden of orthographical and phonetic differences, and read "Mendelssohn" as if the strict rules of spelling and pronunciation did not concern us at all. No less lightly, or light-heartedly, we have dealt with "songs." We have jumped the small hurdles with assurance and speed, and, cheered by our freedom from rules and obligations, we have got as far as "Mendelssohn, Songs . . ." We observe that we do not really owe this easy advance—we came, we saw, we conquered—so much to our ordinary attention as to its relaxation. If we had obeyed the usual laws of attention, if we had not ignored the customary ideas of purpose, we should still be at "Mend," and might have gone on to "stockings" or other fancies. In short, we should have been caught in a tangle of mending wool. But let us suppose that we had disentangled ourselves and turned our voluntary attention to the next step, we should never have found the last syllable of the name "Mendelssohn." If we employ the purposive, active kind of attention that is so necessary, so indispensable in life, the situation would soon have become hopeless. We owe our advance precisely to our escape from the strict demands of attention, which holds all other associations at bay and follows the one train of thought unswervingly.

Our psychical action when we guessed the last element of the riddle—"words"—was of a different nature. When we remember how we beat our brains over that mysterious sign, and how we came to solve it, and then compare the process with that which preceded it, we shall be driven to note a marked difference between the two. At first we wanted to proceed according to the familiar method of solving picture-riddles, and simply guess the word concealed behind the sign. Did it mean boy and girl, boy over girl, girl under boy, or what? It all produced no sense and yet the correct, logical solution was close at hand. Concentrated attention was no help.

We have here one of the cases in which strained attention, conscious, purposive effort, can at best lead us to the conclusion that we are on the wrong track.

Attention, which is intended to facilitate intellectual achievement, or, indeed, to make it in any way possible, has misled us. In those cases in which, in spite of our utmost and most strenuous endeavors and the bracing of our attention, we do not succeed in recalling something, in reproducing a forgotten content, we know that there is a tried remedy: we drop the idea of purpose and stop turning our attention in that particular direction or on that particular set of circumstances.

And what happens? The withdrawal of attention does not give rise to inattention, but to a shifting of attention, to a readiness to receive a variety of stimuli emerging from the unconscious or the unknown. As in the case cited above, a rigid, one-sided attention has detracted from our mental achievement and injured our success because it prevented us from moving in any other direction. We gazed as if spellbound upon the words "boy girl," which we read as if they absolutely had to be a part of what we were seeking. Not until we freed ourselves from this fixation of attention, not until we allowed our attention to turn in other directions, did the solution occur to us.

We often hear patients complain that they fail to concentrate their attention. In analytic investigation we find that this complaint conceals a totally different situation. The attention of these patients is concentrated, though, upon an unconscious content, for instance, certain fantasies. They fail to detach attention from particular psychical contents and direct it to others, which is what life demands of them. We often hear that a patient cannot concentrate his attention, without thinking that it is already concentrated upon a subject, unknown or unconscious to him.

When we beat our brains so long over the last part of the picture-puzzle, we were behaving like people who find it difficult to escape from concentrating on one point and to keep their attention free-floating and unattached. In a sense we were unable to throw off the chain of our concentration and circled, like dancing mice, round the words "boy girl." Analytic practice brings daily proof of what a hindrance any rigid concentration on a particular idea can be to the heuristic task. It is only when we replace it with poised attention that it becomes possible to capture unconscious processes.

In the early days of my work as an analyst, when I was faced with surprising symptoms, puzzling dreams, and incomprehensible trains of thought, just the same thing happened as when we were seeking the last part of the solution of the picture-riddle. Not until I cast off the customary restraint of voluntary attention was I able to get hold of the hidden psychical data. Not until I had left the firm and broad high road did I reach the goal along side paths. The secret meaning escaped my conscious, active attention, and was not found until I had become "inattentive" in the popular meaning of the word, that is, until I gave myself up to unconscious ideas of the goal.

Now of course it would be nonsense to declare that analysts work with poised attention only. The statement would be false if only because at certain points poised attention must be changed to voluntary or active, when the significance of a symptom or a latent relation has been recognized and it has now to be placed and evaluated. Let us return to our comparison with the searchlight. The searchlight that scours the whole foreground equally will, of course, stop at one point if the enemy is sighted there. It must be noted that what we have here is the replacement of one form of attention by another. On such occasions, the original, free-floating attention gives way to the voluntary, direct form.

Another form of substitution is more important. On special occasions attention is definitely withdrawn from the object before it and turns with a jerk, so to speak, to other, seemingly more remote, relations. A special significance attaches to this withdrawal of attention from the immediate aspects of the data. Our thought goes off and reaches a goal by an unusual path that it could have attained by no other. Thus the psychical process of conjecturing the secret meaning of an obsession or part of a dream or mental reaction is often like that of solving the last part of our picture-riddle, "boy girl." The essential thing about it is the withdrawal of attention from what is immediately before it, or at least its slackening, and the fact that in this way the emergence of sudden ideas is facilitated. It is possible to attain an understanding of many unconscious processes only after this temporary switching off of direct attention has prepared the way psychologically. The contents that previously had occupied a central position and were then thrust into the background by the shifting of attention will acquire a new and often undreamed-of significance later.

While we adopted an attitude of poised attention most of the time in solving the picture-riddle, when it came to the solution of the last word our interest was withdrawn from the object for the fraction of a second, and poised attention was interrupted for a moment by "inattention." It is as if a swimmer were suddenly to break off his regular motion through the water in order to plunge into the depths. We can observe two types of distribution of mental energy in analysis, too, and introspection may easily distinguish them. Moreover, the momentary plunge into unconscious depths, hitherto undreamed-of, is akin to the mental phenomenon of the birth of wit. Indeed, the result is sometimes similar: in our rebus the solution had something of the quality of wit. The psychical effect of discovering this last word of the riddle is different from that of solving the others. It partakes of the character of surprise.

Earlier in this chapter, I made a paradoxical statement and I owe it to my conscience to revert to it. I said that attention of that special voluntary kind prevented surprise. People who practice it always find confirmation of what they already know. Attention as a hindrance to the progress of scientific knowledge—assuredly that is a bold assertion. Still, it is not its boldness but its falsity that I dislike. But I have spoken in this derogatory manner, not of attention as such, but of its special active and voluntary form if applied to unconscious data. This latter often leads to a fixation of our minds, which may be called autohypnotic, on the immediate object or on the one relation that happens to be in the forefront of our thoughts. Under certain circumstances this kind of attention may prepare our minds for the reception of knowledge. Its main effect is that of clearing a particular path, disposing of particular possibilities, which must then make way for the consideration of others.

Furthermore, I should disagree if anyone were to say that Isaac Newton's straining of attention when he was struggling with the problem of gravitation was useless or superfluous, because the law did not come to him until he withdrew his attention and saw the apple fall from the tree in the garden. His laborious and consciously directed thought constituted, we may say, an important psychological prerequisite for the idea that occurred to him unforced. In a sense it gave sanction to it inwardly, and had economic and dynamic value. Every serious research-worker knows that voluntary attention in the form of intellectual labor often stimulates ideas, just as unforced ideas sometimes give birth to thoughts. It is true that we cannot produce valuable unforced ideas by an effort of thought, but thought is often their preliminary condition. Tschaikovsky once called inspiration a guest who does not care to visit lazy people. That is equally true of scientific and artistic labor and of attention in association with productive work. If, in the searching labors of analysis, psychical energy must be differently distributed, that is due to special qualities of the region to be investigated and the data to be examined, the most important parts of which seldom reveal themselves to reflection, but usually in an unforced idea. It is the condition that helps the oppressed minorities in the kingdom of the mind to win their rights.

I have said that active attention generally precludes surprise, while poised attention attenuates it as a rule. But this process of momentary slackening of attention and diversion of interest in another direction, with subsequent return to the object, is a preparation for surprise. We shall recur to the question of how this preparation is connected with the effect of surprise; for the present this allusion to the fact may suffice. We had wanted to solve the last part of the picture-riddle separately and in isolation, like the others, without troubling about what had gone before. We failed. The solution did not emerge in our mind until we had abandoned the effort and remembered the previous part of the riddle, which we had already solved. The way to the solution was paved by the words "Mendelssohn Songs." We then saw two words, but they were crossed out. Of course, the solution was *Songs without Words*. Really it ought to have occurred to us at once, we see now, wondering at ourselves.

In not quite the same way, and yet similarly, the surprise is prepared in analysis, and as it dies away we ask ourselves incidentally how it came about. Tracing our mental process backward, it seems to us that we had really no justification for surprise if we had consciously noticed small signs, which we now remember, or if a symptom that now occurs to us had been noted consciously when it first appeared or was repeated in some obscure place. Then a psychical implication, which we now remember, strikes us as a clear indication of what we took so long to recognize. A symptom, the fragment of a dream, a long-forgotten fact suddenly appear in a new light; widely scattered data arrange themselves in a new relation. Retrospective reflection shows that unconsciously we had understood the meaning of the separate facts very well, and that this unconscious comprehension was, so to speak, a necessary preparation for the present surprise. Things that were not in the center of our attention, things that were at the fringe, a passing impression, a fleeting presentiment, now take on importance.

We now discern the great importance of the time factor in appraising the different kinds of attention. Poised attention generally involves the renunciation of the immediate recognition of links of association. It apprehends the several details of the psychical data equally and prepares the way for us to work our way among them later. Free-floating attention provides, so to speak, a storeroom of impressions, from which later knowledge will suddenly emerge. It also creates the prerequisite conditions for those surprising results that appear in analysis as the product of a prolonged unconscious condensation and dissociation of impressions.

We rarely realize that there is a pre-knowledge within us while we wait for illumination. A case gets more impenetrable and everything looks dark and overcast; yet everything is preparing for the coming flash of insight. There are no bolts from the blue in psychoanalysis. Sudden clarity is preceded by increasing darkness. To speak with Nietzsche: "That which will kindle the lightning must for a long time be a cloud."

Alfred Adler

Alfred Adler (1879–1937) became part of Freud's inner circle of psychoanalysts after graduating from medical school in Vienna in 1895. Because of conflicts with Freud, he left the Psychoanalytic Society in 1911, founding his own Society for Individual Psychology. Soon after Adler published his first book, in which he traced neurotic disturbances to feelings of inferiority and implicated aggression. He considered aggression, more than sexuality, as the major factor in mental and emotional disorders.

After World War I, during the reconstruction of war-ravaged Austria, Adler became one of the first psychoanalysts to apply his techniques to treat children and their problems at home and school. In 1935 Adler moved to New York, where he founded clinics and an American branch of the society. Perhaps because Adler was a pioneer in working with children, his methods have been as popular among teachers, counselors, and social workers as among the ranks of psychotherapists.

Adler proposed that each person has a "style of life," stemming from his pattern of family relationships, out of which characteristic disorders develop. The style of life is adopted in a person's childhood in order to achieve a sense of superiority that will compensate for the child's sense of inferiority. For Adler, then, the motivating force in personality was an aggressive drive that propels the person toward an inflated sense of superiority, even if it is won at the cost of neurosis.

Adler saw the therapist's role as "mothering" the patient, giving him an experience of loving contact, and then helping him to transfer the feelings of warmth and affection that spring from therapy to his other relationships. This therapeutic contact should allow the patient to give up his neurotic strivings for a sense of superiority and self-esteem, and substitute more socially beneficial life goals and ways to achieve them. From selfishness, hostility, and maladjustment, the patient should adopt more healthy social attitudes, such as the spirit of give-and-take, cooperation, and interest in others.

The first stages of treatment in Adlerian therapy revolve around discovering the patient's unique goal of superiority and style of achieving it, both of which have their roots in his childhood. The patient's order of birth, his early memories, his fantasy heroes, his career choice, are all seen as sources of clues, as are his bearing, gestures, and other nonverbal behaviors. Adlerians, like Freudians, take a special interest in their patient's dreams. But rather than looking at them in a Freudian framework, the Adlerian interprets them to discover what they might reveal about the patient's inner attitudes toward his present life problems; dreams are a symbolic rehearsal for what the patient will actually do, or would like to.

Adler was one of the first in Freud's circle to discard the couch, preferring instead to converse in a direct and relaxed way with his patients. Adler saw therapy as a cooperative venture between patient and therapist, both working in a good relationship to help the patient understand himself better. During the course of therapy the patient is to be led gently into seeing how he has been striving for a sense of superiority in ways that actually defeat him, and finally to abandon this "useless" goal in favor of more cooperative, socially beneficial ones.

UNDERSTANDING AND TREATING THE PATIENT

by Alfred Adler

A. UNDERSTANDING THE PATIENT

1. METHODS FOR UNDERSTANDING

Individual Psychology is committed to the principle of investigating the system of a psychological disorder along the path which the patient himself has taken. Our work has shown what great significance must be ascribed to the individual material which the patient has at his disposal and, still more, to his own evaluation of this material. Therefore an

understanding of the individual and an individualizing examination became a main requirement.

All the methods of Individual Psychology for understanding the personality take into account the individual's opinion
of his goal of superiority, the strength of his inferiority
feeling, the degree of his social interest, and the fact that the
whole individual cannot be torn from his context with life—
or better said, from his context with society.

According to my experience, so far the most trustworthy
approaches to the exploration of personality are given in a
comprehensive understanding of (1) the earliest childhood
recollections, (2) the position of the child in the birth order,
(3) childhood disorders, (4) day and night dreams, and (5)
the nature of the exogenous factor that causes the illness. All
the results of such an investigation, which also include the attitude toward the physician, must be evaluated with the
greatest caution, and their course must always be examined
for consistency with other findings. In this way we will
succeed in obtaining a faithful picture of the self-consistent
style of life of an individual and in comprehending in the
case of a failure the degree of his deviation, the nature of
which always turns out to be a lack of the ability to make
contact.

2. EMPATHY, INTUITION, AND GUESSING

The partially unconscious course of the neurosis, which
contradicts reality, is explained primarily by the unswerving
tendency of the patient to arrive at his goal. The contradiction
to reality, that is, to the logical demands of society, is related
to the limited experiences and the peculiar human relationships which were effective at the time of the construction of
the life-plan in early childhood. Insight into the meaning of this
plan is best acquired through artistic and intuitive empathy
with the essential nature of the patient. One will then notice
how, unintentionally, one makes comparisons between oneself
and the patient, between different attitudes of the same patient,
or between similar attitudes of different patients. To give an
orientation to one's observations, which include the patient's
symptoms, experiences, manner of life, and development, I
use three devices. The first assumes that the life-plan originated under aggravated conditions, such as organ inferiorities,
pressure in the family, pampering, rivalry, or a neurotic
family-tradition, and directs my attention to childhood reactions similar to the present symptoms. The second device as-

sumes an equation in which the personality ideal is the determining factor of the neurosis and according to which I enter my observation. The third device looks for the largest common denominator for all accessible expressive movements.

Until recent times it was chiefly the poets who best succeeded in getting the clue to a person's style of life. Their ability to show the individual living, acting, and dying as an indivisible whole in closest connection with the tasks of his environment rouses our highest admiration. This power was due to their gift of divination. Only by guessing did they come to see what lies behind and between the expressive movements, namely, the individual's law of movement. Many people call this gift *intuition* and believe that it is the special possession only of the greatest minds. In reality this gift is most human. Everyone makes use of it constantly in the chaos of life, before the abysmal uncertainty of the future. Correct guessing is the first step toward the mastery of our problems. But this correct guessing distinguishes especially the man who is a partner, a fellow man, and is interested in the successful solution of all human problems.

Some day soon it will be realized that the artist is the leader of mankind on the path to the absolute truth. Among poetic works of art which have led me to the insights of Individual Psychology the following stand out as pinnacles: fairy tales, the Bible, Shakespeare, and Goethe.

3. EXPRESSIVE BEHAVIOR AND SYMPTOMS

The glance, the gait, the vigor or weakness of the patient's approach can reveal a great deal. Much may be missed if one becomes accustomed to rules such as assigning a particular place, like a couch, or keeping to a certain time. The first interview, although entirely unconstrained, should already be a test. Even the handshake may suggest a definite problem. One often sees that pampered persons like to lean against something, and that children cling to their mothers. But, just as with everything that requires the ability to guess, so here also one should avoid strict rules and should verify instead. I see an advantage in not interrupting the patient's movements. Let him get up, come and go, or smoke as he likes. I have even occasionally given patients the opportunity to go to sleep in my presence when they proposed this, thus making my task more difficult. Such an attitude spoke as clearly as hostile words. A patient's sidelong glance also clearly indicates his slight inclination to cooperate. This can become conspicuous in other ways as well, as when the patient says little or nothing, when he beats about the bush, or when by incessant talking he prevents the consultant from speaking. For the patient the consultation is a social problem, like every encounter of one person with another. Everyone will introduce himself according to his law of movement. The expert can often tell something of the patient's social feeling at the first glance.

I have found it of considerable value to conduct myself as during a pantomime, that is, for a while not to pay any attention to the words of the patient, but instead to read his deeper intention from his bearing and his movements within a situation. In doing so one will sense the sharp contradiction between the seen and the heard expressions and recognize clearly the meaning of symptoms.

We must remember that the patient has no understanding of his own forms of expression and is thus unable to conceal his true self. We see his personality in action and revealed, not by what he says or thinks about himself, but by his acts interpreted in their context. Not that the patient deliberately wants to lie to us, but we have learned to recognize a vast gulf between a man's conscious thoughts and his unconscious motivations, a gulf which can best be bridged by a disinterested but sympathetic outsider. The outsider, whether he be the psychologist, or the parent, or the teacher, should learn to interpret a personality on the basis of objective facts seen as the expression of the purposive, but more or less unconscious, strivings of the individual.

We look upon symptoms as creations, as works of art. Thus when we try to prove something from any particular symptom we can do so only if we look upon the symptom as a single part of a complete whole, that is, we must find in every symptom something that lies deeper than the outward and visible signs, something that underlies the actual manifestation and form of the complaint itself. We must look behind the headache, the anxiety symptom, the obsession idea, behind the fact of an individual being a thief or a loafer in school. For behind lies something more, something personal and entirely individual. The more we understand of the structure of the psyche, the more will we realize that no symptom observed in two different cases has ever exactly the same significance. But there is one assumption we can make in all cases: a symptom is connected with the individual's struggle to reach a chosen goal.

4. THE ORGANIC COMPONENT

In the first interviews with the patient we must make sure whether it really is a case of neurosis or one of organic disorder. If I do not suspect a real organic disorder, I may temporarily exclude that aspect of the case from consideration, and proceed to investigate the circumstances and style of life. If on the other hand, it is evidently a case of organic disorder, I must consider whether the complaint and suffering are greater than the illness itself would justify, that is, whether there is a combination of organic and psychic illness. In such cases I have often found more pain than the illness warrants, or unaccountable excitement which may increase the fever. In organic illness, also, the appetite varies according to the general outlook, and a serious illness may be prolonged or even fatally influenced if the patient turns pessimistic or becomes psychologically lethargic.

5. VERIFYING THE UNDERSTANDING

To verify my findings, I check one indication by another [for internal consistency], eliciting information of many various kinds. We can thus more easily comprehend the style of life; and if we always check and verify each impression by others, we shall not be misled into mere generalizations.

There are a number of tests for the correctness of a neuropsychiatric opinion. (1) The psychiatrist examines the patient in the presence of the family physician, without asking leading questions or doing any systematic questioning. Yet he must proceed so that the whole personality is illuminated. The family physician, without having been given any explanation previously, will from the questions and answers of the examination usually see the coherence which comes to light, whereas the patient will remain completely unaware of it.

(2) The above method is not incontestable, therefore a second test for the correctness of our view of the symptom is necessary. Set aside the symptom and the actual reason for the treatment completely, and concern yourself only with the personality of the patient. Try to gain information about him, to explore his nature, his intentions in life, and his attitude toward the demands of his family and society. Soon you will achieve a fairly sharply outlined character-picture into which the various traits can be fitted. (3) Look for an assumption according to which the behavior of the patient becomes un-

derstandable. If you have made the correct assumption, you will find that the patient also uses it as his starting point, although he does not comprehend its significance. (4) Ask the patient: What would you do if you were completely well? Most certainly he will name precisely that demand of society which we would expect him to avoid.

I try to note what activities, of a kind normally to be expected, are being excluded by the patient. As soon as I feel I have grasped his circumstances, I inquire whether the patient's thoughts, feelings, actions, and characteristics are all working in the same direction, towards the exclusion or at least the postponement of a present problem. The discussion invariably reveals an accented "if." "I would marry if . . ." "I would resume my work if . . ." "I would take my examination if . . ." and so on. The neurotic has always collected some more or less plausible reasons to justify his escape from the challenge of life, but he does not realize what he is doing.

(5) The correctness of the results is further checked if the guiding lines, which we have deduced from the essential nature of the patient, afford us an understanding of the symptom as necessary, somehow usable, and expedient.

Since the struggle to reach a position of vantage is the key to the whole personality, we shall meet it at every point of the individual's psychological life. To recognize this fact gives us two further great aids in our task of understanding an individual style of life. (6) We can begin wherever we choose: every expression will lead us in the same direction—towards the one motive, the one melody, around which the personality is built. (7) We are provided with a vast store of material. Every word, thought, feeling, or gesture contributes to our understanding. Any mistake we might make in considering one expression too hastily can be checked and corrected by a thousand other expressions. We cannot finally decide the meaning of one expression until we can see its part in the whole; but every expression is saying the same thing, every expression is urging us towards the solution. In a way we are like archaeologists who find fragments of earthenware, tools, the ruined walls of buildings, broken monuments, and leaves of papyrus; and from these fragments proceed to infer the life of a whole city which has perished. Only we are dealing not with something which has perished, but with the inter-organized aspects of a human being, a living personality which can continuously set before us new manifestations of its own meaning.

B. EXPLAINING THE PATIENT TO HIMSELF

1. THE PATIENT'S MISTAKE

The apperception-schema of the patient evaluates all impressions as if they were fundamental matters and dichotomizes them in a purposeful manner into above-below, victor-vanquished, masculine-feminine, nothing-everything, etc. It is due to such a schema that one finds traits in the neurotic similar to those found in the beginnings of culture, where necessity also forced people to such safeguards. This is why we call the neurotic schema primitive. It would be fantastic to suspect in such analogies anything more than mimicry, let alone a repetition of phylogenesis. This apperception-schema must always be traced and unmasked as being immature and untenable, but suited to the purpose of continued fighting.

At the same time there must be uncovered, step by step, the unattainable goal of superiority over all; the purposive concealment of this goal; the all-dominating, direction-giving power of the goal; the patient's lack of freedom and his hostility toward mankind, which are determined by the goal. Similarly we find the proof, as soon as sufficient material is at hand, that all neurotic character traits, the neurotic affects and symptoms, serve as a means to continue along the prescribed path and to make that path more secure.

So long as he does not understand this error, so long as he regards his fictional world as the right one, so long as he finds the real objective world unbearable for his vanity, he will remain a neurotic. If he can abandon his dream of a world, a dream which was born of his vanity and which justifies his vanity, then more and more will it be possible for him to begin to feel himself an equal among equals, and less and less will he feel dependent upon the opinions of others. His courage, too, will mount and his reason and "common sense" will increase and gain control where heretofore he has been under the sway of his "private sense."

In a somnambulistic sort of way the neurotic person is so much involved in the world he has created during his early childhood that he needs the help provided by discussions under objective Individual Psychological direction to enable him to understand himself sufficiently so that he can increase his ability to cooperate. The cure or reorientation is brought about by a correction of the faulty picture of the world and the unequivocal acceptance of a mature picture of the world.

2. HELPING INSIGHT

The uncovering of the neurotic system, or life-plan (or style of life) for the patient, is the most important component in therapy. The reason for this is that the life-plan in its entirety can be kept intact only if the patient succeeds in withdrawing it from his own criticism and understanding. The uncovering of the neurotic life-plan proceeds apace in friendly and free conversation, in which it is always indicated that the patient take the initiative. I have found it best merely to search for the patient's neurotic line of operation in all his expressions and thoughts and to unmask it, and at the same time train the patient unobtrusively to do the same.

The physician must be so convinced of the uniqueness and exclusiveness of the neurotic direction line, that he is able to foretell the patient's disturbing devices and constructions, always to find and explain them, until the patient, completely upset, gives them up—only to put new and better hidden ones in their place. How often this will occur is impossible to say beforehand. But ultimately the patient will give in. He will do so the more readily, the less his relation to the physician has permitted the feeling of a defeat to develop. Just as the neurotic devices lie along the path to the feeling of some superiority, so there are also definite subjective sources of error which are utilized and conserved for the very reason that somehow they deepen the feeling of inferiority and thus furnish stimuli and incentive for further precautions. Such errors together with their purpose must be brought within the vision of the patient.

Among my patients, children and adults, I have never yet found one to whom it would not have been possible to explain his erroneous mechanism. To be sure, my patients are almost always intelligent.

3. EXPLAINING

I always use the simplest and most direct method possible in the treatment of neurotics, but it would be of no use to tell a patient, for example, "You are a domineering woman, and you are now trying to rule by means of illness," for she would be offended. I must win her first, and take her part as far as possible. Every neurotic is partly right. In this particular case, if the woman did not feel deprived of value by her advancing age—a real privation of women in our present culture—she would not cling to her prestige in such unseemly ways. But it is only very gradually that I can bring her to face the truth about what she is doing.

In cases of alcoholism and drug addiction [to give another example], it would be useless merely to take away the poison and say some encouraging words. The patient must realize why he took to drink. But insufficient also would be his recognition of the general principles of Individual Psychology, that those who turn inebriate have lost social courage and interest, or succumbed to fear of an imminent defeat. It is easy for the physician to say, and even for the patient to believe, that he turned to drink because of a sense of inferiority which originated in childhood, yet nothing will come out of the mere phraseology. The physician must grasp the special structure and development of that individual life with such accuracy, and express it with such lucidity, that the patient knows he is plainly understood and recognizes his own mistake.

When patients or practitioners come to me and say: "We have explained everything," or "We quite understand, and yet we cannot succeed," I consider their statements ridiculous. Always if I go into such a case of unsuccessful treatment I find that neither physician nor patient has understood the matter nor explained anything. Sometimes the patient has felt inferior and suppressed by the physician, and resisted all true explanation. Occasionally the tables have been turned and the patient has been treating the doctor! Not infrequently an inexperienced practitioner teaches the patient the theories of Individual Psychology in such phrases as "You lack social courage, you are not interested in others, you feel inferior," and so forth, which may be worse than useless. A real explanation must be so clear that the patient knows and feels his own experience instantly.

Nobody who has understood anything of Individual Psychology would attempt to cure by upbraiding the patient, as if we could do good by taking up a moralistic attitude. A patient has to be brought into such a state of feeling that he likes to listen, and wants to understand. Only then can he be influenced to live what he has understood.

That the patient is under no circumstances to be offended, I need not tell psychologically trained physicians. But this may occur without the knowledge of the physician, as when the patient may purposely revaluate harmless remarks which the physician may make as long as he does not clearly understand the nature of the patient. Therefore, particularly at the beginning, reserve is called for, and it is essential to grasp as quickly as possible the neurotic system. With some experience this may usually be discovered on the first day.

4. THE ACTUAL CURE

The actual change in the nature of the patient can only be his own doing. I have found it most profitable to sit ostentatiously with my hands in my lap, fully convinced that no matter what I might be able to say on the point, the patient can learn nothing from me that he, as the sufferer, does not understand better, once he has recognized his life-line.

From the very beginning the consultant must try to make it clear that the responsibility for his cure is the patient's business, for as the English proverb very rightly says: "You can lead a horse to water, but you can't make him drink." One should always look at the treatment and the cure not as the success of the consultant but as the success of the patient. The adviser can only point out the mistakes, it is the patient who must make the truth living.

[The alleviation of symptoms, as against a complete cure, is also the patient's own doing.] In a considerable portion of neurotics, the turning to a physician, sometimes even to another person, is of itself enough to drive the patient on further. In approximately half of the neurotics, the call on the physician signifies their decision to get better, that is, to give up a symptom which has become superfluous or [too] disturbing. It is this 50 per cent of "cures" that enables all schools of psychiatry to continue to live.

C. THE THERAPEUTIC RELATIONSHIP

1. DEPRECIATION TENDENCY AND RESISTANCE

I expect from the patient again and again the same attitude which he has shown in accordance with his life-plan towards the persons of his former environment, and still earlier towards his family. At the moment of the introduction to the physician and often even earlier, the patient has the same feelings towards him as toward important persons in general. The assumption that the transference of such feelings or that resistance begins later is a mere deception. In such cases the physician only recognizes them later. Often it is then too late, if the patient in the meantime has terminated the treatment while enjoying his hidden superiority, or has created an unbearable situation by a worsening of his symptoms.

It is the depreciation tendency which underlies the phenomenon Freud describes as resistance and erroneously understood as the consequence of the repression of sexual impulses. The neurotic comes to the physician with this tendency, and he carries it away with him after the treatment, but considerably diminished, more like that of the normal person. The increased insight into himself then stands like a guardian over the patient and forces him to find more useful paths for his desire to be above, and to dampen his depreciation tendency.

The following must be understood as forms of the depreciation tendency, which may at times be directed against the psychotherapist: expressions of doubt, criticism, forgetfulness, tardinesses, any special requests by the patient, relapses after initial improvement, persistent silence, as well as stubborn retention of symptoms. These are often most subtle expressions. The therapist must have broad experience with and knowledge of the depreciation tendency not to be taken by surprise.

Since the physician obstructs the neurotic strivings of the patient, the physician is regarded as an obstacle, an obstruc-

tion, preventing the attainment of the superiority-ideal along
the path of the neurosis. Therefore every patient will attempt
to depreciate the physician, to deprive him of his influence,
and to conceal from him the true state of affairs; the patient
will always find new twists aimed at the psychotherapist. Especially as improvement progresses, will the patient attempt
more energetically to jeopardize the success of the treatment
by being unpunctual, wasting time, or staying away. When
there is a standstill, there is usually hearty friendship and
peace—except that the neurotic symptoms continue. At times
a specially marked hostility arises which, like all the phenomena of resistance, can be neutralized only if the patient's attention is drawn again and again to the essential similarity of
all of his behavior.

A patient who had been under treatment for two months
came to me one day and asked whether she could not come
the next time at four o'clock instead of three. No matter how
insistently patients in such cases plead the necessity of their
requests, we are justified in assuming that this is an indication
of intensified aggressiveness directed against the physician.
The patient claimed that she would have to go to the dress-
maker at three o'clock, a rather weak reason which was only
slightly strengthened by the fact that owing to the length of
the treatment, her free time was somewhat restricted. As I
was not free at the hour she requested, I tentatively suggested
five to six. This the patient rejected because her mother
would be free at five and expected her at a friend's house. So
we see that we are justified in assuming that the patient is
showing resistance to the treatment.

The so-called *resistance* is only lack of courage to return to
the useful side of life. This causes the patient to put up a defense against treatment, for fear that his relation with the
psychologist should force him into some useful activity in
which he will be defeated. For this reason we must never
force a patient, but guide him very gently towards his easiest
approach to usefulness. If we apply force he is certain to escape.

2. DISARMING THE PATIENT

It is very necessary to keep from the patient any point
from which he could attack. I can only give a few hints here
designed to prevent the physician from falling into the position of being treated by the patient. For example, one should
never, not even in the most certain cases, promise a cure, but

rather only the possibility of a cure. One of the most important devices in psychotherapy is to ascribe the work and the success of the therapy to the patient at whose disposal one should place onself in a friendly way, as a coworker.

For successful treatment it is absolutely necessary that the physician have a great deal of tact, renounce superior authority, be equally friendly at all times, be alertly interested, and have the cool-headed feeling that he is facing a sick person with whom he must not fight, but who is always ready to start a fight.

"To knock the weapons out of his hand," that is, to have the abnormal means of the neurotic appear ineffectual is the goal of every psychotherapeutic tactic. A patient once asked me, smiling, "Has anyone ever taken his life while being treated by you?" I answered him, "Not yet, but I am prepared for this to happen at any time."

A girl of twenty-seven who came to consult me after five years of suffering said: "I have seen so many doctors that you are my last hope in life." "No," I answered, "not the last hope. Perhaps the last but one. There may be others who can help you too." Her words were a challenge to me; she was daring me not to cure her, so as to make me feel bound in duty to do so. This is the type of patient who wishes to shift responsibility upon others, a common development of pampered children. It is important to evade such a challenge. The patient may have worked up a high tension of feeling about the idea that the doctor is his "last hope," but we must accept no such distinction. To do so would be to prepare the way for a disappointment, or even suicide.

To predict the possibility of an aggravation of the disease in cases of fainting spells, pains, or agoraphobia, saves a great amount of work at the beginning, because the attacks, as a rule, then do not take place. This fact corroborates our view about the marked negativism of neurotics. To show pleasure at a partial success or to boast about it would be a great mistake; the situation would soon take a turn for the worse. It is therefore better to turn one's manifest interest to the difficulties patiently, without annoyance, and in a calm scientific manner.

A basic principle for the therapist is never to allow the patient to force upon him a superior role such as that of teacher, father, or saviour, without contradicting and enlightening the patient. Such attempts represent the beginning of a movement on the part of the patient to pull down, in a manner to which he has been previously accustomed, all persons standing above him, and by thus administering a defeat, to disavow them. To insist upon any superior rank or right is always disadvantageous with neurotic patients.

Special caution is called for in persuading the patient to any kind of venture. If this should come up, the consultant should say nothing for or against it, but, ruling out as a matter of course all generally dangerous undertakings, should only state that, while convinced of the success, he could not quite judge whether the patient was really ready for the venture. Spurring the patient on before he has acquired a greater social interest will usually have to be atoned for by a strengthening or a recurrence of the symptoms.

My own practice, also, is never to advise marriage or free relations. I find that it always leads to bad results. A patient who is told that he should marry or seek sexual experience is quite likely to develop impotence.

In the question of occupation, we can proceed more energetically. This does not mean requesting the patient to take up an occupation, but pointing out to him that he is best prepared for one or another occupation and could accomplish something in it.

The patient may bring complaints about his family. These must be anticipated in order to make it plain to him beforehand that his relations are to blame only so long as he makes them blameworthy by his conduct, and that they will immediately be blameless as soon as he feels himself well; further, that one cannot expect more knowledge from the patient's relatives than he himself possesses; and that he has on his own responsibility used the influences of his environment as building bricks for constructing his mistaken style of life. It is also well to remind him that his parents, in the event of their being at fault, can appeal to the mistakes of their parents, and so on through the generations, so that for this reason there can be no blame in his sense of the word.

On the other hand, I always find the hostile relationship of the patient's relatives to the physician of advantage and sometimes have attempted to stir it up carefully. Since generally the tradition of the patient's entire family is similarly neurotic, one can greatly benefit the patient by disclosing and explaining this.

3. AWAKENING SOCIAL INTEREST

Psychotherapy is an exercise in cooperation and a test of cooperation. We can succeed only if we are genuinely interested in the other. We must be able to see with his eyes and listen with his ears. He must contribute his part to our common understanding. We must work out his attitudes and his difficulties together. Even if we felt we had understood him, we should have no witness that we were right unless he also understood. A tactless truth can never be the whole truth; it shows that our understanding was not sufficient. We must cooperate with him in finding his mistakes, both for his own benefit and for the welfare of others.

All cases of failure which we have seen involve a lack of cooperation. Therefore cooperation between patient and consultant, as the first, serious scientifically conducted attempt to raise social interest, is of paramount importance, and from the start all measures should be taken to promote the cooperation of the patient with the consultant. Obviously this is only possible if the patient feels secure with the physician.

The task of the physician or psychologist is to give the patient the experience of contact with a fellow man, and then to enable him to transfer this awakened social interest to others. This method of winning the patient's good will, and then transferring it to his environment, is strictly analogous to the function of the mother, whose social task it is to interpret society to the individual. If the mother fails in this task, the task is likely to fall much later to the physician, who is heavily handicapped for it. The mother has the enormous advantage of the physical and psychological relation; she represents the greatest experience of love and fellowship that the child will ever have.

For the psychologist the first rule is to win the patient; the second is never to worry about his own success; if he does so, he forfeits it. The psychotherapist must lose all thought of himself and all sensitiveness about his ascendancy, and must never demand anything of the patient. Since his is a belated assumption of the maternal function, he must work with a corresponding devotion to the patient's needs. The patient's social interest, which is always present in some degree, finds its best possible expression in the relation with the psychologist.

The consultee must under all circumstances get the conviction that in relation to the treatment he is absolutely free. He can do or not do, as he pleases.

4. ENCOURAGEMENT

On one occasion I was actually menaced by a weakly man who suffered from dementia praecox and who was completely cured by me after having been declared incurable three years earlier. I knew that he expected to be given up and rejected by me also; this was in accordance with the notion of his fate which he had held since childhood. For three months he remained silent during the treatment. I used this time to give him cautious explanations of his life insofar as I knew about it. I recognized his silence and similar actions as an inclination to obstruct me. Finally as a culmination of his tactics he lifted his hand to strike me, against which I instantly resolved not to defend myself. After a further attack during which a window was smashed, I bound up his slightly bleeding wound in the friendliest way. (I know that my friends will not generalize from this case any more than from any other!) Later, when I was completely assured of the success of the treatment, I asked him: "How in your opinion did we both succeed in making you well?" His answer ought to make a very strong impression in interested circles. He replied: "That's quite simple. I had lost all courage to live. In our consultations I found it again." If one has recognized the Individual Psychology truth that courage is but one side of social interest, one will understand the transformation of this man.

In Individual Psychology treatment we have appreciable help [for building up courage] in that we are always able to draw attention to errors only and never to innate defects, to the possibilities of a cure and to equality with others, and also to the generally low level of social interest.

Altogether, in every step of the treatment, we must not deviate from the path of encouragement. This is in accordance with the conviction of Individual Psychology, by which so much untenable vanity feels offended, that "everybody can do everything" with the exception of amazingly high achievement, about the structure of which we cannot say very much anyway. . . .

Anna Freud

Anna Freud, Sigmund Freud's daughter, has for many years been associated with the Tavistock Institute in London. Anna, true to her father's tradition, is very much in the mainstream of psychoanalysis. Two of her original contributions to the field have been in clarifying the dynamics of defense mechanisms, and in the tailoring of psychoanalysis for children.

In this selection, one of a series of lectures she gave in the 1940s on analysis with children, Anna Freud clarifies some of the key similarities and differences between analytic method with adults and with children. She also focuses on differences of technique she has with another major progenitor of child therapy, Melanie Klein.

Klein pioneered in using play as therapy. For Klein, having children play during therapy offered a valuable opportunity for observing the child's reality through the symbolic meanings of his playing. Klein, however, went further than Anna Freud thought appropriate in reading symbolic meanings into every bit of play activity. If, for example, a child opened the purse of a lady visitor, Klein might interpret that as symbolically expressing curiosity about whether his mother is pregnant. Freud, on the other hand, would read less weighty meanings into it: perhaps, she suggests, there are more innocent causes, such as someone having brought a treat in a purse the previous day.

The style of child therapy Anna Freud developed does use play, as well as drawings and dream recall, in retooling the basics of psychoanalysis with adults for use with children. While she does caution against overinterpretation, she agrees with Klein that what the child does during play often has a deeper significance. "We certainly feel justified," she writes, "in drawing into the analysis all the patient's behaviour towards us during the visit, and all the little voluntary and involuntary actions which we observe him to perform. In this we are relying upon the state of transference in which he finds himself, which can invest even otherwise trivial behaviour with symbolical significance."

But the type of transference that a child in therapy develops, contends Anna Freud, is fundamentally different from that of an adult patient. At the outset, she says, the therapist should take pains to establish a strong, affectionate relationship with the child. Only then will the child make progress in therapy: "The really fruitful work always takes place with a positive attachment." But when the therapist later coaxes the child to face unpleasant repressed material, the therapist will become the object of the child's "hatred and repulsion"—so-called "negative transference."

But while these positive and negative feelings from the child seem to resemble the workings of transference in adults, this is not the case, says Freud. With an adult, transference allows the reenactment with the therapist of childhood conflicts. This cannot occur with children, she points out, because the child is still in the midst of living through those childhood situations that in later life are the stuff of analysis. The therapist does not serve as a screen for the patient's conflicts from childhood—as happens with adults in analysis—but rather as a sort of stand-in parent, providing the experiences that will serve as a therapeutic corrective before the conflicts of childhood can grow into the neurosis of an adult.

THE RÔLE OF TRANSFERENCE IN THE ANALYSIS OF CHILDREN

by Anna Freud

Ladies and Gentlemen. I will go briefly over the ground covered at our last meeting.

We directed attention to the methods of the analysis of children; we remarked that we have to put the case-history together from information furnished by the family, instead of relying exclusively upon that given by the patient; we became familiar with the child as a good dream-interpreter, and evaluated the significance of day dreams and imaginative drawings as technical auxiliaries. On the other hand I had to report that children are not inclined to enter into free association, and by this refusal oblige us to look for some substitute for this most essential of aids in the analysis of adults. We concluded with a description of one of these substitute methods, postponing its theoretical evaluation until to-day.

The play technique worked out by Mrs. Melanie Klein is certainly valuable for observing the child. Instead of taking the time and trouble to pursue it into its domestic environment we establish at one stroke the whole of its known world in the analyst's room, and let it move about in it under the analyst's eye but at first without his interference. In this way we have the opportunity of getting to know the child's various reactions, the strength of its aggressive impulses or of its sympathies, as well as its attitude to the various things and persons represented by the toys. There is this advantage over the observation of real conditions, that the toy environment is manageable and amenable to the child's will, so that it can carry out in it all the actions which in the real world, so much bigger and stronger than itself, remain confined to a phantasy-existence. All these merits make the use of the Klein play-method almost indispensable for familiarisation with small children, who are not yet capable of verbal self-expression.

Mrs. Klein however takes an important further step in the employment of this technique. She assumes the same status for these play-actions of the child as for the free associations of the adult patient, and translates as she goes along the actions undertaken by the child in this way into corresponding thoughts; that is to say, she tries to find beneath everything done in play its underlying symbolic function. If the child overturns a lamp-post or a toy figure she interprets it as something of an aggressive impulse against the father; a deliberate collision between two cars as evidence of an observation of sexual union between the parents. Her procedure consists in accompanying the child's activities with translations and interpretations, which themselves—like the interpretation of the adult's free associations—exert a further influence upon the patient.

Let us examine the justification for equating the child's play activity with the adult's free association. The adult's ideas are "free," that is to say the patient has divested his thoughts of all direction and influence, but his attitude is nevertheless influenced by a certain consideration—that he who is associating has set himself to be analysed. The child lacks this attitude. I think it is possible, as I have explained before, to give the children some idea of the purpose of analysis. But the children for whom Mrs. Klein has worked out her play-technique, in the first infantile period, are too young to be influenced in this way. Mrs. Klein considers it as one of the important advantages of her method that by it she is saved the necessity of such a preparation of the child. But if the child's play is not dominated by the same purposive attitude as the adult's free association, there is no justification for treating it as having the same significance. Instead of being invested with symbolic meaning it may sometimes admit of a harmless explanation. The child who upsets a toy lamp-post may on its walk the day before have come across some incident in connection with such an object; the car collision may be reproducing some happening in the street; and the child who runs towards a lady visitor and opens her handbag is not necessarily, as Mrs. Klein maintains, thereby symbolically expressing its curiosity as to whether its mother's womb conceals another little brother or sister, but may be connecting some experience of the previous day when someone brought it a little present in a similar receptacle. Indeed with an adult we do not consider ourselves justified in ascribing a symbolic significance to every one of his acts or ideas, but only to those which arise under the influence of the analytical situation which he has accepted.

In reply to this objection to the Klein technique it may be said that a child's play is certainly open to the harmless interpretation just suggested, but why does it reproduce just those particular scenes with the lamp-post or the cars? It is not just the symbolic significance behind these observations which cause them to be preferred and reproduced before any others in the analytical hour? It is true, the argument may proceed, that the child lacks in its actions the purposive attitude of the analytical situation, which guides the adult. But perhaps it does not need it at all. The adult must renounce the guidance of his thoughts by a conscious effort of will and leave their direction entirely to his unconscious impulses. But the child may require no such deliberate modification of its situation. Perhaps it is at all times and in every piece of play entirely surrendered to the domination of its unconscious.

It is not easy to determine by an exchange of theoretical arguments the question of whether the equation of children's play with adults' free association is justifiable or not. This is obviously a matter for review in the light of practical experience.

Let us try criticism on another point. We know that Mrs. Klein utilises for interpretation, besides the things which the child does with the toys provided, all its procedure towards the objects found in her room or towards her own person. Here again she follows strictly the example of adult analysis. We certainly feel justified in drawing into the analysis all the patient's behaviour towards us during the visit, and all the little voluntary and involuntary actions which we observe him to perform. In this we are relying upon the state of transference in which he finds himself, which can invest even otherwise trivial behaviour with symbolical significance.

Here the question arises as to whether a child finds itself in the same transference situation as the adult; in what manner and in what forms its transference-impulses come to expression; and in what they lend themselves to interpretation. We have come to the important consideration, of *the rôle of transference as a technical expedient in the analysis of children*. The decision on this question will at the same time furnish fresh material to controvert or support Mrs. Klein's contention.

I explained in the first lecture how I took great pains to establish in the child a strong attachment to myself, and to bring it into a relationship of real dependence on me. I would not have tried so hard to do this, if I had thought the analysis of children could be carried out without a transference of this kind. But the affectionate attachment, the positive transference as it is called in analytical terminology, is the prerequisite for all later work. The child in fact will only believe the loved person, and it will only accomplish something to please that person.

The analysis of children requires much more from this attachment than in the case of adults. There is an educational as well as an analytical purpose with which we shall later be concerned in more detail: Successful upbringing always—not only in children's analysis—stands or falls with the pupil's attachment to the person in charge of it. And we cannot say in regard to the analysis of children that the establishment of a transference is in itself enough for our purpose, regardless of whether it is friendly or hostile. We know that with an adult we can get through long periods with a negative transference, which we turn to our account through consistent interpretation and reference to its origins. But with a child negative impulses towards the analyst—however revealing they may be in many respects—are essentially inconvenient, and should be dealt with as soon as possible. The really fruitful work always takes place with a positive attachment.

I have described the establishment of this affectionate tie during our discussion of the introductory phase to the analysis of children. Its expression in fantasies and small or larger actions is hardly distinguishable from the equivalent processes in adult patients. We are made to feel the negative reactions at every point where we attempt to assist a fragment of repressed material towards liberation from the unconscious, thereby drawing upon ourselves the resistance of the ego. At such a time we appear to the child as the dangerous and to-be-feared tempter, and we bring on ourselves all the expressions of hatred and repulsion with which at other times it treats its own forbidden instinctual impulses.

I will give an account of a positive transference-fantasy from the six-year-old obsessional patient. The external occasion for it was furnished by myself, for I had visited her in her own home and stayed for her evening bath. She opened her visit on the next day with the words, "You visited me in my bath and next time I'll come and visit you in yours." Some while later she retailed for me the daydream which she had composed in bed before going to sleep, after I had gone away. I add her own explanatory asides in brackets.

"All the rich people did not like you. And your father who was very rich did not like you at all. (That means I am angry with your father, don't you think?) And you liked no one and gave lessons to no one. And my father and mother hated me and so did John and Billy and Mary and all the people in the world hated us, even the people we did not know, even the dead people. So you liked only me and I liked only you and we always stayed together. All the others were very rich but we two were quite poor. We had nothing, not even clothes, for they took away everything we had. There was only the sofa left in the room and we slept on that together. But we were quite happy together. And then we thought we ought to have a baby. So we mixed a-a and cissies to make a baby. But then we thought that was not a nice thing to make a baby out of. So we began to mix flower-petals and things that gave me a baby. For the baby was in me. It stayed in me quite a long while (my mother told me that, that babies stay quite a long while in their mothers) and then the doctor took it out. But I was not a bit sick (mothers usually are, my mother said). The baby was very sweet and cunning and so we thought we'd like to be just as cunning and changed ourselves to be very small. I was 'so' high and you were 'so' high. (That is, I think because in our lessons last week we found out that I wanted to be like Billy and Mary.) And as we had nothing at all we started to make ourselves a house out of rose-leaves, and beds out of rose-leaves and pillows and mattresses all out of rose-leaves sewn together. Where the little holes were left we put something white in. Instead of wallpaper we had the thinnest glass and the walls were carved in different patterns. The chairs were made of glass too but we were so light that we were not too heavy for them. (I think I left my mother out because I was angry with her for not coming to see me.)" Then there followed a detailed description of the furniture and all the things that were made for the house. The daydream was obviously spun out in this direction until she went to sleep, laying special emphasis on the point that our initial poverty was finally quite made up for and that in the end we had much nicer things than all the first mentioned rich people.

The same little patient at other times related how she was warned against me from within. The inner voice said, "Don't believe Anna Freud. She tells lies. She will not help you and will only make you worse. She will change your face too, so that you look uglier. Everything she says is not true. Just be tired, stay quietly in bed and don't go to her to-day." But she always told this voice to be silent and said to it that it should be told of first of all in the next appointment.

Another small patient envisaged me, at the time when we were discussing her masturbation, in all sorts of degrading rôles—as a beggar, as a poor old woman, and once as just myself but standing in the middle of my room with devils dancing round me.

You will notice that we become the object towards which the patient's friendly or hostile impulses are directed, just as we do in the case of adults. It might seem from these examples that a child makes a good transference. Unfortunately that is not really true. The child indeed enters into the liveliest relations with the analyst, and evinces a multitude of reactions which it has acquired in the relationship with its parents; it gives us most important hints on the formation of its character in the fluctuation, intensity, and expression of its feelings; but it forms no transference neurosis.

The analysts amongst you will know what I mean by this.

The adult neurotic gradually transforms, in the course of analytic treatment, the symptom on account of which he sought this remedy. He gives up the old objects on which his fantasies were hitherto fixed, and centres his neurosis anew upon the person of the analyst. As we put it, he substitutes transference-symptom for his previous symptoms, transposes his existing neurosis, of whatever kind, into a transference-neurosis, and displays all his abnormal reactions in relation to the new transference person, the analyst. On this new ground, where the analyst feels at home, he can follow up with the patient the origin and growth of the individual symptoms; and on this cleared field of operations there then takes place the final struggle, for gradual insight into the malady and the discovery to the patient of the unconscious processes within him.

There are two possible reasons why this cannot be brought about in the case of a small child. One lies within the psychological structure of the child itself, the other in the child's analyst.

The child is not, like the adult, ready to produce a new edition of its love-relationships, because, as one might say, the old edition is not yet exhausted. Its original objects, the parents, are still real and present as love-objects—not only in fantasy as with the adult neurotic; between them and the child exist all the relations of everyday life, and all its gratifications and disappointments still in reality depend on them. The analyst enters this situation as a new person, and will probably share with the parents the child's love or hate. But there is no necessity for the child to exchange the parents for him, since compared to them he has not the advantages which the adult finds when he can exchange his fantasy-objects for a real person. Let us in this connection reconsider Mrs. Klein's method. She maintains that when a child evinces hostility towards her in the first visit, repulsing or even beginning to strike her, one may see in that a proof of the child's ambivalent attitude towards its mother. The hostile components of this ambivalence are merely displaced onto the analyst. But I believe the truth of the matter is different. The more tenderly a little child is attached to its own mother, the fewer friendly impulses it has towards strangers. We see this most clearly with the baby, who shows only anxious rejection towards everyone other than its mother or nurse. Indeed the converse obtains. It is especially with children who are accustomed to little loving treatment at home, and are not used to showing or receiving any strong affection, that a positive relationship is often most quickly established. They obtain from the analyst what they have up till now expected in vain from the original love objects.

On the other hand, the behaviour of the children's analyst, as we have described him, is not such as to produce a transference that can be well interpreted. We know how we bear ourselves in the analysis of adults for this purpose. We remain impersonal and shadowy, a blank page on which the patient can inscribe his transference-fantasies, somewhat after the way in which at the cinema a picture is thrown upon an empty screen. We avoid either issuing prohibitions, or allowing gratifications. If in spite of this we seem to the patient forbidding or encouraging, it is easy to make it clear to him that he has brought the material for this impression from his own past.

But the children's analyst must be anything but a shadow. We have already remarked that he is a person of interest to the child, endowed with all sorts of interesting and attractive qualities. The educational implications which, as you will hear, are involved in the analysis, result in the child knowing very well just what seems to the analyst desirable or undesirable, and what he sanctions or disapproves of. And such a well-defined and in many respects novel personality is unfortunately a bad transference-object, of little use when it comes to interpreting the transference. The difficulty here is, as though, to use our former illustration, the screen on which a film was to be projected already bore another picture. The more elaborate and brightly-colored it is, the more will it tend to efface the outlines of what is superimposed.

For these reasons the child forms no transference neurosis. In spite of all its positive and negative impulses towards the analyst it continues to display its abnormal reactions where they were displayed before—in the home circle. Because of this the children's analyst is obliged to take into account not only what happens under his own eye but also what occurs in the real scene of the neurotic reactions, i.e. the child's home. Here we come to an infinity of practical technical difficulties in the analysis of children, which I only lay broadly before you without going into actual detail. Working from this standpoint we are dependent upon a permanent news-service about the child; we must know the people in its environment and be sure to some extent of what their reactions to the child are. In the ideal case, we share our work with the persons who are actually bringing up the child, just as we share with them the child's affection or hostility.

Where the external conditions, or the personalities of the parents, do not allow of such co-operative treatment, certain material for the analysis eludes us. On this account I had to conduct some analyses of children almost exclusively by means of dreams and day dreams. There was nothing interpretable in the transference and much of the day-to-day symptomatic neurotic material never became available to me.

But there are ways and means to bring about an equation of the child's situation to that of the adult (so much better suited for the carrying through of analysis); and so to force the child into a transference neurosis. This may become necessary where it is a case of severe neurotic illness in an environment hostile either to analysis or the child. In such a case the child would have to be removed from its family and placed in some suitable institution. As there is no such institution in existence at present we are at full liberty to imagine one, say a home supervised by the children's analyst himself, or—less far-fetched—a school where psycho-analytical principles predominate and the work is attuned to co-operation with the analyst. In both cases a symptom-free period would first occur, in which the child accustoms itself to the new and favourable surroundings. The better it feels at this time, the more unapt and unwilling for analysis shall we find it. We shall probably do best to leave it quite undisturbed. Only when it has "acclimatised itself", that is to say when under the influence of the realities of everyday life it has formed an attachment to the new environment, beside which the original objects gradually pale; when it allows its symptoms to revive again in this new existence, and groups its abnormal reactions around new personages; when it has thus formed its transference-neurosis—will it become analysable once more.

In an institution of the first sort, managed by the children's analyst (and at present we cannot even judge whether such an arrangement is to be desired) it would then be a matter of an actual transference-neurosis in the sense of the adult's, with the analyst as focal object. In the other sort we should simply have artificially bettered the home environment, creating a substitute home which so to say allows us to see into it, as seems necessary for the analytical work, and the reactions of which towards the child we can control and regulate.

Thus the removal of the child from its home might appear

to be the most practical solution. But when we come to consider the termination of a child's analysis, we shall see how many objections there are to it. By this expedient we forestall the natural development at a crucial stage, forcing the child's premature detachment from the parental objects at a time when it neither is capable of any independence in its emotional life, nor has at its disposal, owing to external circumstances, any freedom in the choice of new love-objects. Even if we insist on a very long duration for the analysis of children there still remains in most cases a hiatus between its termination and the development of puberty, during which the child needs education, protection, and guidance in every sense of the words. But what gives us any assurance that after we have secured a successful resolution of the transference the child will find of itself the way to the right objects? It returns home at a time when it has become a stranger there, and its further guidance is now perhaps entrusted to the very persons from whom we have forcibly detached it. On inner grounds it is not capable of self-reliance. We are thus placing it in a position of renewed difficulty, in which it will find again most of the original elements of its conflict. It can now take either once more the path to neurosis or, if this is closed to it by the successful outcome of the analytical treatment, the opposite line of open rebellion. From the purely therapeutical point of view this may seem an advantage; but from that of social adjustment which in the child's case matters most in the end, it is certainly none.

Wilhelm Reich

Wilhelm Reich (1897–1957) became part of the Vienna Psychoanalytic Society before graduating from medical school in Vienna and for several years played an important role within that group. Reich wholeheartedly accepted the primacy of the sex instinct and even extended Freud's views, most particularly in his attempt to rectify what he saw as Freud's neglect of social factors in human development. To Freud's main tenets about sex—that is, that it is controlled by unconscious forces, that it is present in children, that it is repressed by society—Reich added the concept of "orgastic potency," the ability for full and complete sexual gratification, and "orgastic impotence," the burdening of the character structure to avoid sexual gratification. Reich embraced Marxism, and placed among the causes of orgastic impotence the performance of boring, repetitive, and alienating work made necessary and perpetuated by the class structure.

In his attempt to synthesize the works of Freud and Marx, Reich managed to alienate almost everyone. He was expelled from the International Psychoanalytic Association in 1934, one year after he had been expelled from the Communist Party. He emigrated to Scandinavia, and later to the United States. In the 1940s his claims to have found the biological counterpart of psychic energy—and to be able to use it in the treatment of disease, including cancer, resulted in his imprisonment.

Reich argued that in every neurosis dammed-up sexual energy is expressed as anxiety, the major symptom in this kind of disturbance. The dammed-up sexual energy can have three outcomes, according to Reich: one outcome is the development of neurotic symptoms that are indicative of blocked energy; another is anxiety, as Freud originally postulated; the third is character disorder. On a sociological level, Reich extended this view to theorize that in societies where sexuality is repressed there is necessarily more destructive aggression.

One of Reich's major contributions to therapy was in highlighting the importance of interpersonal issues between the therapist and patient. He was one of the first analysts to take such issues seriously; the excerpt included here is a lecture he gave at the 10th International Psychoanalytic Congress in 1927. Reich acknowledged the utility of the psychoanalytic approach, but suggested that patients need to be prepared for analysis.

Reich urged beginning analysis by looking beyond the patient's presenting symptoms to his "character armor," which shows up not so much in what the patient says, but in how he says it and what he does. "Different characters," said Reich, "produce the same material in different ways." A person's character armor is his characteristic way of warding off anxiety. Since analysis threatens to upset the "neurotic balance" armor achieves, it will arouse a style of resistance typical of the type of armoring the person reveals. This "character resistance," Reich contended, must be dealt with at the outset, because it would otherwise be used to sabotage treatment. To this end Reich confronted the patient directly in order to uncover his particular forms of resistance. This was a radical procedure at a time when all psychoanalysis was conducted with therapist sitting out of the patient's line of vision, while the patient lay on a couch. Although this technique is commonly used today, it was an innovation in his day.

Although Reich ended his career in controversy, his views have had a lasting impact on therapy. Apart from his innovations in psychoanalytic practice, Reich was among the first to focus on the role of the body in psychological disorders. This emphasis was later popularized by therapists such as Fritz Perls and Alexander Lowen who developed methods in which talking was secondary to signals from the body. While Reich is today poorly regarded among psychoanalytic circles (except for his technique of character analysis), he has become a patron saint of body-based therapy.

THE TECHNIQUE OF CHARACTER ANALYSIS

by Wilhelm Reich

1. INTRODUCTION

Our therapeutic method is contingent upon the following basic theoretical concepts. The *topographical* point of view determines the principle of technique to the effect that the unconscious has to be made conscious. The *dynamic* point of view dictates that this making conscious of the unconscious must not proceed directly, but by way of resistance analysis. The *economic* point of view and the knowledge of *structure* dictate that, in resistance analysis, each individual case entails a definite plan which must be deduced from the case itself.

As long as the making conscious of the unconscious, i.e., the *topographical* process, was regarded as the sole task of analytic technique, the formula was justified that the patient's unconscious manifestations had to be translated into the language of the conscious *in the sequence in which they appeared*. In this process, the *dynamics* of the analysis were left largely to chance, that is, whether the act of becoming conscious actually released the germane affect and whether the interpretation had anything more than an intellectual influence on the patient. The very inclusion of the dynamic factor, i.e., the demand that the patient had not only to remember but also to experience what he remembered, complicated the simple formula that "the unconscious had to be made conscious." Since the dynamic effect of analysis depends not on the material which the patient produces but on the resistances which he brings into play against this material and on the emotional intensity with which they are mastered, the task of analysis undergoes no insignificant shift. Whereas it is sufficient, from the topographical point of view, to make the patient conscious of the clearest and most easily interpretable elements of the unconscious in the sequence in which they appear, in other words, *to adhere to the pattern of the contents of the material*, it is necessary, when the dynamic factor is taken into consideration, to relinquish this plan as a means of orientation in the analysis. Instead, another must be adopted, which embraces both the content of the material and the affect, namely *the pattern of successive resistances*. In pursuing this plan, however, a difficulty arises in most cases, a difficulty which we have not considered in the foregoing presentation.

2. CHARACTER ARMORING AND CHARACTER RESISTANCE

a) The inability to follow the basic rule

Our patients are seldom capable of analysis at the outset. Only a very small number of patients are prepared to follow the basic rule and to open themselves completely to the analyst. First of all, it is not easy for the patient to have immediate trust in the analyst, if only because he is a stranger. Added to this, however, is the fact that years of illness, the unrelenting influence of a neurotic milieu, bad experiences with mental specialists—in short, the entire secondary fragmentation of the ego—have created a situation that is adverse to the analysis. The elimination of this difficulty becomes a precondition of the analysis, and it could be accomplished easily if it were not complicated by the characteristic, indeed character of the patient, which is itself a part of the neurosis and has developed on a neurotic basis. It is known as the "narcissistic barrier." Fundamentally, there are two ways of getting at these difficulties, especially at the difficulty entailed by the resistance to the basic rule. The first way, and the one usually pursued, I believe, is to prepare the patient for analysis through instruction, reassurance, challenge, exhortation, persuasion, and more of the same. In this case, by establishing a kind of positive transference, the analyst seeks to convince the patient of the necessity of being open and honest in the analysis. This roughly corresponds to the technique suggested by Nunberg. Vast experience has taught us, however, that this pedagogic or active approach is highly uncertain, is dependent upon uncontrollable contingencies, and lacks the secure basis of analytic clarity. The analyst is constantly at the mercy of the oscillations of the transference and treads on uncertain terrain in his efforts to make the patient capable of analysis.

The second method is more complicated, and not yet feasible for all patients. It is a far more secure approach. Here the attempt is made *to replace the instructional measures by analytic interpretations*. There is no question that this is not always possible, yet it remains the ideal goal toward which analysis strives. Instead of inducing the patient to enter into the analysis by persuasion, suggestion, transference maneuvers, etc., the analyst takes a more passive attitude and attempts to get an insight into the *contemporary* meaning of the patient's behavior, *why* he or she doubts, arrives late, speaks in a ranting or confused manner, communicates only every third idea or so, criticizes the analysis, or produces deep material, often in uncommon amounts. In other words, the analyst can do one of two things: (1) attempt to persuade a narcissistic patient who speaks in grandiloquent technical terminology that his behavior is detrimental to the analysis and that he would do better to rid himself of analytic terminology and to come out of his shell; or (2) dispense with any kind of persuasion and wait until he understands why the patient behaves as he does. It may turn out, for instance, that the patient's ostentatious behavior is an attempt to cover up a feeling of inferiority toward the analyst. In this case, the analyst will endeavor to influence him through a consistent interpretation of the meaning of his actions. In contrast to the first, this second approach is entirely in keeping with the principles of analysis.

From this endeavor to use purely analytic interpretations wherever possible in place of all the instructional or otherwise active measures which become necessary as a result of the patient's characteristics, a method of analyzing the *character* emerged in an unsought and unexpected way.

Certain clinical considerations make it necessary for us to designate as *"character resistances"* a special group of the resistances that we encounter in the treatment of our patients. *These derive their special character not from their content but from the specific mannerisms of the person analyzed.* The compulsive character develops resistances whose form is specifically different from that of the hysterical character, the form of whose resistances, in turn, is different from that of the genital narcissistic, impulsive, or neurasthenic character. *The form of the ego's reactions,* which differs from character to character even where the contents of the experiences are the same, *can be traced back to infantile experiences in the same way as the content of the symptoms and fantasies.*

b) *Where do the character resistances come from?*

Some time ago, Glover made an effort to discriminate between character neuroses and symptom neuroses. Alexander also operated on the basis of this distinction. I adhered to it in earlier works, but it turned out, on closer comparison of the cases, that this distinction makes sense only insofar as there are neuroses with circumscribed symptoms ("symptom neuroses") and neuroses without them ("character neuroses"). In the former, understandably, the symptoms are more conspicuous; in the latter, the neurotic character traits stand out. But are there symptoms which do not have a neurotic reaction basis, which, in other words, are not rooted in a neurotic character? The only difference between character neuroses and symptom neuroses is that, in the case of the latter, the neurotic character also produces symptoms, has become, so to speak, concentrated in them. That the neurotic character is at one time exacerbated in circumscribed symptoms and at another time finds other ways of discharging the libido stasis requires more detailed investigation. But if it is acknowledged that the symptom neurosis is always rooted in a neurotic character, then it is clear that, in *every* analysis, we are dealing with resistances that are manifestations of a neurotic character. The individual analysis will differ only with respect to the importance ascribed to the analysis of the character in each case. However, a retrospective glance at analytic experiences cautions us against underestimating this importance in any one case.

From the point of view of character analysis, the differentiation between neuroses which are chronic, i.e., have existed since childhood, and those which are acute, i.e., appeared later, has no importance whatever; it is of no great moment whether the symptoms appear in childhood or later. What matters is that the neurotic character, i.e., the reaction basis for the symptom neurosis, is formed, at least in its principal features, by the time the Oedipal stage comes to a close. We have ample clinical experience to show that the boundary which the patient draws between health and the outbreak of sickness always vanishes in the analysis.

Since the symptom formation does not hold up as a descriptive characteristic, we have to look for others. Two which readily come to mind are *illness insight* and *rationalizations*.

A lack of insight into the illness is not, of course, absolutely reliable but it is certainly an essential indication of character neurosis. The neurotic symptom is sensed as something alien, and it engenders a feeling of being ill. On the other hand, the neurotic character trait, e.g., the exaggerated sense of order of the compulsive character or the anxious shyness of the hysterical character, is organically incorporated into the personality. One might complain of being shy, but one does not feel sick for that reason. Not until the characterological shyness becomes a pathological blushing or until the compulsive-neurotic sense of order becomes a compulsive ceremony, not until, in other words, the neurotic character exacerbates symptomatically, does one feel that one is sick.

Naturally, there are symptoms for which no insight, or insufficient insight, exists. They are regarded by patients as bad habits or something which has to be accepted (e.g., chronic constipation, mild ejaculatio praecox). Then there are some character traits which are sometimes felt to be pathological, e.g., irrational, violent fits of anger, gross negligence, a penchant for lying, drinking, splurging, and other such. Generally, however, an insight into the sickness is indicative to a neurotic symptom, whereas lack of insight points to a neurotic character trait.

In practical terms, the second important difference consists in the fact that symptoms never exhibit such complete and credible *rationalizations* as neurotic character traits. Neither hysterical vomiting nor abasia; neither compulsive counting nor compulsive thinking can be rationalized. There is no question about the senselessness of a sympton, whereas the neurotic character trait has a sufficiently rational motivation so as not to appear pathological or senseless.

Furthermore, there is a justification for neurotic character traits which is immediately rejected as absurd when it is applied to symptoms. We often hear it said: "That's simply the way I am." The implication here is that the person concerned was born that way; he simply cannot behave differently— that's his character. However, this does not tally with the facts, for the analysis of its development shows that the character has to become what it is, and not something else, for very specific reasons. Fundamentally, therefore, it is capable of analysis and of being changed, just like the symptom.

Occasionally, symptoms have become so ingrained in the personality that they are like character traits. An example is compulsive counting that is wholly absorbed within the framework of one's need to be orderly, or compulsive methodicalness that is fulfilled in the rigid subdivisions of each day. The latter is especially true of the compulsion to work. Such modes of behavior are held to be indicative more of eccentricity or excessiveness than of pathology. Hence, we see that the concept of illness is highly flexible, that there are many shades, ranging from the symptom as an isolated foreign body through the neurotic character trait and the "wicked habit" to rationally sound behavior. However, in view of the fact that these shades are not very much help to us, the differentiation between symptom and neurotic character trait recommends itself, even insofar as rationalizations are concerned, notwithstanding the artificiality of all divisions.

With this reservation, another differentiation occurs to us with respect to the structure of the symptom and of the character trait. In the process of analysis, it is shown that, in terms of its meaning and origin, the symptom has a very simple structure compared with that of the character trait. True enough, the symptom too is indeterminate; but the more deeply we penetrate into its reasons, the more we move away from the actual compass of the symptom and the more clearly we perceive its basis in the character. Hence, theoretically, the reaction basis in the character can be worked out from any symptom. The symptom is directly determined by a limited number of unconscious attitudes; hysterical vomiting, for example, is based on a repressed fellatio desire or an oral desire for a child. Each of them is expressed in the character, the former in a kind of childishness, the latter in a maternal attitude. But the hysterical character, which determines the hysterical symptom, is based on a multiplicity of—to a large extent antagonistic—strivings, and is usually expressed in a specific *attitude* or *mode of existence*. It is not nearly so easy to analyze the attitude as it is to analyze the symptom; fundamentally, however, the former, like the latter, can be traced back to and understood on the basis of drives and experiences. Whereas the symptom corresponds solely to one definite experience or one circumscribed desire, the character, i.e., the person's specific mode of existence, represents an expression of the person's entire past. So a symptom can emerge quite suddenly, while the development of each individual character trait requires many years. We must also bear in mind that the symptom could not have suddenly emerged unless a neurotic reaction basis already existed in the character.

In the analysis, the neurotic character traits as a whole prove to be a compact *defense mechanism* against our therapeutic efforts, and when we trace the origin of this character "armor" analytically, we see that it also has a definite economic function. Such armor serves on the one hand as a

defense against external stimuli; on the other hand it proves
to be a means of gaining mastery over the libido, which is
continuously pushing forward from the id, because libidinal
and sadistic energy is used up in the neurotic reaction forma-
tions, compensations, etc. Anxiety is continually being bound
in the processes which are at the bottom of the formation and
preservation of this armor in the same way that, according to
Freud's description, anxiety is bound in the compulsive symptoms. We shall have more to say about the economy of the
character formation.

Since, in its economic function as defensive armor, the
neurotic character trait has established a certain, albeit *neurotic balance,* analysis constitutes a danger to this balance. It
is from this narcissistic defense mechanism of the ego that
the resistances originate which give the analysis of the individual case its special features. If, however, a person's mode
of behavior represents the result of a total development which
is capable of analysis and resolution, then it must also be possible to deduce the technique of character analysis from that
behavior.

c) On the technique of analyzing the character resistance

In addition to the dreams, associations, slips, and other
communications of the patients, the *way in which* they
recount their dreams, commit slips, produce associations, and
make their communications, in short their bearing, deserves
special attention.* Adherence to the basic rule is something
rare, and many months of character-analytic work are required to instill in the patient a halfway sufficient measure of
candidness. The way the patient speaks, looks at and greets
the analyst, lies on the couch, the inflection of the voice, the
degree of conventional politeness which is maintained, etc.,
are valuable cues in assessing the secret resistances with
which the patient counters the basic rule. And once they have
been understood, they can be eliminated through interpretation. It is not only *what* the patient says but *how* he says it
that has to be interpreted. Analysts are often heard to complain that the analysis is not progressing, that the patient is
not producing any "material." By material, what is usually

---

*Footnote, 1945: The *form* of expression is *far more important* than
the ideational *content*. Today we use only the form of expression to arrive at the *decisively* important experiences of childhood. It is the form
of expression and not the ideational content that leads us to the biological reactions which lie at the basis of the psychic manifestations.

meant is merely the content of the associations and communications. But the nature of the patient's silence or sterile repetitions is also material which has to be used fully. There is scarcely a situation in which the patient does not produce *any* material, and we have to lay the blame upon ourselves if we can't make use of the patient's bearing as material.

There is of course nothing new in the statement that behavior and the form of the communications are of analytic importance. What we are concerned with here, however, is the fact that they give us access to the analysis of the character in a very definite and relatively complete way. Bad experiences in the analysis of some neurotic characters have taught us that, *at the outset* of such cases, the form of the communications is of greater importance than the content. We want merely to allude to the concealed resistances produced by the emotionally paralyzed, by the "good" men and women, the excessively polite and correct patients; by those patients, moreover, who always give evidence of a deceptive positive transference or, for that matter, by those who abuse a passionate and monotonous cry for love; those who conceive of analysis as a kind of game; the eternally "armored" who laugh in their sleeve at anything and everything. The list could be extended indefinitely. Hence, one has no illusions about the painstaking work which the innumerable individual problems of technique will entail.

To allow what is essential in character analysis to stand out more clearly in contrast to symptom analysis, and to give a better idea of our thesis in general, let us consider two pairs of cases. The first pair consists of two men being treated for ejaculatio praecox: one is a passive-feminine character, the other a phallic-aggressive character. Two women suffering from an eating disturbance constitute the second pair: one is a compulsive character, the other a hysteric.

Let us further assume that the ejaculatio praecox of the two male patients has the same unconscious meaning: fear of the (paternal) phallus assumed to be in the woman's vagina. On the basis of the castration anxiety which lies at the root of the symptom, both patients produce a negative father transference in the analysis. They hate the analyst (father) because they perceive in him the enemy who limits their pleasure, and each of them has the unconscious desire to dispose of him. While the phallic-sadistic character will ward off the danger of castration by means of vituperations, disparagements, and threats, the passive-feminine character will be-

come more and more confiding, more and more passively
devoted, and more and more accommodating. In both of
them the character has become a resistance: the former
wards off the danger aggressively; the latter gets out of its
way by compromising his standards, by deceptiveness and devotion.

Naturally, the character resistance of the passive-feminine
type is more dangerous, for he works with devious means. He
produces material in abundance, recalls infantile experiences,
appears to adapt himself beautifully—but at bottom he
glosses over a secret obstinacy and hate. As long as he keeps
this up, he will not have the courage to show his true nature.
If the analyst does not pay any attention to his manner and
merely enters into *what* the patient produces, then, according
to experience, no analytic effort or elucidation will change his
condition. It may even be that the patient will recall his
hatred of his father, but he will not *experience* it unless the
meaning of his deceptive behavior is consistently pointed out
to him in the transference, *before* a deep interpretation of the
father-hatred is begun.

In the case of the second pair, let us assume that an acute
positive transference has developed. In both women, the main
content of this positive transference is the same as that of the
symptom, namely an oral fellatio fantasy. However, the
transference resistance ensuing from this positive transference
will be wholly different in form. The woman suffering from
hysteria, for example, will be *apprehensively* silent and behave timidly; the woman having a compulsive neurosis will
be *obstinately* silent or behave in a cold, haughty way toward
the analyst. The transference resistance employs various
means in warding off the positive transference: in the one instance, aggression; in the other, anxiety. We would say that in
both cases the id conveyed the same wish, which the ego
warded off differently. And the form of this defense will always remain the same in both patients; the woman suffering
from hysteria will always defend herself in a way expressive
of anxiety while the woman suffering from a compulsive neurosis will always defend herself aggressively, no matter what
unconscious content is on the verge of breaking through. In
other words the *character resistance always remains the same
in the same patient and disappears only when the neurosis
has been uprooted.*

The character armor is the molded expression of *narcissistic* defenses chronically embedded in the psychic structure. In

addition to the known resistances which are mobilized against each new piece of unconscious material, there is a constant resistance factor which has its roots in the unconscious and pertains not to content but to *form*. Because of its origin in the character, we call this constant resistance factor "character resistance."

On the basis of the foregoing statements, let us summarize the most important features of character resistance.

Character resistance is expressed not in terms of content but formally, in the way one typically behaves, in the manner in which one speaks, walks, and gestures; and in one's characteristic habits (how one smiles or sneers, whether one speaks coherently or incoherently, *how* one is polite and *how* one is aggressive).

It is not what the patient says and does that is indicative of character resistance, but *how* he speaks and acts; not what he reveals in dreams, but *how* he censors, distorts, condenses, etc.

The character resistance remains the same in the same patient, regardless of content. Different characters produce the same material in a different way. The positive father transference of a woman suffering from hysteria is expressed and warded off differently than that of a woman suffering from a compulsive neurosis. Anxiety is the defense mechanism in the former; aggression in the latter.

The character resistance which is manifested in terms of form is just as capable of being resolved, with respect to its content, and of being traced back to infantile experiences and instinctual interests as the neurotic symptom is.*

In given situations, the patient's character becomes a resistance. In everyday life, in other words, the character plays a role similar to the one it plays as a resistance in the treatment: that of a psychic defense apparatus. Hence, we speak of the "character armoring" of the ego against the outer world and the id.

If we trace the formation of the character into early childhood, we find that, in its time, the character armor ensued for the same reasons and for the same purposes the character resistance serves in the contemporary analytic situation. The

---

*In light of this clinical experience, the element of form has been incorporated into the sphere of psychoanalysis, which, until now, has focused predominantly on content.

resistive projection of the character in the analysis mirrors its
infantile genesis. And those situations which seem to appear
by chance but actually are brought about by the character
resistance in the analysis are exact duplicates of those childhood situations which caused the formation of the character.
Thus, in the character resistance, the function of defense is
combined with the projection of infantile relationships to the
outer world.

Economically, the character in everyday life and the character resistance in the analysis serve as a means of avoiding
what is unpleasant (*Unlust*), of establishing and preserving a
psychic (even if neurotic) balance, and finally of consuming
repressed quantities of instinctual energy and/or quantities
which have eluded repression. The binding of free-floating
anxiety or—what amounts to the same thing—the absorbing
of dammed-up psychic energy, is one of the cardinal functions of the character. Just as the historical, i.e., the infantile,
element is embodied and continues to live and operate in the
neurotic symptom, so too it lives and operates and is embodied in the character. This explains why the consistent
loosening of the character resistance provides a sure and
direct approach to the central infantile conflict.

How do these facts bear upon the analytic technique of
character analysis? Is there an essential difference between
character analysis and the usual resistance analysis?

There are differences and they relate to:

a) the sequence in which the material is to be interpreted

b) the technique of resistance interpretation itself

With respect to (*a*): In speaking of "selection of material,"
we shall have to be prepared to encounter an important objection. It will be said that any selection is in contradiction to
the basic principle of psychoanalysis, namely that the analyst
must follow the patient, must allow himself to be led by him.
Every time the analyst makes a selection, he runs the risk of
falling prey to his own inclinations. First of all, we have to
point out that, in the kind of selection we are speaking of
here, it is not a matter of neglecting analytic material. The
whole point here is *to insure* that the material is interpreted
in a *legitimate sequence*, in keeping with the structure of the
neurosis. All material is in turn interpreted; it is only that one
detail is momentarily more important than another. We also
have to realize that the analyst always selects anyhow, for in
the very act of singling out individual details of a dream in-

stead of interpreting them successively, he has made a selection. And as far as that goes, the analyst has also made a biased selection when he considers only the content and not the form of the communications. Hence, the very fact that the patient produces material of the most diverse kinds in the analytic situation forces the analyst to make selections in interpreting this material. It is merely a question of selecting *correctly,* i.e., in keeping with the analytic situation.

With patients who, because of a particular character development, repeatedly disregard the fundamental rule, as well as with all cases in which the character is obstructing the analysis, it will be necessary to single out the germane *character resistance from the welter of material and to work it though analytically by interpreting its meaning.* Naturally, this does not mean that the rest of the material is neglected or disregarded. On the contrary, everything is valuable and welcome which gives us an insight into the meaning and origin of the recalcitrant character trait. The analyst merely puts off the analysis, and, above all, the interpretation of the material which does not have an immediate bearing upon the transference resistance, until the character resistance has been understood and broken through, at least in its basic features. In Chapter III, I tried to point out the dangers of giving deep interpretations before the character resistances have been resolved.

With respect to (*b*): Now we turn our attention to some special problems of the technique of character analysis. First, we must anticipate a likely misunderstanding. We stated that character analysis begins with the singling out and consistent analysis of the character resistance. This does not mean that the patient is enjoined not to be aggressive, not to be deceptive, not to speak in an incoherent manner, to follow the basic rule, etc. Such demands would not only be contrary to analytic procedure, they would be fruitless. It cannot be sufficiently stressed that what we are describing here has nothing whatever to do with the so-called education of the patient and similar matters. In character analysis, we ask ourselves why the patient is deceptive, speaks in an incoherent manner, is emotionally blocked, etc.; we endeavor to arouse his interest in the peculiarities of his character in order to elucidate, with his help, their meaning and origin through analysis. In other words, we merely single out from the orbit of the personality the character trait from which the cardinal resistance proceeds, and, if possible, we show the patient the surface relation between the character and the symptoms. But for the rest, we leave it up to him whether or not he wants to make use of his knowledge to change his character. Fundamentally, our procedure in this is no different from the one followed in the analysis of a symptom; the one exception is that, in character analysis, we have to *isolate* the character trait and put it before the patient *again and again* until he has succeeded in breaking clear of it and in viewing it as he would a vexatious compulsive symptom. In breaking clear of and objectifying the neurotic character trait, the patient begins to experience it as something alien to himself, and ultimately gains an insight into its nature.

In this process, it becomes apparent, surprisingly, that the personality changes—at least temporarily. And as the character analysis progresses, that impetus or disposition which gave rise to the character resistance in the transference automatically comes to the surface in an unconcealed form. Applying this to our example of the passive-feminine character, we can say that the more thoroughly the patient objectifies his inclinations to passive devotion, the more aggressive he will become. For, of course, his feminine, deceptive behavior was, in the main, an energetic reaction against repressed aggressive impulses. Hand in hand with the aggressiveness, however, the infantile castration anxiety also reappears which, at one time, caused the aggression to be transformed into a passive-feminine attitude. Thus, through the analysis of the character resistance, we arrive at the center of the neurosis, the Oedipus complex.

Let there be no illusions, however: the isolation and objectification as well as the analytic working through of such a character resistance usually take many months, demand great effort and, most of all, steadfast patience. Once the breakthrough has been achieved, the analytic work usually proceeds by leaps and bounds, borne by *affective* analytic experiences. If, on the other hand, such character resistances are left untended; if the analyst merely follows the patient, continually interpreting the content of his material, such resistances will, as time goes on, form a ballast that will be almost impossible to remove. When this happens, the analyst begins to feel in his bones that all his interpretations of content were wasted, that the patient continues to doubt everything, to accept it merely *pro forma*, or to laugh in his sleeve at everything. In later stages of the analysis, after the essential interpretations of the Oedipus complex have already been given, the analyst will find himself embroiled in a hopeless situation, if he has neglected to clear away these resistances right from the beginning. . . .

Carl Gustav Jung

Carl Gustav Jung (1875–1961) was the son of a Protestant minister in the small Swiss village of Kesswil. As a youth he was greatly impressed with parapsychology and spiritualism—interests that were formative in the direction and thrust of his later work. After receiving a medical degree, Jung was Joseph Bleuler's assistant in a Zurich mental hospital. With Bleuler's encouragement, he applied Freud's psychoanalytic "talking cure" there and soon became a student of Freud himself.

Jung's association with Freud, though close, was short-lived. On a trip to the United States together, Freud's interpretations of Jung's dreams indicated trouble brewing between them. Soon after the two pioneers separated in dispute over Jung's rejection of Freud's theories of the Oedipus complex and the sexual origins of neurosis.

After almost a decade of inner turmoil, Jung emerged as the head of his own analytic society, and went on to formulate the concepts for which he is now well-known: the polarity of introversion and extraversion; the collective unconscious with its archetypes; the psyche as composed of persona (the social mask) and shadow (the person's hidden aspects), anima (the feminine in men), animus (masculine in women), and self (a person's inmost core). Whereas Freud saw his therapy as a scrubbing away of preconceptions, and thus a return to reality, Jung saw his form of therapy as "individuation," the patient changing from identification with what he was not to what he in fact could become.

As Jung explains in this chapter on the aims of psychotherapy, the way to individuation was through the patient's unconscious. Jung takes pains to point out that this goal of therapy is appropriate for people in the "afternoon" of life, not in its "morning": His treatment is not designed for the neuroses of the young. Two-thirds of his patients, Jung tells us, are past middle age. They suffer not from a clear clinical problem, but rather from the "senselessness and emptiness of their lives." What they seek is not health or normality, but meaning.

This need for meaning, often expressed as a sense of being "stuck," Jung saw as the "general neurosis of our time." To help his patients, Jung relied in part on the techniques of free association he had learned from Freud. But Jung went far beyond the orthodox Freudian techniques. In seeking to plumb the messages offered in his patients dreams and fantasies, for example, Jung urged his patients to paint their symbols. Jung himself read widely in myths, anthropology, and religion to find analogies that might reveal hidden symbolic meanings of his patients' dreams. By interpreting these symbols, said Jung, the patient can discover an "inner truth." By coming to understand the clues offered in his unconscious about his inner being, the patient finally "begins to experiment with his own nature—a state of fluidity, change and growth. . . ."

THE AIMS OF PSYCHOTHERAPY

by Carl G. Jung

I certainly recognize how much my work has been furthered first by Freud and then by Adler; and whenever possible I apply their standpoints to my practical treatment of patients. Nevertheless I insist upon the fact that I have met with failures which I feel could have been avoided had I taken into consideration those empirical data which later forced me into modifications of their views. It is impossible to describe all the situations with which I was confronted, and I must content myself with singling out a few typical cases. It was with older patients that I had the greatest difficulties— that is, with persons over forty. In handling younger people I generally find the familiar viewpoints of Freud and Adler applicable enough, for they offer a treatment which brings the patient to a certain level of adaptation and normality, apparently without leaving any disturbing after-effects. With older people, according to my experience, this is often not the case. It seems to me that the elements of the psyche undergo in the course of life a very marked change—so much so, that we may distinguish between a psychology of the morning of life and a psychology of its afternoon. As a rule, the life of a young person is characterized by a general unfolding and a striving toward concrete ends; his neurosis, if he develops one, can be traced to his hesitation or his shrinking back from this necessity. But the life of an older person is marked by a contraction of forces, by the affirmation of what has been achieved, and the curtailment of further growth. His neurosis comes mainly from his clinging to a youthful attitude which is now out of season. Just as the youthful neurotic is afraid of life, so the older one shrinks back from death. What was a normal goal for the young man, inevitably becomes a neurotic hindrance to the older person. In the case of the young neurotic, what was once a normal dependence on his parents inevitably becomes, through his hesitation to face the world, an incest-relation which is inimical to life. It must be remembered that, despite all similarities, resistance, repression, transference, "guiding fictions" and so forth, have one meaning when we find them in young people, while in older persons they have quite another. The aims of therapy should undoubtedly be modified to meet this fact. The age of the patient seems to me, therefore, a most important *indicium.*

But there are also various *indicia* which we should note within the period of youth itself. Thus, according to my view, it is a blunder in technique to treat from the Freudian standpoint a patient of the type to whom the Adlerian psychology applies, that is, an unsuccessful person with an infantile need for self-assertion. Conversely, it would be a gross error to force the Adlerian viewpoint upon a successful man whose motives can be understood in terms of the pleasure principle. In doubtful cases the resistances of the patient may serve as valuable signposts. I am inclined at the start to take deep-seated resistances seriously, strange as this may sound. For I am convinced that the doctor is not necessarily in a better position to know what is wanted than is the patient's own psychic constitution, which may be quite unconscious to the patient himself. This modesty on the part of the doctor is altogether appropriate in view of the situation today. Not only have we as yet no generally valid psychology, but what is more, the variety of psychic constitutions is untold, and there also exist more or less individual psyches which refuse to fit into any general scheme.

As to this question of psychic constitution, it is well known that I postulate two different basic attitudes in accordance with the typical differences already suspected by many students of human nature—the extraverted and the introverted attitudes. These attitudes also I take to be important *indicia*, as likewise the predominance of a particular psychic function over other functions. The great variability of individual life necessitates constant modifications of theory which are often applied by the doctor quite unconsciously, but which in principle do not at all coincide with his theoretical creed.

While we are on this question of psychic constitution, I must not fail to point out that there are some people whose attitude is essentially spiritual and others whose attitude is essentially materialistic. It must not be assumed that such an attitude is accidentally acquired or springs from some misunderstanding. These attitudes show themselves as ingrained passions which no criticism or persuasion can stamp out; there are even cases where an apparently outspoken materialism has its source in the denial of a religious disposition. Cases of the reverse type are better known today, although they are not more frequent than the others. These attitudes also are *indicia* which, in my opinion, ought not to be overlooked.

When we use the word *indicium* it might appear to mean, as in medical parlance generally, that this or that treatment is indicated. Perhaps this should be the case, but psychotherapy has assuredly reached no such degree of certainty—for which reason our *indicia* are unfortunately not much more than mere warnings against one-sidedness.

The human psyche is highly equivocal. In every single case we must consider the question whether an attitude or a so-called *habitus* exists in its own right, or is perhaps only a compensation for the opposite. I must confess that I have so often been mistaken in this matter, that in any concrete case I am at pains to avoid all theoretical presuppositions as to the structure of the neurosis and as to what the patient can and ought to do. As far as possible, I let pure experience decide the therapeutic aims. This may perhaps seem strange, because it is usually assumed that the therapist should have an aim. But it seems to me that in psychotherapy especially it is advisable for the physician not to have too fixed a goal. He can scarcely know what is wanted better than do nature and the will-to-live of the sick person. The great decisions of human life have as a rule far more to do with the instincts and other mysterious unconscious factors than with conscious will and well-meaning reasonableness. The shoe that fits one person pinches another; there is no recipe for living that suits all cases. Each of us carries his own life-form—an indeterminable form which cannot be superseded by any other.

None of these considerations, of course, prevents our doing everything possible to make the lives of patients normal and reasonable. If this brings about a satisfactory result, then we can let it go at that; but if it is insufficient, then, for better or for worse, the therapist must be guided by the data presented through the patient's unconscious. Here we must follow nature as a guide, and the course the physician then adopts is less a question of treatment than of developing the creative possibilities that lie in the patient himself.

What I have to say begins with the point where treatment ceases and development sets in. My contribution to psychotherapy is confined to those cases in which rational treatment yields no satisfactory results. The clinical material at my disposal is of a special nature: new cases are decidedly in the minority. Most of my patients have already gone through some form of psychotherapeutic treatment, usually with partial or negative results. About a third of my cases are suffering from no clinically definable neurosis, but from the senselessness and emptiness of their lives. It seems to me, however, that this can well be described as the general neurosis of our time. Fully two-thirds of my patients have passed middle age.

It is difficult to treat patients of this particular kind by rational methods, because they are in the main socially well-adapted individuals of considerable ability, to whom normalization means nothing. As for so-called normal people, I am even worse off in their regard, for I have no ready-made life-philosophy to hand out to them. In the majority of my cases, the resources of consciousness have been exhausted; the ordinary expression for this situation is: "I am stuck." It is chiefly this fact that forces me to look for hidden possibilities. For I do not know what to say to the patient when he asks me: "What do you advise? What shall I do?" I do not know any better than he. I know only one thing: that when to my conscious outlook there is no possible way of going ahead, and I am therefore "stuck", my unconscious will react to the unbearable standstill.

This coming to a standstill is a psychic occurrence so often repeated in the evolution of mankind, that it has become the theme of many a fairy-tale and myth. We are told of the Open Sesame to the locked door, or of some helpful animal who finds the hidden way. We might put it in this way: "getting stuck" is a typical event which, in the course of time, has evoked typical reactions and compensations. We may therefore expect with a certain degree of probability that something similar will appear in the reactions of the unconscious, as, for example, in dreams.

In such cases, therefore, my attention is directed more particularly to dreams. This is not because I am tied to the notion that dreams must always be called to the rescue, or because I possess a mysterious dream-theory which tells me how everything must shape itself; but quite simply from perplexity. I do not know where else to go for help, and so I try to find it in dreams; these at least present us with images pointing to something or other, and that is at any rate better than nothing. I have no theory about dreams; I do not know how dreams arise. I am altogether in doubt as to whether my way of handling dreams even deserves the name of "method".

I share all my readers' prejudices against dream interpretation as being the quintessence of uncertainty and arbitrariness. But, on the other hand, I know that if we meditate on a dream sufficiently long and thoroughly—if we take it about with us and turn it over and over—something almost always comes of it. This something is of course not of such a kind that we can boast of its scientific nature or rationalize it, but it is a practical and important hint which shows the patient in what direction the unconscious is leading him. I even *may* not give first importance to the question whether our study of the dream gives a scientifically verifiable result; if I do this, I am following an exclusively personal aim, and one which is therefore auto-erotic. I must content myself with the fact that the result means something to the patient and sets his life into motion again. I may allow myself only *one* criterion for the validity of my interpretation of the dream—and this is that it *works*. As for my scientific hobby—my desire to know why it is that the dream works—this I must reserve for my spare time.

The contents of the initial dreams are infinitely varied—I mean those dreams which the patient relates to me at the beginning of the treatment. In many cases they point directly to the past and bring to mind what is forgotten and lost to the personality. It is from these very losses that one-sidedness results, and this causes the standstill and consequent disorien-

tation. In psychological terms, one-sidedness may lead to a
sudden loss of libido. All our previous activities become unin-
teresting, even senseless, and the goals towards which we
strove lose their value. What in one person is merely a passing mood may in another become a chronic condition. In
these cases it often happens that other possibilities of development of the personality lie somewhere or other in the past,
and no one, not even the patient, knows about them. But the
dream may reveal the clue. In other cases the dream points to
present facts, as for example marriage or social position,
which have never been consciously accepted as sources of
problems and conflicts.

These possibilities fall within the scope of rational explanation, and it is not difficult to make such initial dreams plausible. The real difficulty begins when dreams, as is often the
case, do not point to anything tangible—especially when they
show a kind of foreknowledge of the future. I do not mean
that such dreams are necessarily prophetic, but that they anticipate or "reconnoitre". Such dreams contain inklings of
possibilities, and therefore can never be made plausible to an
outsider. They are often not plausible even to me, and then I
say to my patients: "I don't believe it, but follow up the
clue." As I have said, the stimulating effect is the sole
criterion, and it is by no means necessary that we should understand why such an effect takes place. This is especially
true of dreams containing mythological images which are
sometimes incredibly strange and baffling. These dreams contain something like "unconscious metaphysics"; they are expressions of undifferentiated psychic activity which may often
contain the germs of conscious thought.

In a long initial dream of one of my "normal" patients, the
illness of his sister's child played an important part. She was
a little girl of two. Some time before, this sister really had
lost a boy through illness, but otherwise none of her children
were ill. The image of the sick child in the dream at first
proved baffling to him—undoubtedly because it in no way
fitted in with the facts. Since there was no direct and close
connection between the dreamer and his sister he could find
in this image little that was personal to him. Then suddenly it
occurred to him that two years earlier he had taken up the
study of occultism, and that it was this which had led him to
psychology. The child was evidently his interest in the things
of the psyche, an idea which I should never have hit upon of
my own accord. Looked at from the side of theory, this

dream-image can mean anything or nothing. For that matter, does a thing or a fact ever mean anything in and of itself? We can only be sure that it is always the human being who interprets, that is, gives meaning to a fact. And that is the gist of the matter for psychology. It impressed the dreamer as a new and interesting idea that the study of occultism might have something sickly about it. Somehow the thought struck home. And this is the decisive point: the interpretation *works*, however we may elect to account for its working. For the dreamer this thought contained a criticism, and through it a certain change in attitude was brought about. By such slight changes, which one could never think out rationally, things begin to move and the dead point is overcome.

In commenting upon this example I could say in a figure of speech that the dream *meant* that the occult studies of the dreamer had something sickly about them. And in this sense I may also speak of "unconscious metaphysics", if the dreamer is brought by his dream to this very thought. But I go still further; I not only give the patient an opportunity to see what occurs to him in connection with his dream, but I allow myself to do the the same. I give him the benefit of my guesses and opinions. If, in doing this I should open the door to so-called "suggestion", I see no occasion for regret; it is well known that we are susceptible only to those suggestions with which we are already secretly in accord. No harm is done if now and then one goes astray in this riddle-reading. Sooner or later the psyche rejects the mistake, much as an organism does a foreign body. I need not try to prove that my dream interpretation is correct, which would be a somewhat hopeless undertaking, but must simply help the patient to find what it is that activates him—I was almost betrayed into saying what is actual.

It is of especial importance for me to know as much as possible about primitive psychology, mythology, archæology and comparative religion, for the reason that these fields afford me priceless analogies with which I can enrich the associations of my patients. Working together, we are then able to find the apparently irrelevant full of meaning and vastly increase the effectiveness of the dream. Thus to enter a realm of immediate experience is most stimulating for those who have done their utmost in the personal and rational spheres of life and yet have found no meaning and no satisfaction there. In this way, too, the matter-of-fact and the common-place come to wear an altered countenance, and can even acquire a new glamour. For it all depends on how we look at things, and not on how they are in themselves. The least of things with a meaning is worth more in life than the greatest of things without it.

I do not think that I underestimate the risk of this undertaking. It is as if one began to build a bridge out into space. Indeed, one might even allege—as has often been done—that in following this procedure the doctor and his patient are both together indulging in mere fantasies. And I do not consider this an objection, but quite to the point. I even make an effort to second the patient in his fantasies. Truth to tell, I have a very high opinion of fantasy. To me, it is actually the maternally creative side of the masculine spirit. When all is said and done, we are never proof against fantasy. It is true that there are worthless, inadequate, morbid and unsatisfying fantasies whose sterile nature will be quickly recognized by every person endowed with common-sense; but this of course proves nothing against the value of creative imagination. All the works of man have their origin in creative fantasy. What right have we then to depreciate imagination? In the ordinary course of things, fantasy does not easily go astray; it is too deep for that, and too closely bound up with the tap-root of human and animal instinct. In surprising ways it always rights itself again. The creative activity of the imagination frees man from his bondage to the "nothing but" and liberates in him the spirit of play. As Schiller says, man is completely human only when he is playing.

My aim is to bring about a psychic state in which my patient begins to experiment with his own nature—a state of fluidity, change and growth, in which there is no longer anything eternally fixed and hopelessly petrified. It is of course only by stating its general principles that I can present my technique here. In handling a dream or a fantasy I make it a rule never to go beyond the meaning which has an effect upon the patient; I merely strive in each case to make this meaning as conscious to him as possible, so that he can also become aware of its supra-personal connections. This is important, for when something quite universal happens to a man and he supposes it to be an experience peculiar to himself, then his attitude is obviously wrong, that is, too personal, and it tends to exclude him from human society. We require not only a present-day, personal consciousness, but also a supra-personal consciousness which is open to the sense of historical continuity. However far-fetched it may sound, experience shows that many neuroses are caused by the fact that people blind themselves to their own religious promptings because of a childish passion for rational enlightenment. The psychologist of today ought to realize once and for all that we are no longer dealing with questions of dogma and creed. A religious attitude is an element in psychic life whose importance can hardly be overrated. And it is precisely for the religious outlook that the sense of historical continuity is indispensable.

To return to the question of my technique, I ask myself to what extent I am indebted to Freud. In any case I learned it from Freud's method of free association, and I regard my technique as a further development of this method.

As long as I help the patient to discover the effective elements in his dream, and as long as I try to show him the general meaning of his symbols, he is still, psychologically speaking, in a state of childhood. For the time being he depends on his dreams and is always asking himself whether the subsequent dream will give him new light or not. Moreover, he is dependent on my having ideas about his dreams and on my ability to increase his insight through my knowledge. Thus he is still in an undesirably passive condition in which everything is uncertain and questionable; neither he nor I know the journey's end. Often it is not much more than a groping about in Egyptian darkness. In this condition we must not expect any very marked effects, for the uncertainty is too great. Moreover we constantly run the risk that what we have woven by day, the night will unravel. The danger is that nothing comes to pass; that nothing keeps its shape. It not infrequently happens in these circumstances that the patient has an especially colourful or curious dream, and says to me: "Do you know, if only I were a painter I would make a picture of it." Or the dreams treat of photographs, of paintings, drawings or illuminated manuscripts, or perhaps of the films.

I have turned these hints to practical account, and I now urge my patients at such times actually to paint what they have seen in dream or fantasy. As a rule, I am met with the objection: "I am not a painter." To this I usually reply that neither are modern painters—for which very reason modern painting is absolutely free—and that it is anyhow not a question of the beautiful, but merely of the trouble one takes with the picture. How little my way of painting has to do with "art" I saw recently in the case of a talented portraitist; she had to begin all over again with pitiably childish efforts—

literally as if she had never had a brush in her hand. To paint what we see before us is a different matter from painting what we see within.

Many of my more advanced patients, then, begin to paint. I can well understand that everyone will consider this as an utterly futile sort of dilettantism. However, it must be remembered that we are speaking not of people who have still to prove their social usefulness, but of those who can no longer find significance in their value to society, and who have come upon the deeper and more dangerous question of the meaning of their individual lives. To be a particle in a mass has meaning and charm only for the man who has not yet advanced to that stage, but none for the man who has experienced it to satiety. The importance of individual life may always be denied by the "educator" whose pride it is to breed mass-men. But any other person will sooner or later be driven to find this meaning for himself.

Although from time to time my patients produce artistically beautiful creations which might very well be shown in modern "art" exhibitions, I nevertheless treat them as wholly worthless according to the tests of serious art. It is even essential that no such value be allowed them, for otherwise my patients might imagine themselves to be artists, and this would spoil the good effects of the exercise. It is not a question of art—or rather it should not be a question of art—but of something more, something other than mere art: namely the living effect upon the patient himself. The meaning of individual life, whose importance from the social standpoint is negligible, is here accorded the highest value, and for its sake the patient struggles to give form, however crude and childish, to the inexpressible.

But why do I encourage patients to express themselves at a certain stage of development by means of brush, pencil or pen? My purpose is the same here as in my handling of dreams: I wish to produce an effect. In the childish condition described above, the patient remains in a passive state; but now he begins to play an active part. At first he puts on paper what has come to him in fantasy, and thereby gives it the status of a deliberate act. He not only talks about it, but he is actually *doing* something about it. Psychologically speaking, it is one thing for a person to have an interesting conversation with his doctor twice a week—the results of which hang somewhere or other in mid-air—and quite another thing to struggle for hours at a time with refractory brush and colours, and to produce in the end something which, at its face value, is perfectly senseless. Were his fantasy *really* senseless to him, the effort to paint it would be so irksome that he could scarcely be brought to perform this exercise a second time. But since his fantasy does not seem to him entirely senseless, his busying himself with it increases its effect upon him. Moreover, the effort to give visible form to the image enforces a study of it in all its parts, so that in this way its effects can be completely experienced. The discipline of drawing endows the fantasy with an element of reality, thus lending it greater weight and greater driving power. And actually these crude pictures do produce effects which, I must admit, are rather difficult to describe. When a patient has seen once or twice how he is freed from a wretched state of mind by working at a symbolical picture, he will thenceforward turn to this means of release whenever things go badly with him. In this way something invaluable is won, namely a growth of independence, a step towards psychological maturity. The patient can make himself creatively independent by this method—if I may call it such. He is no longer dependent on his dreams or on his doctor's knowledge, but can give form to his own inner experience by painting it. For what he paints are active fantasies—it is that which activates him. And that which is active within is himself, but not in the sense of his previous error when he mistook his personal ego for the self; it is himself in a new sense, for his ego now appears as an object actuated by the life-forces within. He strives to represent as fully as possible in his picture-series that which works within him, only to discover in the end that it is the eternally unknown and alien—the hidden foundations of psychic life.

I cannot possibly picture to you the extent to which these discoveries change a patient's standpoint and values, and how they shift the centre of gravity of the personality. It is as though the ego were the earth, and it suddenly discovered that the sun (or the self) was the centre of the planetary orbits and of the earth's orbit as well.

But have we not always known all this to be so? I myself believe that we have always known it. But I may know about something with my head which the other man in me is far from knowing, and I may in fact live as though I did not know it. Most of my patients knew the deeper truth, but did not live it. And why did they not live it? Because of that bias which makes us all put the ego in the centre of our lives—and this bias comes from the over-valuation of consciousness.

It is highly important for a young person who is still unadapted and has as yet achieved nothing, to shape the conscious ego as effectively as possible—that is, to educate the will. Unless he is positively a genius he even may not believe in anything active within himself that is not identical with his will. He must feel himself a man of will, and he may safely depreciate everything else within himself or suppose it subject to his will—for without this illusion he can scarcely bring about a social adaptation.

It is otherwise with the patient in the second half of life who no longer needs to educate his conscious will, but who, to understand the meaning of his individual life, must learn to experience his own inner being. Social usefulness is no longer an aim for him, although he does not question its desirability. Fully aware as he is of the social unimportance of his creative activity, he looks upon it as a way of working out his own development and thus benefiting himself. This activity likewise frees him progressively from a morbid dependence, and he thus wins an inner firmness and a new trust in himself. These last achievements in turn serve to further the patient in his social existence. For an inwardly sound and self-confident person will be more adequate to his social tasks than one who is not on good terms with his unconscious.

I have purposely avoided weighting down my essay with theory, for which reason many things must remain obscure and unexplained. But in order to make intelligible the pictures produced by my patients, certain theoretical points must at least be mentioned. A feature common to all these pictures is a primitive symbolism which is conspicuous both in the drawing and in the colouring. The colours are usually quite barbaric in their intensity; often, too, an archaic quality is present. These peculiarities point to the nature of the creative forces which have produced the pictures. They are non-rational, symbolistic currents in the evolution of man, and are so archaic that it is easy to draw parallels between them and similar manifestations in the fields of archaeology and comparative religion. We may therefore readily assume that these pictures originate chiefly in that realm of psychic life which I have called the collective unconscious. By this term I designate an unconscious psychic activity present in all human beings which not only gives rise to symbolical pictures today, but was the source of all similar products of the past. Such pictures spring from—and satisfy—a natural need. It is as if, through these pictures, we bring to expression that part of the psyche which reaches back into the primitive past and reconcile it with present-day consciousness, thus mitigating its disturbing effects upon the latter.

It is true, I must add, that the mere execution of the pictures is not all that is required. It is necessary besides to have an intellectual and emotional understanding of them; they must be consciously integrated, made intelligible, and morally assimilated. We must subject them to a process of interpretation. But despite the fact that I have so often travelled this path with individual patients, I have not yet succeeded in making the process clear to a wider circle and in working it up in a form suitable for publication. This has so far been accomplished only in a fragmentary way.

The truth is, we are here on perfectly new ground, and a ripening of experience is the first requisite. For very important reasons I should like to avoid over-hasty conclusions. We are dealing with a region of psychic life outside consciousness, and our way of observing it is indirect. As yet we do not know what depths we are trying to plumb. As I indicated above, it seems to me to be a question of some kind of centring process, for many pictures which patients feel to be decisive point in this direction. It is a process which brings into being a new centre of equilibrium, and it is as if the ego turned in an orbit round it. What the aim of this process may be remains at first obscure. We can only remark its important effect upon the conscious personality. From the fact that the change heightens the feeling for life and maintains the flow of life, we must conclude that a peculiar purposefulness is inherent in it. We might perhaps call this a new illusion—but what is illusion? By what criterion do we judge something to be an illusion? Does there exist for the psyche anything which we may call "illusion"? What we are pleased to call such may be for the psyche a most important factor of life—something as indispensable as oxygen for the organism—a psychic actuality of prime importance. Presumably the psyche does not trouble itself about our categories of reality, and it would therefore be the better part of wisdom for us to say: everything that *acts* is actual.

He who would fathom the psyche must not confuse it with consciousness, else he veils from his own sight the object he wishes to explore. On the contrary, to recognize the psyche, even, he must learn to see how it differs from consciousness.

It is highly probable that what we call illusion is actual for the psyche: for which reason we cannot take psychic actuality to be commensurable with conscious actuality. To the psychologist there is nothing more stupid than the standpoint of the missionary who pronounces the gods of the "poor heathen" to be illusions. But unfortunately we keep blundering along in the same dogmatic way, as if what we call the real were not equally full of illusion. In psychic life, as everywhere in our experience, all things that act are actual, regardless of the names man chooses to bestow on them. To understand that these happenings have actuality—that is what is important to us; and not the attempt to give them one name instead of another. To the psyche the spirit is no less the spirit even though it be called sexuality.

I must repeat that the various technical terms and the changes rung upon them never touch the essence of the process described above. It cannot be compassed by the rational concepts of consciousness any more than life itself. It is because they feel the whole force of this truth that my patients turn to symbolical expression. In the representation and interpretation of symbols they find something more effective and adequate to their needs than rational explanations.

Karen Horney

Karen Horney (1885–1952) received a medical degree in Berlin in 1913, where, probably through the influence of Alfred Adler, she came to question the biological determinism of Freud's thought. In her own work, Horney placed more emphasis on the role of social and cultural factors in human psychological development. For example, she questioned the role of penis envy in girls and the universality of the Oedipus complex, and brought to light the masculine bias in psychoanalytic thinking.

Horney emigrated to the United States before World War II, where she practiced psychoanalysis and, in 1941, founded the Institute for Psychoanalysis in New York. A prolific and lucid author, she excelled in rendering her psychological thought accessible to the general public.

Horney was a member of the psychoanalytic loyal opposition. While she didn't stray too far from the fold, she offered her own theory of neurosis, from which followed innovations in technique. As Horney put it, "New ways in theory necessarily condition new ways in therapy."

The theory Horney offered to explain neurosis is quite different from Freud's. Horney held that to protect oneself against "basic anxiety," a feeling of helplessness in a hostile world, people seek ways to cope safely with life. Once found, people cling to these ways, which Horney calls "neurotic trends," rigidly adhering to them to avoid feelings of danger and anxiety. The three main strategies people adopt to ward off their basic anxiety are moving toward, against, or away from others. Neurotic trends, says Horney, offer a partial, but precarious, security.

For Horney a main task of therapy is to assess which of these strategies a patient uses, and to wean him from neurotic reliance on it. The course of therapy is directed to that end.

At the outset Horney urges the therapist not to try to arrive at a direct understanding of the patient's presenting symptoms, but to try to grasp their meaning in the context of the patient's character structure. The therapist should not try to tie the patient's current peculiarities and problems directly to specific childhood experiences; glib interpretations and connections to the past can result in resistance in the patient. Key memories will come up spontaneously anyway, with less danger of falsification.

Instead, the therapist should detect the patient's main neurotic trends, exploring the effects they have in the patient's life. By so doing, the therapist can relieve the patient's anxiety, which in turn will help him improve his relations with other people in his life. This will finally allow the patient to relinquish his neurotic trends. Horney, in a large step away from her early psychoanalytic training, urged therapists not to be entirely passive. They should, she said, take risks, steering patients away from blind alleys in therapy by clarifying, pointing out contradictions, making suggestions—and actively supporting the patient's desire for happiness.

PSYCHOANALYTIC THERAPY

by Karen Horney

Psychoanalytic therapy, insofar as it is not intuitive or directed by plain common sense, is influenced by theoretical concepts. To a great extent these concepts determine which factors are observed and which factors are deemed important in creating, maintaining and curing a neurosis, and determine also what is regarded as the therapeutic goal. New ways in theory necessarily condition new ways in therapy. Here . . . the questions I shall discuss will be more or less restricted to the work to be done in analysis, the curative factors, the therapeutic goal, the difficulties involved for patient and analyst, the psychic factors which drive the patient to overcome his disturbances.

In order to understand these factors let us briefly summarize what essentially constitutes a neurosis. The combination of many adverse environmental influences produces disturbances in the child's relation to self and others. The immediate effect is what I have called the basic anxiety, which is a collective term for a feeling of intrinsic weakness and help-lessness toward a world perceived as potentially hostile and dangerous. The basic anxiety renders it necessary to search for ways in which to cope with life safely. The ways that are chosen are those which under the given conditions are accessible. These ways, which I call the neurotic trends, acquire a compulsory character because the individual feels that only by following them rigidly can he assert himself in life and avoid potential dangers. The hold which the neurotic trends have on him is further strengthened by the fact that they serve as his only means of attaining satisfaction as well as safety, other possibilities of attaining satisfaction being closed to him because they are too replete with anxiety. Furthermore, the neurotic trends provide an expression for the resentment which he harbors toward the world.

While the neurotic trends have thus a definite value for the individual they also invariably have far-reaching unfavorable consequences for his further development.

The security they offer is always precarious; the individual is easily subject to anxiety as soon as they fail to operate. They make him rigid, all the more so since further protective means often have to be built up to allay new anxieties. Invariably he becomes entangled in contradictory strivings; these may develop from the beginning, or a rigid drive in one direction may call forth an opposite drive, or a neurotic trend may bear a conflict in itself.* The presence of such incompatible striving adds to the ample possibilities for the generation of anxiety, for their very incompatibility implies the danger that one of them will jeopardize the other. Hence on the whole the neurotic trends render a person still more insecure.

Moreover, the neurotic trends further alienate the individual from himself. This fact, along with the rigidity of his structure, essentially impairs his productivity. He may be able to work, but one live source of creativeness which is in his real spontaneous self necessarily becomes choked. Also, he becomes discontented, for his possibilities of satisfaction are limited, and the satisfactions themselves are usually merely temporary and partial.

---

*A typical example of the first kind is the development of a neurotic ambition simultaneously with a neurotic need for affection; an example of the second kind is the masochistic tendency toward unobtrusiveness, calling forth propensities toward self-inflation; an example of the third kind is the conflicting tendencies toward compliance and defiance which are at the root of the need to appear perfect.

Finally, the neurotic trends, although their function is to provide a basis on which to deal with others, contribute to a further impairment of human relationships. The main reasons for this are that they help to increase dependency on others, and that they precipitate various kinds of hostile reactions.

The character structure which thus develops is the kernel of neuroses. Despite infinite variations it always contains certain general characteristics: compulsory strivings, conflicting trends, a propensity to develop manifest anxiety, impairment in the relation to self and others, marked discrepancy between potentialities and actual attainments.

The so-called symptoms of neuroses, which are usually regarded as the criteria for their classification, are not essential constituents. Neurotic symptoms such as phobias, depressions, fatigue and the like may not develop at all. But if they develop they are an outgrowth of the neurotic character structure and can be understood only on that basis. As a matter of fact, the only distinction between "symptoms" and neurotic character difficulties is that the latter obviously pertain to the structure of the personality while the former are not obviously connected with the character but appear to be, as it were, an extra-territorial growth. A neurotic's timidity is an obvious outcome of his character trends; his phobia of high places is not. Nevertheless, the latter is merely an expression of the former, for in his phobia of high places his various fears have merely been shifted to and focused on one special factor.

In the light of this interpretation of neuroses two kinds of therapeutic approach appear to be erroneous. One is the attempt to arrive at a direct understanding of the symptomatic picture without first having a grasp of the particular character structure. In mere situation neuroses it is possible sometimes to tackle directly the symptom that has emerged by relating it to the actual conflict. But in chronic neuroses we understand at the beginning little if anything of the symptomatic picture because it is the ultimate result of all existing neurotic entanglements. We do not know, for instance, why one patient has a syphilidophobia, another recurring eating spells, a third hypochondriac fears. The analyst should know that the symptoms cannot be directly understood, and why. As a rule, any attempt to make an immediate interpretation of the symptoms proves to be a failure, and means at least a waste of time. It is better to keep them in the background of one's mind and to take them up later on when an understanding of character trends sheds light upon them.

The patient, as a rule, is not content with this procedure. He naturally wants to have his symptoms explained at once, and resents what he feels to be an unnecessary delay. Often a deeper reason for his resentment is that he does not want anyone to intrude into the secrecies of his personality. The analyst does best to explain frankly the reasons for his procedure and to analyze the patient's reactions to it.

The other erroneous way is to relate the patient's actual peculiarities directly to certain childhood experiences and to establish a quick casual connection between two series of factors. In therapy Freud is primarily interested in tracing actual difficulties back to instinctual sources and infantile experiences, and this procedure is consistent with the instinctivistic and genetic character of his psychology.

In accordance with this principle Freud has two objectives in therapy. If—allowing for the inaccuracy involved—we consider what Freud calls instinctual drives and "super-ego" equivalent to what I call neurotic trends, Freud's first objective is to recognize the existence of neurotic trends. He would, for example, conclude from the existence of self-recriminations and self-imposed restrictions that the patient has a severe "super-ego" (need to appear perfect). His next objective is to relate these trends to infantile sources and to explain them on that basis. Concerning the "super-ego" he would be primarily interested in recognizing the kind of parental prohibitions which are still operating in the patient, and in unearthing the oedipal relations (sexual ties, hostilities, identifications) which he believes to be ultimately responsible for the phenomenon.

According to my slant on neuroses, the main neurotic disturbances are the consequences of the neurotic trends. Hence my main objective in therapy is, after having recognized the neurotic trends, to discover in detail the functions they serve and the consequences they have on the patient's personality and on his life. Taking again as an example the need to appear perfect, I would be interested primarily in understanding what this trend accomplishes for the individual (eliminating conflicts with others and making him feel superior to others), and also what consequences the trend has on his character and his life. The latter investigation would make it possible to understand, for example, how such a person anxiously conforms with expectations and standards to the extent of becoming a mere automaton, and yet subversively defies them; how this double play results in listlessness and inertia; how he is proud of his apparent independence, yet actually is entirely dependent on the expectations and opinions of others; how he resents everything that is expected of him, yet feels lost without such expectations to guide him; how he is terrified lest anyone should discover the flimsiness of his moral strivings and the duplicity which has pervaded his life; how this in turn has made him seclusive and hypersensitive to criticism.

I differ from Freud in that, after recognition of the neurotic trends, while he primarily investigates their genesis I primarily investigate their actual functions and their consequences. The intention in both procedures is the same: to diminish the holds the neurotic trends have on the person. Freud believes that by recognizing the infantile nature of his trends the patient will automatically realize that they do not fit into his adult personality and will therefore be able to master them. The sources of error involved in this contention have been discussed. I believe that all the obstacles which Freud holds responsible for therapeutic failures—such as depth of unconscious guilt feelings, narcissistic inaccessibility, unchangeability of biological drives—are really due to the erroneous premises on which his therapy is built.

My contention is that by working through the consequences the patient's anxiety is so much lessened, and his relation to self and others so much improved, that he can dispense with the neurotic trends. Their development was necessitated by the child's hostile and apprehensive attitude toward the world. If analysis of the consequences, that is, analysis of the actual neurotic structure, helps the individual to become indiscriminately friendly toward others instead of indiscriminately hostile, if his anxieties are considerably diminished, if he gains in inner strength and inner activity, he no longer needs his safety devices, but can deal with the difficulties of life according to his judgment.

It is not always the analyst who suggests to the patient that he search for causes in his childhood; often the patient spontaneously offers genetic material. Insofar as he offers data relevant to his development this tendency is constructive. But insofar as he unconsciously uses these data to establish a quick causal connection the tendency is evasive in character. More often than not he hopes thereby to avoid facing trends which actually exist within him. The patient has an understandable interest in not realizing either the incompatibility of such trends or the price he pays for them: up to the time of analysis both his safety and his expectations of satisfaction rested on the pursuit of these strivings. He would prefer to preserve a muddled hope that his drives are not so imperative and not so incompatible as they seem, that he can have his cake and eat it, that nothing has to be changed. Therefore he has good reasons to resist when the analyst insists on working through the actual implications.

As soon as the patient himself is able to realize that his genetic endeavors lead to a dead-end, it is best to interfere actively and to point out that even though the experiences he recalls may have a bearing on the actual trend, they do not explain why the trend is maintained today; it should be explained to him that it is usually more profitable to postpone curiosity as to causation and study first the consequences which the particular trend entails for his character and for his life.

The emphasis I lay on the analysis of the actual character structure does not imply that data concerning childhood should be neglected. In fact, the procedure I have described—a procedure which desists from artificial reconstructions—even leads to a clearer understanding of childhood difficulties. In my experience, regardless of whether I work with the old or with the modified technique, it is comparatively rare that entirely forgotten memories creep up. More frequently falsifications of memories are corrected, and incidents which were regarded as irrelevant are given significance. The resultant understanding which the patient gradually acquires of his particular course of development helps to restore him to himself. Furthermore, through understanding himself he becomes reconciled to his parents or to their memory; he understands that they too were caught in conflicts and could not help harming him. What is more important, when he no longer suffers from the harm done him, or at least sees a way of overcoming it, old resentments are mitigated.

The tools with which the analyst operates during this procedure are to a large extent those which Freud has taught us to use: free associations and interpretations, as a means of lifting unconscious processes into awareness; a detailed study of the relationships between patient and analyst, as a means of recognizing the nature of the patient's relationships to others.

In this regard my differences from Freud concern basically two groups of factors.

One is the kind of interpretations given. The character of interpretations depends on the factors which one deems to be essential . . . this point need only be mentioned here.

The other group concerns factors which are less tangible and hence more difficult to formulate. They are implicit in the analyst's way of handling the procedure: his activity or passivity, his attitude to the patient, his making or refraining from value judgments, the attitudes he encourages and discourages in the patient. The outstanding considerations may here be briefly summarized.

According to Freud the analyst should play a comparatively passive role. Freud's advice is that the analyst should listen to the patient's associations with an "evenly-hovering attention," avoiding deliberate attentiveness to certain details and avoiding conscious exertion.

Naturally, even in Freud's view, the analyst cannot be altogether passive. He exerts an active influence on the patient's associations by the interpretations he gives. When, for instance, the analyst tends to make reconstructions of the past, the patient is thereby implicitly directed to search in the past. Also, every analyst will actively interfere when he notices that the patient persistently avoids certain topics. Nevertheless, the ideal, in Freud's view, is that the analyst be guided by the patient and merely interpret the material when he sees fit to do so. That in this procedure he also influences the patient is, as it were, an effect which though desirable is only reluctantly admitted.

My view, on the other hand, is that the analyst should deliberately conduct the analysis. This statement, however, like Freud's emphasis on passivity, is to be taken with a grain of salt, because it is always the patient who indicates the general line by showing, through his associations, the problems which are uppermost in his mind. Also, according to my view, there will be many hours in which the analyst does nothing but interpret. Interpretation may imply many things: clarifying the problems which the patient, because he is unaware of their existence, presents in involved and disguised forms; pointing out existing contradictions; making suggestions as to possible solutions for a problem on the basis of insights already achieved concerning the patient's structure, and the like. These are hours in which the patient follows a profitable path. But as soon as I believe that the patient is running into a blind alley I would not hesitate to interfere most actively and to suggest another way, though of course I would analyze why he prefers to proceed along a certain line, and would present the reasons why I prefer that he try to search in another direction.

As an example let us assume that a patient has realized that it is imperative for him to be right. He has realized this sufficiently to begin to wonder about it and to ask why it is so important. My method would be to point out deliberately that as a rule one does not get very far with an immediate search for reasons, that it is more profitable to recognize first in detail all the consequences this attitude has for him and to understand what functions if fulfills. Of course the analyst takes more risk and more responsibility this way. Responsibility, however, rests on the analyst anyhow, and the risk of making wrong suggestions and thereby losing time is, according to experience, less than the risk entailed in non-interference. When I feel uncertain about a suggestion made to the patient I point out its tentative character. If then my suggestion is not to the point, the fact that the patient feels that I too am searching for a solution may elicit his active collaboration in correcting or qualifying my suggestion.

The analyst should exercise a more deliberate influence not only on the direction of the patient's associations but also on those psychic forces which may help him eventually to overcome his neurosis. The work the patient has to accomplish is most strenuous and most painful. It implies no less than relinquishing or greatly modifying all the strivings for safety and satisfaction which have hitherto prevailed. It implies relinquishing illusions about himself which in his eyes have made him significant. It implies putting his entire relations to others and to himself on a different basis. What drives the patient to do this hard work? Patients come for analytical help because of different motivations and with different expectations. Most frequently they want to get rid of manifest neurotic disturbances. Sometimes they wish to be better able to cope with certain situations. Sometimes they feel arrested in their development and wish to overcome a dead point. Very rarely do they come with the outright hope for more happiness. The strength and constructive value of these motivations vary in each patient, but all of them can be actively used in effecting a cure.

One has to realize, however, that these driving forces are not entirely what they seem. The patient wants to achieve his

ends on his own terms. He may wish to be freed of suffering
without his personality being touched. His wish for greater ef-
ficency or for a better development of his talents is almost always determined largely by an expectation that analysis will
help to maintain more perfectly his appearance of infallibility
and superiority. Even his quest for happiness, in itself the
most effective of all motivations, cannot be taken at its face
value, because the happiness the patient has in mind secretly
entails the fulfillment of all his contradictory neurotic wishes.
During the analysis, however, all of these motivations are reinforced. This occurs in a very successful analysis without
the analyst paying special attention to it. But since their
reinforcement, or we might say their mobilization, is of
paramount importance for effecting a cure, it is desirable for
the analyst to know what factors bring this about, and to conduct the analysis in such a way as to make these factors oper-
ative.

In analysis the wish to become free from suffering gains in
strength, because, even though the patient's symptoms may
decrease, he gradually realizes how much intangible suffering
and how many handicaps his neurosis entails. A painstaking
elaboration of all the consequences of the neurotic trends
helps the patient to recognize them and to acquire a constructive discontentment with himself.

Also, his desire to improve his personality is put on a more
solid basis as soon as his pretenses are removed. Perfectionistic drives, for example, are replaced by a genuine wish to develop inherent potentialities, regardless of whether these
concern special gifts or general human faculties, such as the
faculty for friendship and love, the faculty to do a good job
and enjoy it for its own sake.

Most important of all, the quest for happiness becomes
stronger. Most patients have known merely the partial satisfaction attainable within the boundaries set by their anxieties;
they have never experienced true happiness nor have they
dared to reach out for it. One reason for this is that the neurotic has been altogether engrossed in his pursuit of safety
and has felt content when merely free of haunting anxiety,
depressions, migraine and the like. Also, in many cases, he
has felt bound to maintain, in his own as in other's eyes, the
appearance of misunderstood "unselfishness"; hence despite
his actual egocentricity he has not dared to have outright
wishes for himself. Or it may be that he has expected happiness to shine upon him like sunrays from the sky without

his own active contribution. Deeper than all of these reasons and probably their ultimate cause, the individual has been a puffed-up balloon, a marionette, a success hunter, a stowaway, but never himself. And it seems that a precondition for happiness is to have the center of gravity within oneself.

There are several ways in which analysis reinforces the desire for happiness. By removing the patient's anxieties analysis frees energies and wishes for something more positive in life than mere riskless safety. Also it unmasks the "unselfishness" as a pretense maintained because of fears and a thirst for distinction. The analysis of this part of the façade deserves special attention because it is especially here that a wish for happiness may be liberated. Furthermore, analysis helps the patient to realize gradually that he is following the wrong path in expecting happiness to come to him from without, that the enjoyment of happiness is a faculty to be acquired from within. It is of no use merely to tell this to him, because he knows it anyhow as an age-old and undisputed truth, and because it would remain for him an abstract fact without bearing on reality. The way it gains life and reality in analysis is through psychoanalytic means. For instance, a patient who desires happiness through love and companionship realizes in analysis that for him "love" unconsciously signifies merely a relationship in which he will obtain everything he wants from a partner and have him at his beck and call, that he expects to receive "unconditional love" while he keeps his inner self entirely apart and remains wrapped up in himself. By becoming aware of the nature of his demands, by becoming aware of the intrinsic impossibility of their ever being fulfilled, and particularly by becoming aware of what consequences these demands and his reactions to their frustrations have actually had on his relationships, he realizes eventually that he need not despair of obtaining happiness through love but can obtain it if only he works sufficiently at regaining his own inner activity. Finally, the more a patient can dispense with his neurotic trends the more he becomes his own spontaneous self and can be trusted to take care of his quest for happiness himself.

There is still another possibility of mobilizing and reinforcing the patient's desire to change. Even if he is familiar with psychoanalysis the patient almost invariably harbors the illusion that being analyzed means only becoming aware of certain unpleasant things in himself, particularly those lying in the past, and that such awareness, as if by magic, will set him right with the world. If he considers at all the fact that analysis aims at a change in his personality, he expects the change to happen automatically. I shall not embark upon the philosophical question as to the relationship between an insight into some undesirable trend and a will impulse to change that trend. At any rate, the patient unwittingly distinguishes between awareness and change, because of subjective reasons which are readily understandable. In principle he accepts the necessity for becoming aware of repressed trends—though in detail, naturally, he fights every step in this direction—but he refuses to accept the necessity for change. None of this is clearly thought out, but he may be greatly shocked when the analyst confronts him with the necessity for an eventual change.

While some analysts point out this necessity to the patient, others in some way share the patient's attitude. An incident which occurred when I was supervising an analysis by a colleague may serve as an illustration. The patient had reproached the colleague for wanting to make him over, to change him, at which the colleague retorted that that was not his intention, that he merely wanted to uncover certain psychic facts. I asked the colleague whether he was convinced of the truth of his answer. He admitted that it was not quite true, but he felt that it was not right to wish the patient to change.

This question involves a seeming contradiction. Every analyst is proud to hear from others that a patient of his has changed immensely, yet he would hesitate to admit or to express to the patient a deliberate wish to effect a change in the patient's personality. He is prone to insist that all he does or wants to do is to lift unconscious processes into awareness, that what the patient does with his better knowledge of himself is the patient's own business. This contradiction is accounted for by theoretical reasons. There is, first, the general ideal that the analyst is a scientist whose only task is to observe, to collect data and to present these data. There is, furthermore, the doctrine of the limited functions of the "ego." At best it is accredited with a synthetic function operating automatically but with a will power of its own, because all energies are supposed to arise from instinctual sources. Theoretically the analyst does not believe that we can will something because our judgment tells us it is the right or sensible thing to do if we wish to attain certain things. Hence he refrains from deliberately mobilizing will power in a constructive direction.

It would not be correct, though, to say that Freud does not recognize at all the role which the patient's will power plays in therapy. He does so indirectly when he asserts that repression has to be replaced by judgment, or that we work with the patient's intelligence, which implies that the patient's intelligent judgment sets off a will impulse toward a change. Every analyst factually relies on such impulses operating in the patient. When, for instance, he can demonstrate to the patient the existence of an "infantile" trend, like greediness or obstinacy, and its harmful implications, he certainly mobilizes a will impulse toward overcoming this trend. The question is only whether it is not preferable to be aware of doing so and to do it deliberately.

The psychoanalytic way of mobilizing will power is to bring certain connections or motivations to the patient's awareness and thereby enable him to judge and to decide. To what extent this result occurs depends on the depth of the insight gained. In psychoanalytic literature a distinction is made between a "merely" intellectual and an emotional insight. Freud states explicitly that the intellectual insight is too weak to enable patients to make a decision.* It is true that there is a difference in value when a patient only concludes the existence of an early experience and when he feels it emotionally, when he merely talks of death wishes and when he really feels them. But while this distinction has its merits, it does insufficient justice to the intellectual insight. In this context "intellectual" has inadvertently acquired the connotation of "superficial."

An intellectual insight can be a powerful motor, provided it carries sufficient conviction. The quality of insight I have in mind is illustrated by an experience which probably every analyst has had. The patient at some time is aware of having certain trends, for instance, sadistic ones, and really feels them. But several weeks later they appear to him as an en-

---

*"If the patient is to fight the normal conflict that our analysis has revealed against the suppressions, he requires a tremendous impetus to influence the desirable decision which will lead him back to health. Otherwise, he might decide for a repetition of the former issue and allow those factors which have been admitted to consciousness to slip back again into suppression. The deciding vote in this conflict is not given by his intellectual penetration—which is neither strong nor free enough for such an achievement—but only by his relation to the physician" (Sigmund Freud, *A General Introduction to Psychoanalysis*, 1920).

tirely new discovery. What has happened? It was not the emotional quality that was lacking. We could say rather that the insight into the sadistic trends did not carry any weight because it remained isolated. In order for it to be integrated the following steps are necessary: knowledge of disguised manifestations of sadistic trends and of their intensity; knowledge of what situations provoke them and of their consequences, such as anxiety, inhibitions, guilt feelings, disturbances in relationships to others. Only an insight of this scope and precision is strong enough to engage all the patient's available energies for a determination to change.

What is achieved through eliciting the patient's wish to change is similar to some extent to what a physician achieves by telling a diabetes patient that in order to overcome his illness he has to adhere to a certain diet. The physician too mobilizes energies by giving the patient an insight into the consequences which indiscriminate eating would have for him, his constitution being what it is. The difference is that the analyst's task is incomparably more difficult. The internist knows exactly what ails the patient and what the latter must avoid or must do in order to get rid of the illness. But neither the analyst nor his patient realizes what trends cause what disturbances; both of them, in addition to being engaged in an incessant struggle with the patient's fears and sensitivities, have to wind their way through a bewildering network of rationalizations and seemingly strange emotional reactions, in order finally to get hold of some connection illuminating the way.

A determination to change, though immeasurably valuable, is not, however, the equivalent of an ability to do so. In order for the patient to be able to give up his neurotic trends, those factors in his structure which made the trends necessary have to be worked through. Hence the psychoanalytic way of using this newly mobilized energy is to direct it toward further analysis.

The patient may take this further step spontaneously. He may, for instance, make more accurate observations concerning the conditions which provoke sadistic impulses, and be eager to analyze these conditions. Others, however, who are still compelled to eradicate every unpleasant trend at once, may exert efforts to control the sadistic impulses immediately, and when failing to do so become disappointed. In this case I would explain to the patient that his attempts to control the sadistic trends cannot possibly succeed as long as inwardly he still feels weak, downtrodden, easily humiliated, that as long as he feels that way he is bound to feel tempted to triumph vindictively over others, and that therefore if he wishes to overcome the sadistic trends he must analyze the psychic sources which generate them. The more an analyst is aware of this further work still to be done, the more he is able to spare a patient futile disappointment, and the more he can direct his efforts into rewarding channels.

Harry Stack Sullivan

Harry Stack Sullivan (1892–1949) was the first major theorist of the "interpersonal" school of psychotherapy. For Sullivan, emphasis was not on the person alone, but on his interpersonal situation, real or symbolic, or a blend of both. The rationale for this is that given a biological substrate, personality is shaped by social factors—especially the influence of "significant others" such as parents.

Sullivan underwent a brief classical psychoanalysis at the beginning of his career, and was thus influenced by Freud—as well as American thinkers like William Alanson White, William James, and John Dewey. He then worked chiefly with schizophrenics, whom at that time no major theorist except Adolf Meyer saw as either curable or treatable. He worked under Meyer at Johns Hopkins, and soon after started an innovative "special ward" at Sheppard Hospital in Baltimore. In the special ward, staff members were trained by Sullivan to treat each patient as a person, rather than a case, and to bear in mind that their task was to assist in the redevelopment of self-esteem. In this milieu, Sullivan practiced a variant of psychoanalysis in which no couch was used and free association and classical interpretations were relegated to "timely occasions." Interpretations were delivered in such a way as to foster self-esteem—an important Sullivanian contribution to therapy.

From his experiences with schizophrenics, Sullivan concluded people share two interrelated strivings. He believed that the "pursuit of security" or the striving to maintain self-esteem is one of the goals in life. The other major life goal he called the "pursuit of satisfactions."

Sullivan developed a theory of personality in which (although he rejected most of Freud's theory of psychosexual development) he attributed much to childhood and to points of fixation or arrested development. He paid particular attention to obsessive-compulsive disorders, which he viewed as a possible prelude to schizophrenia. In Sullivan's theory, the concept of "self" occupies a central role. The infant personifies the "good me," the "bad me," and the "not me," later organizing these into what Sullivan calls the "self-system," which is embedded in a social network of rational and irrational elements.

The therapist, said Sullivan, must be alert for the patient's inadequate and inappropriate "personifications" of the self and of others, for these provide the key to the patient's disorder. The psychiatric interview was designed to reveal the patient's personification by focusing on patterns of living that are assets or liabilities in his interpersonal relations. To this end, Sullivan asked questions with great care, noting both the content and such subtleties as tone of the voice, posture, and general demeanor.

In addition, whatever the ostensible purpose of the interview—e.g., to overcome fear of public speaking, to solve a family conflict—the actual purpose is always to convey "more feeling of capacity" and brighter prospects for living to the patient.

As Sullivan notes in the following description of the psychiatric interview, in exploring the patient's life, the interview may be complicated by "parataxic distortions," in which the patient sees and reacts to the interviewer as if he or she were someone else (much like the Freudian transference). Of special importance are what the patient esteems about himself and what he disparages, what threatens his self-esteem, and what security operations he uses to protect it. Another unique contribution is Sullivan's active engagement of the patient in forming clinical impressions. Not only would Sullivan summarize his impressions for the patient, but he would also invite the patient to add to or amend them.

BASIC CONCEPTS IN THE PSYCHIATRIC INTERVIEW

by Harry Stack Sullivan

Since the field of psychiatry has been defined as the study of interpersonal relations, and since it has been alleged that this is a perfectly valid area for the application of scientific method, we have come to the conclusion that the data of psychiatry arise only in participant observation. In other words, the psychiatrist cannot stand off to one side and apply his sense organs, however they may be refined by the use of apparatus, to noticing what someone else does, without becoming personally implicated in the operation. His principal instrument of observation is his self—his personality, *him* as a person. The processes and the changes in processes that make up the data which can be subjected to scientific study occur, not in the subject person nor in the observer, but in the situation which is created between the observer and his subject. . . .

A DEFINITION OF THE PSYCHIATRIC INTERVIEW

As a point of reference for comments often somewhat rambling, it may be useful to attempt a definition of what I have in mind when I speak of the psychiatric interview. As I see it, such an interview is a situation of primarily *vocal* communication in a *two-group*, more or less *voluntarily integrated*, on a progressively unfolding *expert-client* basis for the purpose of elucidating *characteristic patterns of living* of the subject person, the patient or client, which patterns he experiences as particularly troublesome or especially valuable, and in the revealing of which he expects to derive *benefit*. Of course, any person has many contacts with other people which are calculated to obtain information—if only the directions for how to get where he wants to go; but these are not properly regarded as instances of the psychiatric, or serious, highly technical inquiry.

THE VOCAL NATURE OF THE COMMUNICATION

The beginning of my definition of the psychiatric interview states that such an interview is a situation of primarily vocal communication—not verbal communication alone. If one assumed that everyone who came to a psychiatrist or other interviewer had to be pinned down, as one too often hears in psychiatry, or cross-examined to determine what was fact and what was fiction, then interviews would have to go on for many, many hours in order to make any sense of the other person. But if consideration is given to the nonverbal but nonetheless primarily vocal aspects of the exchange, it is actually feasible to make some sort of crude formulation of many people in from an hour and a half to, let us say, six hours of serious discourse (I might add, not six consecutive hours, though I've even done that). Much attention may profitably be paid to the telltale aspects of intonation, rate of speech, difficulty in enunciation, and so on—factors which are conspicuous to any student of vocal communication. It is by alertness to the importance of these things as signs or indicators of meaning, rather than by preoccupation only with the words spoken, that the psychiatric interview becomes practical in a reasonable section of one's lifetime.

The experience that gives me a peculiar, if not an important, slant on this whole matter is that I was initially intensely interested in schizophrenic patients. Schizophrenics are very shy people, low in self-esteem and subject to the suspicion that they are not particularly appreciated or respected by strangers. Like many other people, they are rather sensitive to scrutiny, to inspection, and to being "looked in the eye." Perhaps in all too many cases they are full of ancient traditional hokum from the culture about the eyes being the windows of the soul, and things being seen in them that might not otherwise be revealed—which seems to be one of the most misguided ideas I've ever known. In brief, schizophrenics are embarrassed by being stared at.

As I wished to learn as much as I could about schizophrenics (and with good fortune, perhaps about other humans as well), I very early in my psychiatric research work abandoned the idea of watching people while they talked with me. For years, seven and a half at least, I sat at an angle of ninety degrees from the people whom I interviewed, and usually gazed at something quite definitely in front of me—very clearly not at them. Since the field of vision is so great that one can observe motor movement in another person over an extraordinarily wide range, I think I missed few of my patient's starts, sudden changes of posture, and one thing and another, but certainly I could not see the fine movements of their faces.

In order to become somewhat at ease about what was going on, I necessarily developed further an already considerable auditory acuity so that I could hear the kind of things which, perhaps, most people are inclined to deceive themselve into thinking that they can only see. I do believe that the majority of clues to what people actually mean reach us via the ears. Tonal variations in the voice—and by "tonal variations" I mean, very broadly and generically, changes in all the complex group of things that make up speech—are frequently wonderfully dependable clues to shifts in the communicative situation. For example, if somebody is attempting to describe his work as a journeyman electrician, things may go on quite well until he is on the verge of saying something about the job which pertains to a field in which he has been guilty of gross disloyalty to his union, at which time his voice will sound altered. He may still give the facts about what a journeyman electrician should be and do, but he will sound different in the telling.

In the psychiatric interview a great part of the experience which one slowly gains manifests itself in a show of mild interest in the point at which there is a tonal difference. Thus the interviewer would perhaps say, "Oh, yes, and the payment of exactly 2½ per cent of one's income to this fund for the sick and wounded is almost never neglected by good union members, I gather"; to which the other might reply, again sounding quite different from the way he had earlier, "Exactly! It's a very important part of membership." And then, if the interviewer feels sure of the situation, he might say, "And one, of course, which you have never violated." Whereupon the other person sounds very different indeed, perhaps quite indignant, and says, "Of course not!" If the interviewer is extremely sure of the way things are going, he might even say, "Well, of course you understand I have no suspicion about you, but your voice sounded odd when you mentioned it, and I couldn't help but wonder if it was preying on your mind." At this the other person may sound still more different, and say, "Well, as a matter of fact, early in my journeymanship I actually did pocket a little of the percentage, and it has been on my conscience ever since."

Thus the psychiatric interview is primarily a matter of vocal communication, and it would be a quite serious error to presume that the communication is primarily verbal. The sound-accompaniments suggest what is to be made of the verbal propositions stated. Of course, a great many of these verbal propositions may be taken as simply matters of routine data, subject to the ordinary probabilities and to such further inquiries as will make clear what the person means.

I do not believe that I have had an interview with anybody in twenty-five years in which the person to whom I was talking was not annoyed during the early part of the interview by my asking stupid questions—I am certain that I usually correctly read the patient's mind in this respect. A patient tells me the obvious and I wonder what he means, and ask further questions. But after the first half-hour or so, he begins to see that there is a reasonable uncertainty as to what he meant, and that statements which seem obvious to him may be remarkably uncommunicative to the other person. They may be far worse than uncommunicative, for they may permit the inexperienced interviewer to assume that he knows something that is not the case. Only belatedly does he discover that he has been galloping off on a little path of private fantasy which clearly could not be what the patient was talking about, because now the patient is talking about something so obviously irrelevant to it. Thus part of the skill in interviewing comes from a sort of quiet observation all along: "Does this sentence, this statement, have an unquestionable meaning? Is there any certainty as to what this person means?"

For example, during an interview one may learn that a person is married, and if one is feeling very mildly satirical, one can say, "And doubtless happily?" If the answer is "Yes," that "Yes" can have anything in the way of implication from a dirge to a paean of supreme joy. It may indicate that the "Yes" means "No," or anything in between. The logical question, I suppose, after learning how happily the person is married, might be, "Was it your first love?" The answer may be "Yes," at which one may say, "Is that so? That's most unusual." Now, nobody cares whether it's most unusual or not. In fact, it is *fairly* unusual, but it isn't *most* unusual. The "most unusual" makes it an issue, with the result that the informant feels that it requires a little explanation; he is not quite sure whether or not it is something to be proud of. And at this point the interviewer may begin to hear a little about the interviewee's history of interpersonal intimacy with the other sex. Frequently, for example, in cases of marriage to the first love, there is a very open question of whether love has ever entered the patient's life, and one discovers that the marriage is nothing very delightful.

THE TWO-GROUP

To return to my definition of the interview, the next point is that this communication is in a two-group, and in that suggestion there certainly is a faint measure of irony. While it is practically impossible to explore most of the significant areas of personality with a third person present, it is also true that even though only two people are actually in the room, the number of more or less imaginary people that get themselves involved in this two-group is sometimes really hair-raising. In fact, two or three times in the course of an hour, or more, whole new sets of these imaginary others may also be present in the field. Of that, more later when I discuss what I call parataxic distortion.

VOLUNTARY INTEGRATION OF THE PARTICIPANTS

The next point I would like to make concerns the patient's more or less voluntary entrance into this therapeutic situation on an expert-client basis. Psychiatrists are accustomed to dealing with people of all degrees of willingness, all the way from those who are extremely unwilling to see them but are required to do so by process of law, to those who are seriously interested in getting the benefits of modern psychiatry. I think that these startling extremes only accentuate the fact that probably most people go into any interview with quite mixed motivations; they wish they could talk things over frankly with somebody, but they also carry with them, practically from childhood, ingrained determinations which block free discussion. As a result, people often expect that the psychiatrist will be either a great genius or a perfect ass.

Now, the other side of the picture: There are some more or less voluntary elements in the psychiatrist's attitude. He may vary from enthusiasm for what he is about to discover, to a bored indifference about the patient—and these attitudes unhappily may be determined very early in the interview. The attitudes of the interviewee are data. But any striking emotion on the part of the interviewer is an unhappy artifact which amounts to a psychiatric problem. For example, any intense curiosity about the details of another person's life, particularly his sexual life or drinking habits, or something like that, is a very unfortunate ingredient in a psychiatric interview. On the other hand, a more or less disdainful indifference to what the patient may have to offer amounts to a quite serious evidence of morbidity on the part of an interviewer.

As I shall presently suggest, there is no fun in psychiatry. If you try to get fun out of it, you pay a considerable price for your unjustifiable optimism. If you do not feel equal to the headaches that psychiatry induces, you are in the wrong business. It is work—work the like of which I do not know. True, it ordinarily does not require vast physical exertion, but it does require a high degree of alertness to a sometimes very rapidly shifting field of signs which are remarkably complex in themselves and in their relations. And the necessity for promptness of response to what happens proves in the course of a long day to be very tiring indeed. It is curious, but there are data that suggest that the more complicated the field to which one must attend, the more rapidly fatigue sets in. For example, in dealing with a serious problem in a very competent person, the psychiatrist will find that grasping the nuances of what is reserved, and what is distorted, and what unknown by the communicant but very relevant to the work at hand, is not easy. So an enthusiasm about psychiatry is preposterous—it shows one just hasn't grown up; but at the same time, for the psychiatrist to be indifferent toward his work is fatal. The more dependable attitude of the psychiatrist in a psychiatric interview is probably simply to have a very serious realization that he is earning his living, and that he must work for it.

Whether the patient thinks at the beginning that he is very eager to see the psychiatrist or the interviewer, or whether he thinks he is bitterly opposed to it all, is less important. This does make some slight difference at the start, because one tries to accommodate, insofar as one readily can, to the mood of the patient. In other words, if a person comes to you quite angrily, it is not particularly helpful to beam on him and say, "Why, my dear fellow, you seem upset. Do tell me what's troubling you!" That is probably too reminiscent of the worst of his past experience with maiden aunts and so on. When people approach you angrily, you take them very seriously, and, if you're like me, with the faint suggestion that you can be angry too, and that you would like to know what the shooting is about.

Thus the initial attitude—be it willingness or unwillingness, hesitancy or reservation—of the client determines somewhat the attitude, and perhaps the pattern, of the interviewer's initial inquiries. But the client's attitude is not in itself to be taken very seriously; many very resistant people prove to be

remarkably communicative as soon as they discover that the
interrogator makes some sense and that he is not simply dis-
tributing praise, blame, and so on. . . .

THE PATIENT'S CHARACTERISTIC PATTERNS OF LIVING

To return again to my definition of the psychiatric interview,
I said that it is for the purpose of elucidating characteristic
patterns of living. Personality very strikingly demonstrates
in every instance, in every situation, the perduring effects
of the past; and the effects of a particular past event are
not only perhaps fortunate or unfortunate, but also extensively intertwined with the effects of a great many other
past events. Thus there is no such thing as learning what *ails*
a person's living, in the sense that you will come to know
anything definite, without getting a pretty good idea of who it
is that's doing the living, and with whom. In other words, in
every case, whether you know it or not, if you are to correctly understand your patient's problems, you must understand him in the major characteristics of his dealing with
people. Now, this relationship of difficulty in living to all the
rest of the important characteristics of a personality is a thing
which I must stress, because we are such capable creatures,
we humans, that we do not always know anywhere near what
we have experienced. Psychiatrists know a great deal about
their patients that they don't know they know. For example,
caught off guard by the offhand question of a friendly colleague—"Yes, but damn his difficulties in living! What sort of
person is this patient of yours?"—the psychiatrist may rattle
off a description that would do him honor if he only knew it.
   And do you think that this is restricted to psychiatrists?
What you know about the people whom you know at all well
is truly amazing, even though you have never formulated it.
It may never have been very important for you to formulate
it; it hasn't been worth anything to you, you might say. All
that it's worth, of course, is that it makes for better understanding; but, if your interest lies in what the person does and
not in understanding him, you probably don't know how
much you know about him.
   In the psychiatric interview, it is a very good idea to know
as much as possible about the patient. It is very much easier
to do therapy if the patient has caught on to the fact that you
are interested in understanding something of what he thinks

ails him, and also what sort of person his more admiring friends regard him to be, and so on. Thus the purpose of the interview is to elucidate the characteristic patterns of living, some of which make trouble for the patient.

Many people who consult psychiatrists regard themselves as the victims of disease, or hereditary defect, or God knows what in the way of some sort of evil, fateful entity that is tied to them or built into them. They don't think of their troubles, as they call them, as important, but not especially distinguished, parts of their general performance of living in a civilized world with other people. Many problems are so thoroughly removed from any connection with other people—when they are reported by the patient—that the young psychiatrist would, I think, feel rather timid about suggesting to the patient that perhaps he did not experience these problems in his relations with everybody, but only with some particular people; and I think that even the very experienced psychiatrist would scarcely wish to expose the patient to such unnecessary stress. But one can always ask *when* the trouble occurs—in what setting it is most likely to be seen. Remarkably often one of these patients who has an "organic" or "hereditary" neurosis that has nothing to do with other people can produce instances of his neurosis in which five or six different people have been involved—and for the life of him can't think of any other settings in which it has been demonstrated. It is only when he has come to this point that the psychiatrist can say, "In other words, you don't have this difficulty, so far as you know, with your wife and her maiden sister, and so on and so forth?" The patient stops, and thinks, and quite honestly says, "No, I don't believe I ever do." Only then is he on the verge of realizing that perhaps the other fellow *does* have something to do with the difficulty; only after being led around to making that discovery from his own data can he begin to realize that it is the interpersonal context that calls out many troubles.

I am not attempting to say here that there is nothing that makes living difficult except other people and one's inadequate preparation for dealing with them. There are a vast number of things, such as blindness in one or both eyes, and harelip, and poor education, which make difficulties in living. But the psychiatric interview is primarily designed to discover *obscure* difficulties in living which the patient does not clearly understand: in other words, that which for cultural reasons—reasons of his particular education for life—he is foggy about, chronically misleads himself about, or misleads others about. Such difficulties stand out more clearly and more meaningfully as one grasps what sort of person he is, and what that person does, and why.

To sum up, a patient's patterns of difficulty arise in his past experience and variously interpenetrate all aspects of his current interpersonal relationships. Without data reflecting many important aspects of the patient's personality, the patient's statement of symptoms and the psychiatrist's observation of signs of difficulty are unintelligible.

THE PATIENT'S EXPECTATION OF BENEFIT

This brings me to the final portion of my definition—that the patient has at least some expectation of improvement or other personal gain from the interview. This statement may not sound particularly impressive; yet I have participated in long interviews that have been very unpleasant to the patient but which have come to some end useful to him and satisfactory to me only because he caught on to the fact that there was something in it for him. The *quid pro quo* which keeps people going in this necessarily disturbing business of trying to be foursquare and straightforward about one's most lamentable failures and one's most chagrining mistakes is that one is learning something that promises to be useful. Insofar as the patient's participation in the interview situation inspires in the patient a conviction that the psychiatrist is learning not only *how* the patient has trouble,* but *who* the patient is and *with whom* he has trouble, the implied expectation of benefit is in process of realization.

I wish to put a good deal of emphasis on this, because there are interview situations in which there is no attention paid whatever to what the interrogee—the victim, one might say—gets out of it. Instead, it is a wholly one-sided interrogation. Questions are asked and the answers are received by a person who pays no attention to all the anxiety or the feeling of insecurity of the informant, and who gives no clue to the meaning of the information elicited. These one-sided interrogations are all right for certain very limited and crudely defined purposes. For example, if you want to accumulate in fifteen minutes some clues as to whether or not a person will probably survive two years in the Army under any circumstances that are apt to transpire in two years in the Army, then you can use this type of interrogation. But, out of a large number of people interviewed in this way, the percentage of error in your judgment will be high. How high this percentage is, nobody has yet very adequately determined, for even the people who set out to use one-sided interrogation undoubtedly interpret a good deal that goes on besides the answering itself.

One can, in a rather brief interview, reach certain limited objectives. For example, an interviewer can determine that a person should not be given a job as a telephone operator by discovering that he has no capacity for righting himself after a misunderstanding, or that he is unnerved by someone's being unpleasant to him. But for purposes anything like those of the psychiatric interview, in which one is actually attempting to assess a person's assets and liabilities in terms of his future living, some time is required, and a simple question-answer technique will not work.

The interviewer must be sure that the other person is getting something out of it, that his expectation of improving himself (as he may put it), of getting a better job, or of attaining whatever has motivated him in undergoing the interview, gets encouragement. As long as this personal objective receives support, the communicative situation improves, and the interviewer comes finally to have data on which he can make a formulation of some value to himself as an expert, and to the other person concerned.

· · · · ·

THE PSYCHIATRIST AS A PARTICIPANT OBSERVER

As I said at the beginning, psychiatry is peculiarly the field of participant observation. The fact is that we cannot make any sense of, for example, the motor movements of another person except on the basis of behavior that is meaningful to us—that is, on the basis of what we have experienced, done ourselves, or seen done under circumstances in which its purpose, its motivation, or at least the intentions behind it were communicated to us. Without this past background, the observer cannot deduce, by sheer intellectual operations, the meaning of the staggering array of human acts. As an example of this, almost all the things pertaining to communication form such highly conventionalized patterns and are so fixed within the culture that if my pronunciation of a word deviates from yours, you may wonder what in the world I am talking about. Things having to do with your own past experience and with proscriptions of the culture and so on that were common in your home; activities which are attached to you as the person concerned in their doing, and activities to which you respond as if you were the person primarily, directly, and simply concerned in them—all these are the data of psychiatry. Therefore, the psychiatrist has an inescapable, inextricable involvement in all that goes on in the interview; and to the extent that he is unconscious or unwitting of his participation in the interview, to that extent he does not know what is happening. This is another argument in favor of the position that the psychiatrist has a hard enough job to do without any pursuit of his own pleasure or prestige. He can legitimately expect only the satisfaction of feeling that he did what he was paid for—that will be enough, and probably more than he can do well.

The psychiatrist should never lose track of the fact that all the processes of the patient are more or less exactly addressed at him, and that all that he offers—his experience—is more or less accurately aimed at the patient, with a resulting wonderful interplay. For example, one realizes that statements are not things that can be rigidly fixed as to meaning by Webster's or the Oxford Dictionary, but that they are only approximations, sometimes remote approximations, of what is meant. But that is just the beginning of the complexities of the participant character of the psychiatric interview—for that matter, of all attempts at communication between people, of which the psychiatric interview is an especially characterized example.

That does not mean, as some of our experts in semantics might lead us to suppose, that before a psychiatrist starts talking with his patient he should give him a list of words that are not to be used. It simply means, as I said earlier, that the psychiatrist listens to all statements with a certain critical interest, asking, "Could that mean anything except what first occurs to me?" He questions (at least to himself) much of what he hears, not on the assumption that the patient is a liar, or doesn't know how to express himself, or anything like that, but always with the simple query in mind, "Now, could this mean something that would not immediately occur to me? Do I know what he means by that?" Every now and then this leads to the interviewer's asking questions, but it certainly does not imply the vocal questioning of every statement. So if the patient says, "The milkman dropped a can of milk last night and it woke me up," I am usually willing to presume that it is simply so.

On the other hand, a patient may say, "Well, he's my dearest friend! He hasn't a hostile impulse toward me!" I then assume that this is to explain in some curious fashion that this other person has done him an extreme disservice, such as running away with his wife—or perhaps it was a great service; I have yet to discover, from the interview, which it was. And I say, "Is that so? It sounds amazing." Now when I say a thing sounds amazing, the patient feels very much on the spot; he feels that he must prove something, and he tells me more about how wonderful his friend's motivation is. Having heard still more, I am able to say, "Well, is it possible that you can think of nothing he ever did that was at least unfortunate in its effect?" At this the poor fellow will no doubt remember the elopement of his wife. And thus we gradually come to discover why it is necessary for him to consider this other person to be such a perfect friend—quite often a very illuminating field to explore. God knows, it may be the nearest approach to a good friend this man has ever had, and he feels exceedingly the need of a friend.

The more conventional a person's statements are, of course, the more doubtful it is that you have any idea of what he really means. For example, there are people who have been trained to cultivate virtue (and the cultural motives that provided this training were horrible) to such an extent that they are truly almost incapable of saying any evil of anybody.

The psychiatrist, the interviewer, plays a very active role in introducing interrogations, not to show that he is smart or that he is skeptical, but literally to make sure that he knows what he is being told. Few things do the patient more good in the way of getting toward his more or less clearly formulated desire to benefit from the investigation than this very care on the part of the interviewer to discover exactly what is meant. Almost every time one asks, "Well, do you mean so and so?" the patient is a little clearer on what he does mean. And what a relief it is to discover that his true meaning is anything but what he at first says, and that he is at long last uncovering some conventional self-deception that he has been pulling on himself for years.

Let me illustrate this last by telling you of a young man who had been clearly sinking into a schizophrenic illness for several months and who was referred to me by a colleague. Among the amazing things I extracted from this poor citizen was that, to his amazement and chagrin, he spent a good deal of his time in the kitchen with his mother making dirty cracks at her, saying either obscure or actually bitter and critical things to her. He thought he must be crazy, because he was the only child and his mother, so he said, was perfect. As a matter of fact, he had two perfect parents. They had done everything short of carrying him around on a pillow. And now he had broken down just because he was engaged in a couple of full-time courses at one of our best universities. In other words, he was a bright boy, and had very healthy ambitions which represented the realization of the very fine training that he had been given by these excellent parents. I undertook to discover what was so surprising to him about this business of his hostile remarks to his mother, and he made it quite clear that the surprising thing was that she had never done him any harm, and had actually enfolded him in every kind of good. To all this I thought, "Oh yeah? It doesn't sound so to me. It doesn't make sense. Maybe you have overlooked something."

By that time I was actually able to say something like this: "I have a vague feeling that some people might doubt the utility to you of the care with which your parents, and particularly your mother, saw to it that you didn't learn how to dance, or play games, or otherwise engage in the frivolous social life of people of your age." And I was delighted to see the schizophrenic young man give me a sharp look. Although he was seated where I didn't have to look directly at him, I could see that. And I said, "Or was that an unmitigated blessing?" There was a long pause, and then he opined that when he was young he might have been sore about it.

I guessed that that wasn't the whole story—that he was still sore about it, and with very good reason. Then I inquired if he had felt any disadvantage in college from the lack of these social skills with which his colleagues whiled away their evenings, and so on. He recalled that he had often noticed his defects in that field, and that he regretted them. With this improvement in intelligence, we were able to glean more of what the mother had actually done and said to discourage his impulse to develop social techniques. At the end of an hour and a half devoted more or less entirely to this subject, I was able to say, "Well, now, is it really so curious that you're being unpleasant to your mother?" And he thought that perhaps it wasn't.

A couple of days later the family telephoned to say that he was greatly benefited by his interview with me. As a matter of fact, he unquestionably was. But the benefit—and this is perhaps part of why I tell the story—arose from the discovery that a performance of his, which was deeply distressing to him because it seemed irrational and entirely unjust, became reasonably justified by a change in his awareness of his past and of his relationship with the present victim of his behavior. Thus the feeling was erased that he was crazy, that only a madman would be doing this—and, believe me, it is no help to anybody's peace of mind to feel that he is mad. His peace of mind was enhanced to the extent that is was no longer necessary for him to feel chagrin, contempt for himself, and all sorts of dim religious impiety; but on the other hand he could feel, as I attempted to suggest in our initial interview, that there wasn't anything different in his behavior from practically anybody else's except the accents in the patterns of its manifestation. As he was able to comprehend that the repulsive, queer, strange, mystifying, chagrining, horrifying aspects of his experience reflected defects in his memory and understanding concerning its origins, the necessity to manifest the behavior appeared to diminish, which actually meant that competing processes were free to appear, and that the partitioning of his life was to some degree broken down. The outwardly meaningless, psychotic attacks on his mother did not give him the satisfaction that came from asking her more directly why in the devil she had never let him learn to play bridge. With the substitution of the possibility of a more direct approach, the psychotic material disappeared and he was better.

Thus whenever the psychiatrist's attempt to discover what the patient is talking about leads to be somewhat more clear on what he is thinking about or attempting to communicate or conceal, his grasp on life is to some extent enhanced. And no one has grave difficulties in living if he has a very good grasp on what is happening to him.

Everything in that sentence depends on what I mean by "grave," and let me say that here I am referring to those difficulties unquestionably requiring the intervention of an expert. It is my opinion that man is rather staggeringly endowed with adaptive capacities, and I am quite certain that when a person is clear on the situation in which he finds himself, he does one of three things: he decides it is too much for him and leaves it, he handles it satisfactorily, or he calls in adequate help to handle it. And that's all there is to it.

When people find themselves recurrently in obscure situations which they feel they should understand and actually don't, and in which they feel that their prestige requires them to take adequate action (a somewhat hypothetical entity, since they do not know what the situation is), they are clearly in need of psychiatric assistance. That assistance is by way of the participant observation of the psychiatrist and the patient, in which the psychiatrist attempts to discover what is happening to the patient. A great many questions may be asked and answered in the psychiatric interview before the patient sees much of what the psychiatrist is exploring; but, in the process, the patient will have experienced many beginning clarifications of matters which will subsequently take on considerable personal significance.

As an example of such an obscure situation which seemed to demand action, I would like to mention a patient whom I saw for a brief interview a number of years ago in New York. She was a young lady of forty-three or so who presented, as her trouble in life, the fact that at night her breasts were frightfully tampered with by her sister who lived in Oklahoma. Now, such a statement is a reasonable sign of something being a little the matter with the mind. It also developed that the pastor of one of the more important New York churches gave the only help that she had ever been able to obtain in this cursed nuisance perpetrated by her sister. Since I always appreciate any help that anybody can get, particularly from somebody besides me, I was pleased to learn this and wondered why she had sought me out.

At this I learned that there were other difficulties. She was coming to suspect that a woman who worked in her office had been employed by her sister to spy on her—this nice psychotic lady, like many others, was earning a living. I said, "Aha! Now we are getting somewhere! Tell me about that." Whereupon she bridled, realizing that it was risky to admit psychotic content to a psychiatrist. It developed that she had been controlling increasing rage against this woman in her office for weeks, and that she had been consulting her pastor with increasing frequency about the problem. I didn't ask what he did. But I did happen to look at the clock at that point and discovered that I had been keeping another patient waiting twenty minutes. So I said to the young lady, "Well, look here. I don't believe it would be practicable for me to attempt to substitute for the friendly adviser who is considerable comfort and support to you. But I do want to say one thing, which I have to say both as a psychiatrist and as a member of society: If you feel impelled to do something physical to square yourself with this persecutor in your office, then, madam, before you do it, go to the psychopathic pavilion at Bellevue and apply for voluntary admission for two or three days. In the end that will be much better." And she said, "Oh, you're like all the other psychiatrists!" With which the interview was over. I am quite certain that she derived considerable benefit from the finish of that interview.

THE CONCEPT OF PARATAXIC DISTORTION

Now let us notice a feature of all interpersonal relations which is especially striking in the intimate type of inquiry which the psychiatric interview can be, and which is, in fact, strangely illustrated in the case I have just mentioned. This is the parataxic, as I call it, concomitant in life. By this I mean that not only are there quite tangible people involved (in this case the patient's sister living in Oklahoma and a fellow employee in the patient's office), but also somewhat fantastic constructs of those people are involved, such as the sister tinkering with the patient's breasts in her Manhattan room at night, and the fellow employee acting as an emissary or agent of her sister. These psychotic elaborations of imaginary people and imaginary personal performances are spectacular and seem very strange. But the fact is that in a great many relationships of the most commonplace kind—with neighbors, enemies, acquaintances, and even statistically determined people as the collector and the mailman—variants of such distortions often exist. The characteristics of a person that would be agreed to by a large number of competent observers may not appear to you to be the characteristics of the person toward whom you are making adjustive or maladjustive movements. The *real* characteristics of the other fellow at that time may be of negligible importance to the interpersonal situation. This we call *parataxic distortion*.

Parataxic distortion as a term may sound quite unusual; actually the phenomena it describes are anything but unusual. The great complexity of the psychiatric interview is brought about by the interviewee's substituting for the psychiatrist a person or persons strikingly different in most significant re-

spects from the psychiatrist. The interviewee addresses his behavior toward this fictitious person who is temporarily in the
ascendancy over the reality of the psychiatrist, and he interprets the psychiatrist's remarks and behavior on the basis of
this same fictitious person. There are often clues to the occurrence of these phenomena. Such phenomena are the basis for
the really astonishing misunderstandings and misconceptions
which characterize all human relations, and certain special
precautions must be taken against them in the psychiatric interview after it is well under way. Parataxic distortion is also
one way that the personality displays before another some of
its gravest problems. In other words, parataxic distortion may
actually be an obscure attempt to communicate something
that really needs to be grasped by the therapist, and perhaps
finally to be grasped by the patient. Needless to say, if such
distortions go unnoted, if they are not expected, if the possibility of their existence is ignored, some of the most important things about the psychiatric interview may go by default.

Eric Berne

Eric Berne (1910–1970) was a Canadian-born psychiatrist with psychoanalytic training, who rebelled against what he saw as the elitism and complexity of psychoanalysis. He undertook to provide therapy that would be simple to understand and apply by laymen. The result is a translation of psychoanalysis into "transactional analysis," or TA.

Berne postulated that the human personality is composed of "ego states," which are coherent organizations of intellect and emotion. The "Parent" ego state consists of introjected parental values and admonitions; the "Adult" ego state is shaped by objective contact with the enviroment; and the "Child" ego state contains the spontaneous childlike aspects of the personality. Criticism and orthodoxy are associated with the Parent, detached calculation of the rewards of various responses with the Adult, and irrational fears and joy with the Child.

Berne proposed that these ego states influence interactions and that what people say can be classified as coming from one or another ego state. Transactions, in Berne's view, can be seen as taking place between ego states. There is the possibility of "complementary" transactions, where the ego state addressed "replies," or "crossed" transactions, where an ego state other than the one addressed replies. Complementary transactions foster communication, while crossed transactions interfere with it. Transactions can occur simultaneously on overt and covert levels: for example, a seemingly Parent-Parent transaction may contain an even more important hidden Child-Child transaction. With every transaction there is a "pay-off" for each party in the form of pleasant or unpleasant emotions.

What Berne called "games" are transactions that include

overt and covert exchanges and afford well-defined payoffs for the players. The initiator of a game begins by evoking certain feelings in the other, implying that these will be accepted and praised. When these feelings are evoked, the initiator then either criticizes these feelings or uses them to gain a superior moral position.

The preconscious organization of one's entire life is called the "lifescript." According to Berne, the lifescript is laid down in the Child ego state between the ages of three and seven, and is typically one of the following:

> I'm OK and you're OK
> I'm OK and you're not OK
> I'm not OK and you're OK
> I'm not OK and you're not OK

Such feelings are adapted by the child from his parents' opinions at such an early age that he can't make a reasoned evaluation; the child accepts the lifescript wholesale.

The first step in transactional analysis is instruction in these concepts. As therapy progresses—often in a group—the therapist listens carefully for clues to the patient's lifescript and points out the roles of ego states in his transactions. At one point the therapist may explain the patient's lifescript and instruct him in another, more realistic script. The therapist resists becoming involved in the games that have led to neurotic suffering in the patient's life, pointing out that these games are not only frustrating but unnecessary. However, the therapist makes no attempt to destroy these ego states (in fact, it is considered impossible) or to criticize their activity. Instead, the therapist tries to protect the patient from the criticisms of the Parent and the impulsive actions of the Child, while encouraging the influence of the Adult. In the patient-therapist relationship, for example, the patient is rewarded for Adult-Adult transactions.

Much of TA is one-to-one, but the patient may also participate in group sessions. In group sessions the therapist maps the nature of the transactions among patients, and shows how they arise either from lifescripts or from new emerging productive modes of interaction. In the selection that follows Berne describes, for other therapists, the major tenets of TA; although this presentation is couched in sophisticated language, he emphasizes that, in practice, a patient need only master four concepts—Parent, Child, Adult, and game—to benefit from TA. Berne tells how TA can be used in therapy groups, but the same basic principles apply in one-to-one therapy.

GENERAL CHARACTERISTICS OF TRANSACTIONAL ANALYSIS

by Eric Berne

A transactional analyst makes a point of keeping the patient informed of what is happening to him as he goes along, thus often earning his gratitude as well as his improvement. This runs counter to the institutionalized dogma that the patient is not supposed to know what is happening to him, and will get better to more advantage if he is kept in the dark. Thus far, no untoward effects have been noticed from patients having a clear understanding of what is going on in the therapeutic situation, of exactly how far they have progressed, and of how much still remains to be done. The specialized vocabulary of five words can often be taught in a sound way in two or three sessions, with clinical demonstrations from the immediate proceedings of the group.

Since most patients are eager to learn, their alternatives lie between a small vocabulary of well-assimilated operational and experiential terminology which they have personally verified at the clinical level under planned guidance, or a larger vocabulary of ill-digested concepts which they have acquired adventitously of surreptitiously. The "danger of intellectualization" is another fear which has been institutionally exaggerated, so that the word "intellectualization" is often used carelessly as an epithet which derogates not only the specific defence, but also the patient's useful application of his intelligence to the solution of his problems. In practice, there is little difficulty in making the distinction by those who give it their unbiased attention, so that not only the therapist, but the patients as well can soon learn to recognize the difference between intellectualization and using intelligence.

After the patients begin to feel more comfortable in a transactional therapy group and affective expression becomes more vigorous, the therapist must learn, as in all forms of therapy, to distinguish between melodrama, institutionally encouraged acting-out, and authentic expressions of feeling; nor must he succumb to a popular misconception of psychoanalytic treatment, which is sometimes thought of by outsiders as a continual storm of affective expression. Transactional analysis, like psychoanalysis, clears the way to expression of genuine affect rather than encouraging mere abreaction or dramatic incidents based on spurious motivation, which often serve mainly as a relief of boredom in patient and therapist. "Affectivization" of the proceedings is no more helpful than their "intellectualization;" both encourage isolation. Affectivization isolates intelligence, just as intellectualization isolates affect. The goal of transactional analysis is to establish the most open and authentic communication possible between the affective and intellectual components of the personality.

Transactional analysis does not pretend to be a restatement of Freudian, Jungian, or other psychology. Superego, ego, and id are concepts, whereas ego states are experiential and behavioral realities, and are even civil realities in a sense. The colloquialism here is that you can't find the telephone number of a superego, an ego, or an id, but you can find the telephone number of a Parent (such as the patient's father), or of an Adult (the patient himself), or of a Child (his telephone number when he was a little boy). The most fruitful application of psychoanalytic thinking finds its place in group treatment after the patient has been properly prepared by transactional analysis. It is also a profitable preparation for Jungian, Adlerian, existential, and other specialized terminologies and ways of therapeutic thinking. Transactional analysis, then, claims (and this claim has been filed elsewhere in more detail) to be more general than any of these, and hence leaves room for all of them in appropriate contexts.

Transactional theory is simpler and more scientifically economical in its statements than many other psychotherapeutic theories, but its clinical use requires conscientious study, and in the advanced stages where it begins to overlap with psychoanalytic and existential therapies it takes on increased complexity. Nevertheless, its principles can be understood and appreciated by any well-trained psychotherapist, since it deals with the same phenomena as any other approach: human psychopathology. Many others have made observations in passing that resemble transactional statements. What is new here is the manner of ordering and dealing with these phenomena, and the systematic exploration and clarification of certain kinds of statements. The difference between an acute observation and a systematic theory is the difference between a poultice of bread with mold on it and a penicillin injection: they both contain the same essential ingredient, but one is more useful than the other.

Illustrations Two applications of transactional analysis will now be offered for consideration, one heuristic and the other clinical.

First, the therapeutic "poker face," which in unsophisticated circles is considered the hallmark of the trained therapist, is not always easy to justify. The reasons commonly given for maintaining this impassivity in group treatment can be sorted into five classes, which in increasing order of cogency and authenticity are as follows:

1. The therapist is "supposed" to keep a poker face, because everybody knows it is so and the books say so. This amounts to playing a role with the poker face as a physiological uniform.

2. A therapist may be subject to critical questioning at staff conferences if he does not keep a poker face, so that there is some implication that immobility or restrained token mimicry is as far as it is safe to go.

3. Sometimes it appears that the real reason for the poker face is that the therapist does not know what to do next and remains frozen hour after hour in the hope that some clue will be forthcoming.

4. In order for the patient to form a pure transference, it is essential that the therapist not reveal his own reactions to what the patient says.

5. The therapist does not react overtly because it is his task to keep from becoming involved in the patient's manipulations: first, so that he can retain control of the situation; secondly, so that he can observe the patient's reactions better; and thirdly, because it is important to know what the patient does when his manipulations fail.

The last explanation is the most valid one for those therapists who understand it clearly enough to know when relaxations are indicated. As to the other four, the first case signifies an act of compliance, the second an undue vulnerability, the third a deficiency in knowledge, and the fourth a misconception which does not distinguish clearly between psychotherapy and formal psychoanalysis. It will be noted that even in the fifth category, the therapist has not clearly defined his criteria for relaxing his immobility. This whole problem can be solved quite concisely in transactional terms.

From that standpoint, there are three types of therapy. In the first, as with certain schizophrenics, the therapist plays a Parental role and can exhibit his Parental ego state advantageously. In the second, as in analytic work with grownups, his task is to process data, which he can do most efficiently by maintaining a strictly Adult ego state. In the third, as in play therapy with children, the therapist may have to participate in the play at times, and will do that most naturally in his own Child ego state. It is immediately apparent that the prolonged maintenance of a poker face is appropriate only to the second type, and appropriate relaxations are clearly indicated by the nature of the other two kinds of therapy. Furthermore, relaxations are also indicated in "Adult" therapy whenever other considerations take precedence over data-processing; there may be occasions when reassurance, or sagacity from the Parent or humor or liveliness from the Child are indicated.

In the second example of transactional analysis, one supplied by Dr. Robert Goulding from a relatively new group of alcoholic patients, the rapid and clear-cut effects of structural analysis (the first phase of transactional analysis) are nicely demonstrated. Selma was originally Patricia's sponsor in Alcoholics Anonymous. When they came to the treatment group, Patricia reacted like a rebellious child toward Selma, and Selma fought back. With structural analysis, they soon preceived that it was Patricia's Child fighting with Selma's Parent. Patricia recognized her particular sensitivity, based on her own childhood, to Selma's mother Parent. Selma then recognized the irritating quality of Patricia's Child as reminiscent of her own little sister. Once this structure was clarified by them and historically validated, they lost interest in fighting and left the meeting arm in arm for the first time, laughing. This manner of exit also answered operationally their question "What can one do instead of drinking?" by giving them the experience of being friends with people even when sober.

The challenge in this situation lies in the fact that Selma and Patricia are getting better faster then they are supposed to and that this is happening without undue strain on either the therapist's or the patients' part. Rapid improvements with structural analysis may be quite stable and enduring if the patients have authentic insight into the structure of their transactions, and are not merely "making with the interpretations."

THE FORMAL ASPECTS OF
TRANSACTIONAL ANALYSIS

The formal exposition of the principles of transactional analysis has been set down in three previous volumes, and will be given here only in the barest outline. Those principles were first derived from actual clinical material in treatment groups and only later stated formally and supported by documentation. This process will be reversed here; the principles will be given first and the clinical aspects clarified later.

STRUCTURAL ANALYSIS

Ego States   Every human being has at his disposal a limited repertoire of ego states, which fall into three types. Parental ego states are borrowed from parental figures and reproduce the feelings, attitudes, behavior, and responses of those figures. Adult ego states are concerned with the autonomous collecting and processing of data and the estimating of probabilities as a basis for action. Child ego states are relics from the individual's childhood and reproduce his behavior and state of mind at a particular moment or epoch of his development, using, however, the increased facilities at his disposal as a grown-up. It is assumed that there are three organs which mediate the organization and implementation of these three types of ego states. The exteropsyche is concerned with Parental ego states, the neopsyche with Adult ego states, and the archaeopsyche with Child ego states.

The superego, ego, and id as defined by Freud are regarded as determinants of special characteristics of each type of ego state, but neither the ego states themselves nor the organs that "give rise" to them correspond to the Freudian "agencies." Superego, ego, and id are inferential concepts, while ego states are experiential and social realities. The descriptive study of ego states takes precedence over the study of the influences that determine them. In doctrinal terms, structural analysis precedes psychoanalysis. In structural language, psychoanalysis is essentially a process of de-confusing the Child ego state, but that ego state must first be isolated and described, and the Adult ego state must simultaneously be decontaminated and recathected so that it is free to assist with the subsequent analytic work.

The term "transactional analysis" is used to describe the system as a whole, which is divided into a logical and clinically useful sequence of phases: structural analysis, transactional analysis proper, game analysis, and script analysis. The diagnosis of ego states has been described elsewhere, and is a special art to be cultivated by the therapist. A Parental ego state exhibited by a patient is referred to colloquially as his "Parent," an Adult ego state is called his "Adult," and an archaic ego state is called his "Child." Gratifying therapeutic results may be obtained from structural analysis alone, hence it is worth while for its own sake; the fact that it builds a solid foundation for further progress is an additional advantage.

The "Weak Ego"   Two special features of structural analysis should be mentioned. First, there is nothing in this approach which corresponds exactly to the "weak ego" of conventional terminology. Every human being (except perhaps some with the most severe types of organic brain injuries) is regarded as possessing the complete neurological apparatus for neopsychic functioning. In certain cases the Adult ego state may be spoken of as "weakly cathected," but it is never dealt with as though there were some inherent defect in its structure. In clinical practice it can be verified that even mentally retarded people and "deteriorated" schizophrenics possess the complete apparatus of Adult ego functioning, and the therapeutic problem is to cathect this apparatus in order that it may take its normal place in the patient's psychic organization. As an analogy: if no radio is heard in someone's house, that does not means he lacks one; he may have a good one, but it needs to be turned on and warmed up before it can be heard clearly.

In this respect, then, structural analysis is more optimistic than other therapeutic systems, and this optimism is warranted by the results. If a patient is treated as though he had a "weak ego," he is likely to respond accordingly; if he is treated as though he had a perfectly good ego which only needs to be activated, experience shows that there is a good chance that his Adult ego state will become more and more active in his life: that is, he will become more rational and objective toward the outside world and toward himself.

"Mature" and "Immature"   The second distinguishing feature is that the words "mature" and "immature" are never used in transactional analysis. Some of the reasons for this have already been implied in the previous paragraph. In general those are rather fatuous conceptions based on an essentially patronizing attitude. It is not that one person is

"mature" and another "immature"; it is merely that one person chooses to exhibit his Child ego state more often than another. To take two rather clear-cut examples, an alcoholic may have a high capacity for processing certain kinds of data during his working hours, but when he relaxes his Adult ego state after work, he may behave in a child-like way. On the other hand one who is thought of as "mature" by his associates—a steady, "co-operative" community leader—may one day turn out to be an embezzler or a murderer, taking almost everyone by surprise. The question raised by these commonplace cases is as follows: is the responsible man who commits indiscretions when he is intoxicated to be called "immature," and the man who lives compliantly until he commits a crime to be thought of as "mature?"

Special Distinctions   The structural analyst must be familiar with certain functional distinctions in the Parent and Child. What is loosely spoken of as "the Parent" may signify either the Parental ego state—that is, a reproduction of nurturing, angry, or critical behavior on the part of one or both parents—or the Parental influence—that is, behavior historically determined by borrowed parameters. In the Parental ego state, a woman is behaving as mother behaved; under the Parental influence, she is behaving as mother would have liked; and this includes specific maternal permissions or instigations as well as the specific maternal prohibitions generally included under the concept of superego. Hence this purely transactional, behavioral approach avoids the complications and limitations imposed by words like "identification" and "superego," impositions which are largely irrelevant to therapeutic progress, at least in group treatment. The Child similarly is exhibited in two phases: the adapted Child, who is acting under the Parental influence, as evidenced by such adaptations as compliance or withdrawal; and the expressive Child, who acts autonomously in expressing creative, angry, or affectionate tendencies.

Second-order Structural Analysis   At a late stage in treatment, second-order structural analysis may be indicated. This will reveal that the Parent has its own internal structure, such as that shown in Figure 1, where that aspect of the patient's personality structure is divided into "mother" and "father" segments, each of these in turn having Parent, Adult, and Child components, since the actual mother and father, being human beings, also have the usual repertoires of ego states.

For patients in an advanced stage of structural analysis, each subdivision of Figure 1 may have clinical and historical significance. Correspondingly, the Child ego state, at the time it was originally fixated, already had Parent, Adult, and Child components, so that second-order structural analysis may reveal an even more archiac ego state embedded in the Child ego state as currently exhibited by the patient. Thus a woman who ordinarily talks and acts like a ten-year-old girl may under stress feel and respond like a confused ("schizophrenic") two-year-old.

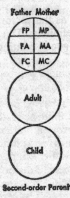

Fig. 1. Structural diagram of a personality

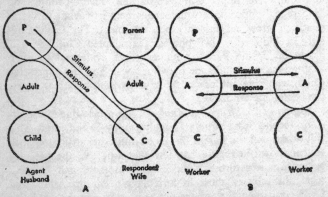

Fig. 2. Complementary transactions

TRANSACTIONAL ANALYSIS

Complementary Transactions Transactional analysis consists of determining which ego state is active at a given moment in the exhibition of a transactional stimulus by the agent, and which ego state is active in the response given by the respondent. Complementary transactions are those in which the vectors are parallel; that is, the response complements the stimulus. A Parental husband speaking to a Childlike wife will expect a Child-like response from her, as shown in Figure 2A. An Adult stimulus anticipates an Adult response, as shown in Figure 2B. This principle gives the first rule of communication: as long as the vectors are parallel, communication can proceed indefinitely. This is a necessary but not the sole condition for a "good" relationship; if the transactions become unpalatable enough, the relationship may deteriorate even though the vectors remain parallel.

Crossed Transactions If an Adult stimulus, such as an interpretation or comment, elicits a Child-to-Parent reaction, the vectors are crossed. This type of crossing is the commonest source of difficulty in social, occupational, and domestic life, and is known as Crossed Transaction Type I. In therapy it constitutes the typical transference reaction. An Adult-to-Adult stimulus eliciting a Parent-to-Child response forms Crossed Transaction Type II (Figure 3). This is the classical counter-transference reaction. It will be apparent that there are seventy-two varieties of crossed transactions, but I and II are the commonest types found in clinical work. The study of crossed transactions gives rise to the second rule of communication: if the vectors are crossed, communication is broken off, and the relationship is "bad"; or in its clinical converse, if communication is broken off, there has usually (or always?) been a crossed transaction.

Ulterior Transactions Both complementary and crossed transactions are simple transactions. Ulterior transactions are of two types. The angular transaction (Figure 4) is most commonly used by professionals who deal with people in their daily work. Here an ostensible Adult-to-Adult stimulus conceals another stimulus directed at the Child (or sometimes the Parent) of the respondent. The desired response comes from the respondent's Child, while the agent is in the clear because his stimulus was factually Adult. In the classical example a professional salesman who knew exactly what he was doing was showing some stoves to a housewife. She asked:

"How much is that one over there?" The salesman replied: "You can't afford that one." The housewife declared defiantly: "That's the one I'll take." Here the salesman's answer to her question (his transactional stimulus) was factual, since his estimate of her financial standing was correct. As a professional salesman, however, he knew that her Child would be listening to his Adult judgment and would respond on the basis of some child-like feeling (although he used other terminology). She disregarded his accurate factual statement of what she could afford and responded the way he wanted her to.

The second type of ulterior transaction is the duplex transaction (Figure 5) in which at the social or overt level—the

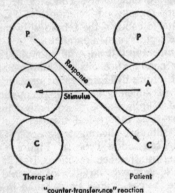

Therapist   Patient
"counter-transference" reaction

Fig. 3. A transactional diagram: crossed transaction type II

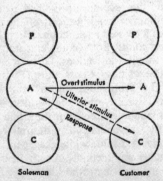

Salesman   Customer

Fig. 4. An angular transaction

level found on the tape recording or the transcript—the stimuli and responses are Adult-to-Adult; but it is evident to a sophisticated observer that below the surface there is another and more meaningful level, the psychological or covert level, where there is Child-to-Child or Parent-to-Child communication. This duplicity gives rise to the third rule of communication: the behavioral outcome of an ulterior transaction is determined at the psychological and not at the social level. In its pragmatic (e.g. research) inverse, this rule reads: No kind or amount of processing of the social level can predict the behavioral outcome of an ulterior transaction; prediction is universally contingent on a knowledge of the psychological level.

GAME ANALYSIS

A game is a series of ulterior transactions with a gimmick, leading to a usually well-concealed but well-defined pay-off. For a detailed discussion the reader is referred to the writer's volume *Games People Play.* . . . The most important thing to remember is that the definition of a game is quite precise, and unless a series of transactions is ulterior and has a definite pay-off it does not constitute a game. On the other hand, transactional games should not be confused with the types of games dealt with in mathematical game theory, although there are certain similarities.

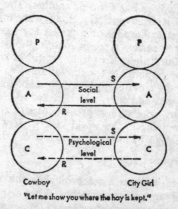

"Let me show you where the hay is kept."

Fig. 5. A duplex transaction

SCRIPT ANALYSIS

The script, or unconscious life plan of the individual, may not come to light except in very advanced groups. It will then be found that the patient is actually spending his whole life in a predetermined way based on decisions he made in early childhood, when he was much too young to make such serious commitments. These decisions remain unconscious, and choices of partners and action are rationalized on grounds which are actually irrelevant since the chief function of partners is to play roles in the protagonist's script, and the ultimate goal of human behavior (under ordinary civil conditions offering the possibility of choice) is to bring about the desired culmination of the script, which may be either tragic or constructive.

In clinical work the tragic scripts are the ones most often found, since people with constructive scripts do not usually feel the need for psychotherapy. In general a script is based on a childhood theory that somewhere there is a kind of Santa Claus who will bring the individual a magic gift to crown his life. People wait varying lengths of time before they fall into despair about the appearance of this Santa Claus, and it is this despair which, other things being equal, determines when they seek treatment—some at 20, some at 40, and some at 60. Failing "Santa Claus," there are four alternatives from which the individual can choose. The most decisive is suicide in one form or another. The second choice is sequestration from society, along with other people in despair, in a state hospital or a prison (or sometimes in isolated areas or in certain types of rooming-houses found in big cities). The third alternative is to get rid of the people who are held to be responsible for the failure—by divorce, homicide, sending the children to boarding school, etc. The fourth alternative is getting better, which means to give up the hope of Santa Claus, to abandon previous destructive games, and to start anew living in the world as it is. It will be apparent that script analysis by its very nature has an existential quality.

TIME STRUCTURING

In order to analyse most profitably the proceedings of groups, there are two approaches. The first is descriptive, dividing the proceedings into discussion, description, and expression. Discussion is concerned with events that are removed from the current group meeting in time or place, including discussions of what happened at the last meeting. In some new groups a definite geographical and temporal progression can be noted. The members begin by talking about things that happened far away and years ago, in Philadelphia or in Alaska, and gradually approach the place and time of the current group meeting. When they arrive there, the discussion takes on a more personal nature, typically beginning with shoes and working upward. Discussion is usually an evasive maneuver. Description is an intellectual way of handling feelings. In structural language the Adult tells the group what the Child is feeling, but the Child himself does not show in such a description. Expression means the direct expression of affect concerning the here and now at the time the affect is felt. Discussion and description are essentially pastimes, and expression may be part of a game or it may signify progress toward genuine game-free intimacy. The last distinction is crucial for therapeutic progress.

Time structuring in groups is based on particular needs. (1) The least differentiated is stimulus hunger, which drives the individual to social action in order to avoid sensory deprivation. (2) More specific is recognition hunger, an Adult's version of the infant's need to be touched, in which "verbal touching" replaces physical touching. The unit of recognition is called a "stroke," by analogy to physical caressing in infancy, where the units more literally take the form of strokes. (3) Structure hunger expresses the antipathy to monotony, stereotypy, and boredom. People are willing to pay almost any price to have their time structured for them, since few are capable of structuring their own time autonomously for very long. Hence the large salaries paid to entertainers. (4) A derivative of structure hunger is leadership hunger. One of the most important functions of a leader is to supply purposeful programs on the basis of which the members can structure their time. A psychotherapist satisfies this hunger, for example, by structuring the group in such a way as to promote the most economical, stable, and speedy recoveries.

The options open to a member for structuring his time at any kind of gathering (roughly in order of safeness) are as follows:

1. Withdrawal. There are three kinds of withdrawal.

   a. Extraneous fantasies, in which the individual mentally leaves the gathering to indulge in fantasies of what he would do elsewhere.

   b. Autistic transactions. There may be either *unadapted*

or *adapted*. Unadapted autistic transactions are those which are impractical under the circumstances, such as fantasies of rape and killing involving members of the gathering. Adapted autistic transactions are found in inhibited individuals who may have something to say which is quite appropriate to the situation, but who are too shy to say it.

2. Rituals. These are stereotyped, predictable exchanges such as greeting and farewell rituals. The unit of ritualistic exchanges is the stroke.

3. Pastimes. Pastimes are similar to rituals except that the transactions are less stereotyped and take the less ceremonial form of multiple-choice sentence-completion transactions as in the pastime called "General Motors": "I like a (Chevrolet, Ford, Plymouth) better than a (Chevrolet, Ford, Plymouth) because (complete in 25 words or less.)." The respondent then says: "Yes, very true, but might I just add one item: *I* like a (Chevrolet, Ford, Plymouth) better than a (Chevrolet, Ford, Plymouth) because (complete in 25 words or less.)."

4. Activity. An activity is what is commonly called work. Since the kind of therapy group we are interested in here does not engage in such activities, they do not present a problem to the therapist. Briefly, activities are programmed by the external material of the activity itself so that the transactions are based on the needs of the moment; e.g. "Pass me the hammer" is said when the external material demands that a hammer be used.

5. Games. Since the experienced transactional therapist will quickly break up rituals and pastimes to move on to games, and since, on the other hand, real intimacy rarely occurs in groups, most of the proceedings of transactional groups will consist of games and game analysis. These will be amply illustrated below.

6. Intimacy. Intimacy is a game-free exchange of internally programmed affective expressions, and must be sharply distinguished from pseudo-intimacy, which is common in institutionalized forms of group therapy where affective expression is encouraged without careful assessment of its authenticity. In the latter case the affective expression is largely socially (externally) rather than internally programmed, and is usually part of a game in which the patient compliantly participates. It is different from the poignant experience which ensues when real intimacy, on the rarest of occasions, occurs in a group.

One advantage of transactional analysis, as previously

noted, is that the technical vocabulary needed to handle the proceedings of a treatment group is relatively small. A clear understanding of four words—Parent, Adult, Child, and game—is the primary requirement for a short-term group or for the first phase of a long-term group, and selections from the secondary vocabulary (such as "script") can be added as need arises.

Abraham Levitsky
and
Frederick S. Perls

Frederick S. Perls (1893–1970) was born in Berlin and received an M.D. there. Trained as a psychoanalyst, Perls was analyzed by Wilhelm Reich. Perls came to the United States in 1946 with his wife, Laura, a psychologist who participated in writing his seminal works on Gestalt therapy.

Gestalt therapy is not an outgrowth of Gestalt psychology exclusively. It is heavily indebted to Freud, Wilhelm Reich, and Otto Rank, and to existential thought as well. Gestalt therapy leans heavily toward humanistic psychology, accepting its positive view of the human being.

The theoretical underpinnings of Gestalt therapy lie in Gestalt psychology, which theorizes that looking at a part of anything leaves out its essential characteristics, present only in the whole. When the whole is experienced, all is in balance; when parts are omitted, the organism makes efforts to restore balance and "complete the Gestalt." Perls sees the person as engaged in a similar struggle for balance, as his life is disturbed by inner needs or outer demands. These needs and demands create tensions. As balance is restored, a person's tension is reduced.

In healthy experience a person can perceive and react to the whole inner and outer situation. But being out of balance engenders in a person fear and avoidance of full awareness, so that the activity and excitement that characterize healthy experience are not available. Regaining full awareness, according to Perls, is crucial to restoring the balance. The techniques of Gestalt therapy are largely designed to open up a person to his direct, immediate experience—what he is thinking, feeling, and doing right now. Through this experience the person can recognize just how he operates—how he defeats, deceives, and frustrates himself. He sees an example of his self-destructive style right in front of him; he encounters himself.

In Gestalt therapy a person's conflicts are dealt with by exaggerating each side. The patient takes first one position, then the other, often speaking to an empty chair or moving back and forth from one seat to another. However painful it may be, the patient must own the disowned in himself, and out of these fragments forge a unified whole. Dreams may be acted out in the same fashion, with the patient giving each part of the dream a separate voice, from the peripheral elements to the central characters. The therapist avoids interpretation, so that the patient can spontaneously discover what the dream reveals about him.

Other techniques of Gestalt therapy are spelled out in the following chapter, written by Perls and his colleague Abraham Levitsky. Levitsky and Perls depict a range of methods used in Gestalt therapy, all of which make the therapist far more active and directive than in the psychoanalytic tradition where Perls received his early training. The goal of Gestalt therapy, though, is in accord with that of analysis: "to help us dig out resistances, promote heightened awareness—to facilitate the maturation process." These Gestalt techniques, note Levitsky and Perls, "will often provide considerable shock value and thus demonstrate to the patient the many and subtle ways in which he prevents himself from fully experiencing himself and his environment."

THE RULES AND GAMES
OF GESTALT THERAPY

by Abraham Levitsky and Frederick S. Perls

The techniques of Gestalt therapy revolve largely around two sets of guidelines which we will call "rules" and "games." The rules are few in number and are usually introduced and described formally at the outset. The games, on the other hand, are numerous and no definitive list is possible since an ingenious therapist may well devise new ones from time to time.

If we are to do justice at all to the spirit and essence of

Gestalt therapy, we must recognize clearly the distinction between rules and commandments. The philosophy of rules is to provide us with effective means of unifying thought with feeling. They are designed to help us dig out resistances, promote heightened awareness—to facilitate the maturation process. They are definitely *not* intended as a dogmatic list of *do's* and *don'ts*; rather, they are offered in the spirit of experiments that the patient may perform. They will often provide considerable shock value and thus demonstrate to the patient the many and subtle ways in which he prevents himself from fully experiencing himself and his environment.

When the intention of the rules is truly appreciated, they will be understood in their inner meaning and not in their literal sense. The "good boy," for instance, totally incapable of understanding the liberating intent of the rules, will frequently follow them exactly but to absurdity, thus endowing them with his own bloodlessness rather than with the vitality they seek to promote.

True to its heritage in Gestalt psychology, the essence of Gestalt therapy is in the perspective with which it views human life processes. Seen in this light, any particular set of techniques such as our presently used rules and games will be regarded merely as convenient means—useful tools for our purposes but without sacrosanct qualities.

THE RULES

The principle of the now. The idea of the now, of the immediate moment, of the content and structure of present experience is one of the most potent, most pregnant, and most elusive principles of Gestalt therapy. Speaking from my own experience [A.L.], I have been at various times intrigued, angered, baffled, and exhilarated by the implications of the seemingly simple idea "being in the now." And what a fascinating experience it is to help others become aware of the manifold ways in which they prevent themselves from having true immediate awareness.

In order to promote *now* awareness, we encourage communications in the present tense. "What is your present awareness?" "What is happening now?" "What do you feel at this moment?" The phrase "What is your *now*?" is an effective one from therapist to patient.

It would not be accurate to say that there is no interest in historical material and in the past. This material is dealt with actively when it is felt to be germane to important themes of the present personality structure. However, the most effective means of integrating past material into the personality is to bring it—as fully as possible—into the present. In this way we avoid the bland, intellectualized "aboutisms" and strive vigorously to give all material the impact of immediacy. When the patient refers to events of yesterday, last week, or last year, we quickly direct him to "be there" in fantasy and to enact the drama in present terms.

We are active in pointing out to the patient how easily he leaves the now. We identify his need to bring into the dialogue absent individuals, the nostalgic urge to reminisce, the tendency to get preoccupied with fears and fantasies of the future. For most of us, the exercise of remaining in present awareness is a taxing discipline that can be maintained only for short periods. It is a discipline to which we are not accustomed and which we are inclined to resist.

I and thou. With this principle, we strive to drive home as concretely as possible the notion that true communication involves both sender and receiver. The patient often behaves as if his words are aimed at the blank wall or at thin air. When he is asked, "To whom are you saying this?" he is made to face his reluctance to send his message directly and unequivocally to the receiver, to the *other*.

Thus the patient is often directed to invoke the other's name—if necessary, at the beginning of each sentence. He is asked to be aware of the distinction between "talking to" and "talking at" the listener. He is led to discover whether his voice and words are truly reaching the other. Is he really touching the other with his words? How far is he willing to touch the other with his words? Can he begin to see that this phobic avoidance of relating to others, of making genuine contact with others is also manifested in his voice mechanisms and his verbal behavior? If he has slight or insufficient contact, can he begin to realize his serious doubts as to whether others actually exist for him in this world; as to whether he is truly *with* people or feeling alone and abandoned?

"It" language and "I" language. This rule deals with the semantics of responsibility and involvement. It is common for us to refer to our bodies and to our acts and behaviors in distantiated, third-person, *it* language:

What do you feel in your eye?
  It is blinking.

What is your hand doing?
  It is trembling.

What do you experience in your throat?
  It is choked.

What do you hear in your voice?
  It is sobbing.

Through the simple—and seemingly mechanical—expedient of changing *it* language into *I* language we learn to identify more closely with the particular behavior in question and to assume responsibility for it.

Instead of "It is trembling," "*I* am trembling." Rather than "It is choked," "*I* am choked." Going one step further, rather than "I am choked," "I am choking myself." Here we can immediately see the different degree of responsibility and involvement that is experienced.

Changing *it* to *I* is an example in microcosm of many of the Gestalt game techniques. As the patient participates, he is far more likely to see himself as an active agent who does things rather than a passive creature to whom things somehow "happen."

A number of other semantic games are available. If the patient says, "I can't do that," the therapist will ask, "Can you say, I *won't* do that?" As the patient accepts and uses this formulation, the therapist will follow with "And what do you experience now?"

T.: What do you hear in your voice?

P.: My voice sounds like it is crying.

T.: Can you take responsiblity for that by saying, "I am crying"?

Other gambits in the semantics of responsibility are having the patient substitute verbs for nouns and frequently use the imperative mode of speech as the most direct means of communication.

Use of the awareness continuum.   The use of the so-called awareness continuum—the "*how*" of experience—is absolutely basic to Gestalt therapy. With it we often achieve effects both striking and startling. The frequent return to and reliance on the awareness continuum is one of the major innovations in technique contributed by Gestalt therapy. The method is quite simple:

T.: What are you aware of now?

P.: Now I am aware of talking to you. I see the others in the room. I'm aware of John squirming. I can feel the tension in my shoulders. I'm aware that I get anxious as I say this.

T.: How do you experience the anxiety?

P.: I hear my voice quiver. My mouth feels dry. I talk in a very halting way.

T.: Are you aware of what your eyes are doing?

P.: Well, now I realize that my eyes keep looking away—

T.: Can you take responsibility for that?

P.: —that I keep looking away from you.

T.: Can you be your eyes now? Write the dialogue for them.

P.: I am Mary's eyes. I find it hard to gaze steadily. I keep jumping and darting about. . . .

The awareness continuum has inexhaustible applications. Primarily, however, it is an effective way of guiding the individual to the firm bedrock of his experiences and away from the endless verbalization, explanations, interpretations. Awareness of body feelings and of sensations and perceptions constitutes our most certain—perhaps our only certain—knowledge. Relying on information provided in awareness is the best method of implementing Perl's dictum to "lose your mind and come to your senses."

The use of the awareness continuum is the Gestalt therapist's best means of leading the patient away from the emphasis on the *why* of behavior (psychoanalytic interpretation) and toward the *what* and the *how* of behavior (experiential psychotherapy):

P.: I feel afraid.

T.: How do you experience the fear?

P.: I can't see you clearly. My hands are perspiring. . . .

As we help the patient rely on his senses ("return to his senses"), we also help him distinguish between the reality *out there* and the frightening goblins he manufactures in his own fantasies:

P.: I'm sure people will despise me for what I just said.

T.: Go around the room and look at us carefully. Tell me what you *see*, what your eyes—not your imaginings—tell you.

P.: (*after some moments of exploration and discovery*) Well, actually people don't *look* so rejecting! Some of you even look warm and friendly!

T.: What do you experience now?

P.: I'm more relaxed now.

No gossiping. As is the case with many Gestalt techniques, the no-gossiping rule is designed to promote feelings and to prevent avoidance of feelings. Gossiping is defined as talking about an individual when he is actually present and could just as well be addressed directly. For example, let us say the therapist is dealing with Bill and Ann:

P.: (*to therapist*) The trouble with Ann is she's always picking on me.

T.: You're gossiping; say this to Ann.

P.: (*turning to Ann*) You're always picking on me.

We often gossip about people when we have not been able to handle directly the feelings they arouse in us. The no-gossiping rule is another Gestalt technique that facilitates direct confrontation of feelings.

Asking questions. Gestalt therapy gives a good deal of attention to the patient's need to ask questions. The questioner is obviously saying, "Give me, tell me . . ." Careful listening will often reveal that the questioner does not really need information, or that the question is not really necessary, or that it represents laziness and passivity on the part of the patient. The therapist may then say, "Change that question into a statement." The frequency with which the patient can actually do this validates the action of the therapist.

Genuine questions are to be distinguished from hypocritical questions. The latter are intended to manipulate or cajole the other into seeing or doing things a particular way. On the other hand, questions in the form of "How are you doing?" and "Are you aware that . . ." provide genuine support.

THE GAMES

Following is a brief description of a number of "games" used in Gestalt therapy. They are proposed by the therapist when the moment—in terms of either the individual's or the group's needs—seems appropriate. Some of the games, such as the "I have a secret" game or the "I take responsibility" game are particularly useful as group warm-ups at the beginning of a session.

It is, of course, no accident that some of the major techniques of Gestalt therapy are couched in game form. This is evidently a basic metacommunication on the part of Perls, highlighting one of the many facets of his philosophy of personality functioning. The game language (itself a game) can be seen as a commentary on the nature of all or most of social behavior. The message is *not* to stop playing games, since every form of social organization can be seen as one or another game form. Rather the message is to be aware of the games we play and to be free to substitute satisfying for nonsatisfying games. Applying this view to any two-person relationship (love, marriage, friendship), we would not be inclined to seek out a partner who "does not play games" but rather one whose games fit comfortably with our own.

Games of dialogue. In trying to effect integrated functioning, the Gestalt therapist seeks out whatever divisions or splits are manifested in the personality. Naturally, whatever "split" is found is a function of the therapist's frame of reference and his observational powers. One of the main divisions postulated is that between the so-called *top-dog* and *under-dog*. Top-dog is roughly the equivalent of the psychoanalytic superego. Top-dog moralizes, specializes in *shoulds*, and is generally bossy and condemning. Under-dog tends to be passively resistant, makes excuses, and finds reasons to delay.

When this division is encountered, the patient is asked to have an actual dialogue between these two components of himself. The same game of dialogue can, of course, be pursued for any significant split within the personality (aggressive versus passive, "nice guy" versus scoundrel, masculine versus feminine, etc.). At times the dialogue game can even be applied with various body parts such as right hand versus left, or upper body versus lower. The dialogue can also be developed between the patient and some significant person. The patient simply addresses the person as if he were there, imagines the response, replies to the response, etc.

Making the rounds. The therapist may feel that a particular theme or feeling expressed by the patient should be faced vis-à-vis every other person in the group. The patient may have said, "I can't stand anyone in this room." The therapist will then say, "OK, make the rounds. Say that to each one of us, and add some other remark pertaining to your feelings about each person."

The "rounds" game is of course infinitely flexible and need not be confined to verbal interaction. It may involve touching, caressing, observing, frightening, etc.

Unfinished business. Unfinished business is the Gestalt therapy analogue of the perceptual or cognitive incomplete task of Gestalt psychology. Whenever unfinished business (unresolved feelings) is identified, the patient is asked to complete it. Obviously all of us have endless lists of unfinished business in the realm of interpersonal relations, with, for instance, parents, siblings, friends. Perls contends that resentments are the most common and important kinds of unfinished business.

"I take responsibility." In this game we build on some of the elements of the awareness continuum but we consider all perceptions to be acts. With each statement, we ask patients to use the phrase, ". . . and I take responsibility for it." For example, "I am aware that I move my leg . . . and I take responsibility for it." "My voice is very quiet . . . and I take responsibility for it." "Now I don't know what to say . . . and I take responsibility for not knowing."

What seems at first blush a mechanical, even foolish procedure is soon seen as one heavily laden with meaning.

"I have a secret." This game permits exploration of feelings of guilt and shame. Each person thinks of a well-

guarded personal secret. He is instructed *not* to share the secret itself but to imagine (project) how he feels others would react to it. A further step can then be for each person to boast about what a terrible secret he nurses. The unconscious attachment to the secret as a precious achievement now begins to come to light.

Playing the projection. Many seeming perceptions are projections. For instance, the patient who says, "I can't trust you," may be asked to play the role of an untrustworthy person in order to discover his own inner conflict in this area. Another patient may complain to therapist, "You're not really interested in me. You just do this for a living." He will be told to enact this attitude, after which he might be asked whether this is possibly a trait he himself possesses.

Reversals. One way in which the Gestalt therapist approaches certain symptoms or difficulties is to help the patient realize that overt behavior commonly represents the reversal of underlying or latent impulses. We therefore use the reversal technique. For example, the patient claims to suffer from inhibition or excessive timidity. He will be asked to play an exhibitionist. In taking this plunge into an area fraught with anxiety, he makes contact with a part of himself that has long been submerged. Or, the patient may wish to work on his problem of extreme touchiness to criticism. He will be asked to play the role of listening very carefully to everything that is said to him—especially criticism—without the need to defend or counterattack. Or, the patient may be unassertive and overly sweet; he will be asked to play the part of an uncooperative and spiteful person.

The rhythm of contact and withdrawal. Following its interest in the totality of life processes, in the phenomena of figure and ground, Gestalt therapy emphasizes the polar nature of vital functioning. The capacity for love is impaired by the inability to sustain anger. Rest is needed to restore energy. A hand is neither open nor closed but capable of both functions.

The natural inclination toward withdrawal from contact, which the patient will experience from time to time, is not dealt with as a resistance to be overcome but as a rhythmic response to be respected. Consequently when the patient wishes to withdraw, he is asked to close his eyes and withdraw in fantasy to any place or situation in which he feels secure. He describes the scene and his feelings there. Soon he is asked to open his eyes and "come back to the group." The on-going work is then resumed, usually with new material provided by the patient, who has now had some of his energies restored by his withdrawal.

The Gestalt approach suggests that we accept withdrawal needs in any situation where attention or interest has lagged but that we remain aware of where our attention goes.

"Rehearsal."   According to Perls, a great deal of our thinking consists of internal rehearsal and preparation for playing our accustomed social roles. The experience of stage fright simply represents our fear that we will not conduct our roles well. The group therefore plays the game of sharing rehearsals with each other, thus becoming more aware of the preparatory means employed in bolstering our social roles.

"Exaggeration."   This game is closely allied to the principle of the awareness continuum and provides us with another means of understanding body language. There are many times when the patient's unwitting movement or gesture appears to be a significant communication. However, the gestures may be abortive, undeveloped, or incomplete—perhaps a wave of the arm or a tap of the leg. The patient will be asked to exaggerate the movement repeatedly, usually making the inner meaning more apparent. Sometimes the patient will be asked to develop the movement into a dance to get more of his self into integrative expression.

A similar technique is used for purely verbal behavior and can well be called the "repetition" game. A patient may make a statement of importance but has perhaps glossed over it or in some way indicated that he has not fully absorbed its impact. He will be asked to say it again—if necessary a great number of times—and, where necessary, louder and louder. Soon he is really hearing himself and not just forming words.

"May I feed you a sentence?"   In listening to or observing the patient, the therapist may conclude that a particular attitude or message is implied. He will then say, "May I feed you a sentence? Say it and try it on for size. Say it to several people here." He then proposes his sentence, and the patient tests out his reaction to the sentence. Typically, the therapist does not simply interpret for or to the patient. Although there

is obviously a strong interpretative element here, the patient must make the experience his own through active participation. If the proposed sentence is truly a key sentence, spontaneous development of the idea will be supplied by the patient.

Marriage counseling games. We will mention only a few of the great number of possible variations on these games.

The partners face each other and take turns saying sentences begining with, "I resent you for . . ." The resentment theme can then be followed by the appreciation theme, "What I appreciate in you is . . ." Then the spite theme, "I spite you by . . ." Or, the compliance theme, "I am compliant by . . ."

Lastly, there is the discovery theme. The partners alternate describing each other in sentences beginning with "I see . . ." Many times this process of discovery involves actually seeing each other for the first time. Since, as Perls points out, the most difficult problem in marriage is that of being in love with a concept rather than an individual, we must learn to distinguish between our fantasied image and the flesh-and-blood person.

Finally, we should mention a particular approach that does not fall under the heading of either rules or games but which can well be included at this point. It is an important gambit in Gestalt therapy and symbolizes much of Perls's underlying philosophy. We might call it the principle of "Can you stay with this feeling?" This technique is invoked at key moments when the patient refers to a feeling or mood or state of mind that is unpleasant and that he has a great urge to dispel. Let us say he has arrived at a point where he feels empty or confused or frustrated or discouraged. The therapist says, "Can you stay with this feeling?"

This is almost always a dramatic moment and a frustrating one for the patient. He has referred to his experience with some sourness and an obviously impatient desire to get on with it, to leave this feeling well behind him. The therapist however asks him deliberately to remain with whatever psychic pain he has at the moment. The patient will be asked to elaborate the *what* and *how* of his feelings. "What are your sensations?" "What are your perceptions, fantasies, expectancies?" At these moments, it is frequently most appropriate and necessary to help the patient distinguish between what he imagines and what he perceives.

The stay-with-it technique illustrates par excellence Perls's emphasis on the role of phobic avoidance in all of neurotic behavior. In his view, the neurotic has habitually avoided vigorous contact with a variety of unpleasant and dysphoric experiences. As a result avoidance has become ingrained, a phobic anxiety has been routinized, and major dimensions of experience have never been adequately mastered.

It is interesting, in this connection, to be reminded of the title of Perls's first book, *Ego, Hunger and Agression.* The title was chosen carefully to carry the message that we must adopt toward psychological and emotional experiences the same active, coping attitudes that we employ in healthy eating. In healthy eating we bite the food; then we effectively chew, grind, and liquefy it. It is then swallowed, digested, metabolized, and assimilated. In this way we have truly made the food a part of ourselves.

The Gestalt therapist—most especially with the stay-with-it technique—encourages the patient to undertake a similar "chewing up" and painstaking assimilation of emotional dimensions of life that have hitherto been unpleasant to the taste, difficult to swallow, and impossible to digest. In this way the patient gains improved self-confidence and a far greater capacity for autonomy and for dealing energetically with the inevitable frustrations of living.

Albert Ellis

Albert Ellis developed rational-emotive therapy (RET) out of his practice as a psychoanalyst, and it reflects his dissatisfactions with that approach. RET approaches neurotic problems, in a direct and straightforward way, by convincing the patient of their irrationality. The core issues are located and directly attacked rather than allowed to emerge slowly as in conventional psychotherapy. The therapist is very directive and takes the stance of an expert, in charge of the process at all times.

Emotional disturbances, according to Ellis, are the result of illogical thinking. Without being clearly aware of it, the patient indoctrinates himself repeatedly with "self-talk" that governs his behavior. The task of RET is to make these inner statements explicit, confront the patient with their irrationality, and force him thereby to abandon them. For example, Ellis contends many neurotics believe one or more of the following:

—it is essential that a person be loved and/or approved of by everyone

—one must be perfectly adequate and competent at all times in order to consider oneself worthwhile

—it is easier to avoid difficulties in living than to face them

—there is always a perfect solution to every problem, and unless it is found, the results will be catastrophic.

According to Ellis, if a person accepts such sentiments, they lead to neurotic suffering. Ellis' approach emphasizes reason, rationality, and logic as principal therapeutic weapons. The RET therapist isolates the patient's key sentence or phrase, demonstrates its irrationality, and replaces it with another. Therapy sessions alone are not enough to change behavior, so the patient is instructed to replace neurotic

sentences with useful ones whenever they may occur. RET
is merely the beginning in the struggle for mental self-correc-
tion that the patient must wage on his own.

Ellis sees RET as a "re-education," where the patient un-
learns the self-defeating attitudes he had ingrained in him
during childhood. The therapist's objective is to replace such
credos with more rational attitudes that will lead to a more
productive and happier life. The patient is held responsible
for his attitudes. On the one hand, he is seen as having made
himself disturbed; on the other, he is encouraged to take control, "to change and substitute more efficient cognitions." In
the following chapter Ellis explains the rationale underlying
RET, describes its basic techniques, and reviews a successful
case.

From THE ESSENCE OF RATIONAL-EMOTIVE THERAPY

by Albert Ellis

It is the central theme of rational-emotive therapy (RET)
that several basic irrational ideas, and many corollaries to
which they normally lead, cause most emotional disturbances.
For once humans believe the kind of nonsense included in
these notions, they will tend to become inhibited, hostile, defensive, guilty, anxious, ineffective, inert, uncontrolled, or unhappy. If, on the other hand, they become thoroughly
released from these kinds of illogical thinking, it would be
difficult for them to become intensely emotionally upset, or at
least to sustain their disturbances for any extended period.

Does this mean that all the other so-called basic causes of
neurosis, such as the Oedipus complex or severe maternal rejection in childhood, are invalid and the Freudian and other
psychodynamic thinkers of the last sixty years have been
barking up the wrong tree? Not necessarily. It means, if the
main hypotheses of this approach are correct, that these psychodynamic thinkers have been emphasizing secondary causes
or results of emotional disturbances rather than truly prime
causes.

Let us take, for example, an individual who acquires, when
he is young, a full-blown Oedipus complex: that is to say, he
lusts after his mother, hates his father, is guilty about his sex

desires for his mother, and is afraid his father is going to castrate him. This person, when he is a child, will certainly be disturbed. But, if he subsequently surrenders the basic illogical ideas we have been discussing, he will not *remain* disturbed.

For this individual's disturbance, when he is a child, does not consist of the *facts* of his Oedipal attachment to his mother but of his *attitudes*—his guilt and his anxiety—about these facts. He is not guilty, moreover, *because* he lusts after his mother, but because *he thinks it is criminal and awful* for him to lust after her. And he is not anxious *because* his father disapproves of his sexual attachment to his mother, but because *he thinks it is horrible* to be disapproved by his father.

It may be very "natural"—meaning *quite common*—for a child to think himself a criminal when he lusts after his mother; but there is no evidence that he is born with this idea or that he *has* to acquire it. In fact, considerable autobiographical and clinical evidence regarding individuals reared even in our own very anti-incestuous society shows that many boys are able to lust after their mothers quite consciously and openly without becoming guilty about their lusting or terribly fearful of their father's opposition.

So Oedipal *attachments* do *not* have to result in Oedipal *complexes*. Even if, in a given case, a boy does become disturbed about his sexual feelings for his mother, he does not, as the Freudians stoutly and erroneously contend, have to remain neurotic in his adult life. For if he is reared (as, alas, he rarely is in our society) to be truly rational, he will not, as an adult, be too concerned if his parents or others do not approve all his actions, since he will be more interested in *his own* acceptance than in *their* approval. He will not believe that his lust for his mother (even should it continue to his adolescent and adult years) is wicked or villainous, but will accept it as a normal part of being a fallible human whose sex desires may easily be indiscriminate. He will realize that the actual danger of his father castrating him is exceptionally slight, and will have few fears on that account. And he will not feel that because he was *once* afraid of his Oedipal attachment he need *forever* remain so.

If this individual, when he is adult, still believes that it would be improper for him to have sex relations with his mother, instead of castigating himself for even thinking of having such relations, he will merely resolve not to carry his desires into practice and will stick determinedly to his resolve. If (by any chance) he weakens and actually has incestuous relations, he will again refuse to castigate himself mercilessly for being weak but will keep showing himself how self-defeating his behavior is and will actively work and practice at changing it.

Under these circumstances, if this individual has a truly rational approach to life, he will take an equally sane approach to Oedipal feelings. How, then, can he possibly *remain* disturbed about any Oedipal attachment that he may have?

Take, by way of further illustration, the case of a woman who, as a child, is continually criticized by her parents, who then feels loathsome and inadequate, who refuses to take chances at trying and possibly failing at difficult tasks, and who comes to hate herself more for being evasive and cowardly. Such a person, during childhood, would of course be disturbed. But how would it be possible to *sustain* her disturbance if she began to think, later in life, in a truly rational manner?

For if this person begins to be consistently rational, she will stop being overconcerned about what others think and will care primarily about what *she* wants to do in life. Consequently, she will stop avoiding difficult tasks and, instead of blaming herself for making mistakes, will say to herself something like: "Now this is not the right way to do things; let me stop and figure out a better way." Or: "There's no doubt that I made a mistake this time; now let me see how I can benefit from making it, so that my next performance will be improved."

This person, if she thinks straight in the present, will not blame defeats on external events, but will realize that she is causing them by inadequate or incompetent behavior. She will not believe that it is easier to avoid than to face difficult life problems, but will see that the so-called easy way is usually the harder and more idiotic procedure. She will not think that she needs someone greater or stronger than herself on whom to rely, but will independently buckle down to hard tasks. She will not feel, because she once defeated herself by avoiding doing things the hard way, that she must always continue to act in this self-defeating manner.

How, with this kind of thinking, could originally disturbed people maintain and continually revivify their emotional upsets? They wouldn't. Similarly, the spoiled brat, the worry-wart, the egomaniac, the autistic stay-at-home—all these disturbed individuals would have the devil of a time indefinitely prolonging their neuroses if they did not continue to believe utter nonsense: namely, the kinds of basic irrational postulates listed in rational-emotive writings.

Will not people's experiences during early childhood frequently *make* them think illogically, and thereby cause disturbance? No, not exactly. For even during childhood, humans *accept* the ideas that are pounded into them, and *need* not (at least technically speaking) automatically take them over. They *can* choose to reject these notions.

Thus, it is statistically probable that the great majority of children, if taught that they are monstrous if they do not behave well, will accept the idea that this is true, and will come to despise themselves for their misdeeds. But all children *need* not accept this belief; and a few, at least, do not seem to do so. These few, apparently, can and do challenge the notion that they are worthless, and somehow manage to grow up thinking of themselves as acceptable, even though their parents or others teach them the contrary.

Moreover, even when young children tend to accept parent-inculcated irrational thinking, they are quite able, in many instances, to challenge and contradict these views during their adolescence and adulthood, and to think otherwise—just as they are able to give up the religious views of their parents at this time. It is certainly *difficult* for adolescents or young adults to disbelieve the nonsense about themselves (or about religion) that their parents teach. But it is hardly impossible! Childhood training, then, is an exceptionally strong influence in helping individuals to think irrationally. But it is not a fatal or irrevocable influence.

Neurosis, in sum, seems to originate in and be perpetuated by some fundamentally unsound, irrational ideas. People come to adopt unrealistic, impossible, often perfectionistic goals—especially the goals that they should be approved by everyone who is important to them, should do many things perfectly, and should never be frustrated in any major desires. Then, in spite of considerable contradictory evidence, they refuse to surrender these anti-empirical beliefs.

Why do so many millions of intelligent, well-educated, potentially rational people act in such a "nutty" manner today? A full answer to this question will eventually be given in a volume of its own. Part of this answer is summarized in the final chapter of my book, *Reason And Emotion In Psychotherapy* (1962). Suffice it to say here that even the most intelligent and capable persons in our society tend *also* to be, because of their biological tendencies, amazingly suggestible, unthinking, overgeneralizing, and strongly bound to the low-level kinds of ideation which it is so easy for them to become addicted to as children; and, perhaps more importantly, we bring up our citizens so that, instead of counteracting their normal tendencies toward irrationality, we deliberately and forcefully encourage them to keep thinking in childish, non-sensical ways.

By innate predisposition, therefore, as well as by powerful social propaganda (especially that promulgated by our families, schools, churches, and governmental institutions), even the brightest human beings often tend to become and to remain disturbed—that is, to behave stupidly and self-de-featingly when they are potentially able to behave more sanely and constructively.

Some "crazy" philosophies, such as the idea that people should be approved or loved by all the significant people in their lives, are not entirely inappropriate to childhood; but they are decidely inappropriate to adulthood. Since most irra-tional ideas are specifically taught by our parents and other social agencies, and since these same irrational notions are held by the great majority of others in our community, let's acknowledge that neurotics tend to be *statistically* normal. In many respects, they have what may be called a cultural or philosophic rather than a psychiatric disturbance (Paul Meehl and William Schofield, personal communications). As Victor Frankl (1966) has pointed out "neurosis" today is usually "noetic"—that is, related to *value* inconsistencies and false-hoods.

Ours, in other words, is a generally neuroticizing civiliza-tion, in which most people are more or less emotionally dis-turbed partly because they are brought up to believe, and then to internalize and to keep reinfecting themselves with, errant nonsense which leads them to become ineffective, self-defeating, and unhappy. Nonetheless, it is not absolutely *necessary* that humans believe the irrational notions which, in point of fact, most of them seem to believe today; and the task of psychotherapy is to get them to disbelieve their irra-tional ideas, to change their self-sabotaging attitudes.

This, precisely, is the task rational-emotive therapists as-sume. Like other therapists, they frequently resort to some of the usual techniques of therapy which I have outlined else-where—including the techniques of relationship, expressive-emotive, supportive, and insight-interpretative therapy. But they view these techniques, as they are commonly employed, largely as preliminary strategies, designed to gain rapport with clients, to let them express themselves fully, and to show them that they have the ability to change.

Many therapeutic techniques, in other words, wittingly or unwittingly show clients *that* they are illogical and how they presumably *originally* became so. But they fail to show how they are presently *maintaining* illogical thinking and precisely what to do to change it and replace it with more rational philosophies of life. And where many therapists passively or indirectly show clients that they are behaving illogically, the rational therapist goes beyond this point to make a forthright, unequivocal *attack* on clients' irrational ideas and to try to *induce* them to adopt more rational views.

Rational-emotive psychotherapy makes a concerted attack on self-defeating positions in two main ways: (a) The therapist serves as a frank counter-propagandist who directly contradicts and denies the self-defeating propaganda and superstitions which clients learned and are now self-instilling. (b) The therapist encourages, persuades, cajoles, and directs clients to engage in some activity (such as doing something they are afraid to do) which itself will serve as a forceful counter-propaganda agency against the nonsense they believe.

Both these main therapeutic activities are consciously performed with one main goal in mind: namely, that of finally inducing clients to internalize a rational philosophy of life just as they originally learned and internalized irrational views.

The rational therapist, then, assumes that clients somehow imbibed irrational modes of thinking and literally *made* themselves disturbed. It is the therapist's function not merely to show clients that they have these low-level thinking processes but to encourage them to change and substitute more efficient cognitions.

If, because clients are exceptionally upset when they come to therapy, they are first to be approached in a cautious, supportive, permissive, and warm manner, and sometimes allowed to ventilate feelings in free association, abreaction, role playing, and other expressive techniques, that may be an effective part of effective therapy. But the rational therapist is not deluded that these relationship-building and expressive-emotive methods are likely to really get to the core of irrational thinking and induce clients to cogitate more rationally.

Occasionally, this is true: since clients may, through experiencing relationship and emotive-expressive aspects of therapy, come to see they are acting illogically; and may therefore resolve to change and actually work at doing so. More often than not, however, illogical thinking will be so ingrained from constant self-repetitions and will be so inculcated in motor pathways (or habit patterns) by the time they come for therapy, that simply showing them, even by direct interpretation, *that* they are illogical will not greatly help. They will often, for example, say to the therapist: "All right: now I understand that I have castration fears and that they are irrational. But I *still* feel afraid of my father."

Therapists, therefore, had usually better keep pounding away, time and time again, at the illogical ideas which underlie clients' fears and hostilities. They'd better show clients that they are afraid, really, not of their father, but of being blamed, of being disapproved, of being unloved, of being imperfect, of being failures. And he'd better convincingly demonstrate how and why such fears (for some of the reasons explained in other rational-emotive writings) *are* irrational and will lead to dreadful results.

If the therapist, moreover, merely tackles the individual's castration fears, and shows how ridiculous *they* are, what is to prevent this person's showing up, a year or two later, with some *other* illogical fear—such as the horror of his being sexually impotent? But if the therapist tackles his *basic* irrational thinking processes, which underlie *all* kinds of serious anxiety, it is going to be most difficult for this client to turn up with a new neurotic sympton some months or years hence. For once an individual truly surrenders ideas of perfectionism, of the horror of failing at something, of the dire need to be approved by others, of the world's owing him a living, and so on, what else is there to be severely anxious or disturbed about?

To give some idea of precisely how the rational-emotive therapist works, it might be well to outline an illustrative case.

Mervin Snodds, a 23-year-old male, came into his therapeutic session a few weeks after he had begun therapy and said that he was very depressed but did not know why. A little questioning showed that this severely neurotic client, whose main presenting problem was that he had been doing too much drinking during the last two years, had been putting off the inventory-keeping he was required to do as part of his job as an apprentice glass-staining artist. "I know," he reported, "that I should do the inventory before it keeps piling up to enormous proportions, but I just keep putting it off and off. To be honest, I guess it's because I resent doing it so much."

"But why do you resent it so much?"

"It's boring. I just don't like it."

"So it's boring. That's a good reason for *disliking* this work, but is it an equally good reason for *resenting* it?"

"Aren't the two the same thing?"

"By no means. Dislike equals the belief, 'I don't enjoy doing this thing and therefore I don't want to do it.' And that's a perfectly sane sentence in most instances. But resentment is the belief, '*Because* I dislike doing this thing, I shouldn't *have* to do it.' And that's invariably a very crazy belief."

"Why is it so crazy to resent something that you don't like to do?"

"For several reasons. First of all, from a purely logical standpoint, it just makes no sense at all to say to yourself, 'Because I dislike doing this thing, I shouldn't *have* to do it.' The second part of this sentence just doesn't follow in any way from the first part. For the full sentence that you are saying actually goes something like this: 'Because *I* dislike doing this thing, *other people* and the *universe* should be so considerate of me that they should never make me do what I dislike.' But, of course, this belief doesn't make any sense: for why *should* other people and the universe be that considerate of you? It might be nice if they were. But why the devil *should* they be? In order for your belief to be true, the entire universe, and all the people in it, would really have to revolve around and be uniquely considerate of you."

"Am I really asking that much? It seems to me that all I'm asking, in my present job, is that I don't have to do the inventory-keeping. Is that too much to ask?"

"Yes, from what you've told me, it certainly is. For the inventory-keeping *is* an integral part of your job, isn't it? You *do* have to do it, in order to keep working at your present place, don't you?"

"Yes. I guess I do."

"And you do, from what you told me previously, want to keep working at this place, for your own reasons, do you not?"

"Yes. As I told you before, in my field I must have an apprenticeship for at least a year. And they agreed to take me on as an apprentice, if I'd work pretty long hours and do the work—"

"—including the inventory-keeping?—"

"Yes, including the inventory-keeping. If I did that and worked long hours, they'd take me on for the year I'd need toward the apprenticeship."

"All right, then. Because *you* wanted to learn the art of glass-staining and *you* can only learn it by having a year's apprenticeship, *you* decided to take on this job, with all its onerous aspects, especially including inventory-keeping. You had, in other words, a logical choice between graciously accepting this job, in spite of the onerous parts of it, or giving up trying to be a glass-stainer. But then, after presumably taking the first of these alternatives, you're now resentful because you can't get the second alternative without this onerous first part."

"Oh, but it isn't the work itself that I resent, in toto; but just the inventory-keeping part."

"But that still doesn't make sense. For the work, in toto, *includes* the inventory-keeping; and your choice of accepting the work in toto obviously includes accepting this part of it, too. So, again, instead of selecting one of two logical alternatives—doing the onerous work, including the inventory-keeping, or giving up trying to be a glass-stainer—you are resentfully and grandiosely refusing the first of these and yet insisting that you should not *have* to give up the second one, too. You are thereby actually insisting, as I said before, that the universe and the people in it should really revolve around *your* wishes rather than be what it and they actually are."

"It sounds, the way you're putting it, like I really haven't got a leg to stand on logically. But what about the fact that my boss *could*, if he wanted to be really fair with me—since I do quite a bit of work for him at a very low rate of pay—get someone else to do the inventory-keeping? After all, he knows perfectly well how I feel about it; and it is *not* work that is necessary for my glass-staining apprenticeship."

"True. Your boss *could* arrange matters differently and *could* let you off from this work that you so abhor. And let's even assume, for the moment, that he is wrong about *not* arranging things more this way and that any decent kind of boss would let you, say, do more glass-staining and less inventory-keeping work."

"Oh, that would be fine! Then I wouldn't gripe at all."

"No, probably you wouldn't. But even assuming that your

boss *is* completely in the wrong about this inventory-keeping matter, your resenting him for *being* wrong still makes no sense."

"Oh? How come?"

"Because, no matter how wrong he is, every human being has the right to be wrong—and you're not giving him that right."

"But why does every human being have the right to be wrong?"

"Simply because he *is* human; and because he is human, is fallible and error-prone. If your boss, for example, is wrong about making you do this inventory work—and let's still assume that he is dead wrong about it—then his wrongdoing would obviously result from some combination of his being stupid, ignorant, or emotionally disturbed; and he, as a fallible human being, has every right to be stupid, ignorant, or disturbed—even though it would be much better, perhaps, if he weren't."

"He has a right, you say, to be as nutty or as vicious as he may be—even though I and others might very much like him to be less nutty or vicious?"

"Correct. And if you are blaming him for being the way he is, then you are denying his right to be human and you are expecting him—which is certainly silly, you'll have to admit!—to be superhuman or angelic."

"You really think that's what I'm doing?"

"Well, isn't it? Besides, look again at how illogical you are by being resentful. Whether your boss is right or wrong about this inventory deal, resenting him for being, in your eyes, wrong is hardly going to make him be any righter, is it? And your resentment, surely, is not going to do *you* any good or make you feel better. Then what good is it—your resentment—doing?"

"No good, I guess. If I take the attitude that—well, it's too bad that inventory-keeping is part of my job, and that my boss sees it this way, but that's the way it is, and there's no point in resenting the way it is, I guess I'd feel a lot better about it, wouldn't I?"

"Yes, *wouldn't* you? On still another count, too, your resentful attitude doesn't make sense."

"On what ground is that?"

"The ground that no matter how annoying the inventory-keeping may be, there's no point in making it still *more* irksome by your continually telling yourself how *awful* it is. As we consistently note in rational-emotive therapy, you're not merely being annoyed by the inventory-keeping job itself, but you're making yourself annoyed *at* being annoyed—and you're thereby creating at least two annoyances for the price of one. And the second, the one of your own creation, may well be much more deadly than the first, the one that is being created by the circumstances of your job."

"Because I'm refusing to gracefully *accept* the inherent annoyingness of doing the inventory, I'm giving myself an even harder time than *it* is giving me—is that right?"

"Quite right. Where the inventory-keeping is a real pain in the neck to you, you are a much bigger pain in the neck to yourself."

"Yeah. And since I have to do this kind of clerical work anyway, since I know darned well that the boss is not going to take it away from me, I would be doing myself much more good if I calmly and quickly got it out of the way, instead of making this terrible to-do about it."

"Right again. Can you see, then, the several points at which your resentment is thoroughly illogical in this situation, even though your dissatisfaction with doing the bookkeeping procedure may well be justified?"

"Let's see, now. First, I make a decision to take the job, in spite of its disadvantages, because I really want to be an apprentice, and then I try to go against my own decision by refusing to accept these disadvantages that I had first presumably accepted."

"Yes, that's illogical point number one."

"Then, second, I go to work for a human being, my boss, and then I refuse to accept him as human, and insist that he be a goddamn angel."

"Exactly. That's illogical point number two."

"Third—let's see—I get quite wrapped up in my resentment, and give myself a start on an ulcer, when it's not likely at all to get my boss to change his mind or to do me any good."

"Right."

"And fourth. Now what was fourth? I don't seem to remember?"

"Fourth: you make yourself annoyed at being annoyed and put off doing work that you'll have to do, sooner or later, anyway, and with your annoyed-at-being-annoyed attitude, almost certainly make that work become considerably *more* onerous than it otherwise doubtless would be."

"Oh, yes. To my real annoyance I add to and imagine up a fake annoyance. And I make an unpleasant job more unpleasant than ever."

"Yes. Now can you see, not just in this case, but in every case of this kind, how your resenting someone is highly irrational?"

"Hm. I think so. But how can I stop being resentful? Just by seeing that is doesn't pay for me to be so?"

"No, not exactly. That's too vague. And too easy. More concretely, track down the exact sentences which you are saying to yourself to cause your resentment; and then question and challenge these sentences, until you specifically see how silly they are and are prepared to substitute much saner sentences for them."

At this point, I helped this client to see that he was telling himself sentences like these in order to be upsetting himself: "My boss makes me do inventory-keeping . . . I do not like to do this . . . There is no reason why I have to do it . . . He is therefore a blackguard for making me do this kind of boring, unartistic work. So I'll fool him and avoid doing it . . . And then I'll be happier."

But these beliefs were so palpably foolish that Mervin could not really believe them, so he began to finish them off with sentences like this: "I'm not really fooling my boss, because he sees what I'm doing. So I'm not solving my problem this way . . . I really should stop this nonsense, therefore, and get the inventory-keeping done . . . But I'll be damned if I'll do it for him! . . . However, if I don't do it, I'll be fired . . . But I still don't want to do it for him! . . . I guess I've got to, though . . . Oh, why must I always be persecuted like this? . . . And why must I keep getting myself into such a mess? . . . I guess I'm just no good . . . And people are against me . . . Especially that son-of-a-bitch boss of mine . . . Oh, what's the use?"

Employing these irrational beliefs, Mervin soon became depressed, avoided doing the inventory-keeping, and then became still more resentful and depressed. Instead, I pointed out to him, he could tell himself quite different sentences, on this order: "Keeping inventory is a bore . . . But it is presently an essential part of my job . . . And I also may learn something useful by it . . . Therefore, I'd better go about this task as best I may and thereby get what *I* want out of the job, and later what *I* want out of the profession of glass-staining."

I also emphasized that whenever Mervin found himself intensely angry, guilty, or depressed, he was thinking irrationally and could immediately question himself as to what was the irrational element in his thinking, and set about replacing it. I used his current dilemma—that of avoiding inventory-keeping—as an illustration of his general disturbance, which largely took the form of severe alcoholic tendencies. He was shown that his alcoholic trends, too, resulted from his trying to do things the easy way and from his resentment against people, such as his boss, who kept making him toe the line and blocking his easy-way-out patterns of response.

Several previous incidents of irrational thinking leading to emotional upheaval in Mervin's life were then reviewed, and some general principles of rational thought were discussed. Thus, the general principle of self-damnation was raised and he was shown precisely why it is illogical for one person to damn anyone else (or himself) for anything.

The general principle of inevitability was brought up, and Mervin was shown that when a frustrating or unpleasant event is inevitable, it is only reasonable to accept it uncomplainingly instead of dwelling on its unpleasant aspects. The general principle of hostility was discussed, and he was shown that accepting oneself and trying to do what one is truly interested in doing in life is far more important than being obsessed with others' behavior and resentfully trying to get back at them.

In this manner, by discussing with Mervin some of the general rules of rational living, I tried to go beyond his immediate problem and to help him devise a generalized mode of thinking or problem solving that would enable him to deal effectively with almost any future similar situation that might arise.

After 47 sessions of RET (mainly in group,) spread out over a two-year period, Mervin was able to solve his work problems, to finish his apprenticeship, and to go on to high-level activity in his profession. More importantly, he cut out almost all drinking and restricted himself to a half-dozen glasses of beer a week. His hostilities toward his bosses and his other associates became minimal, and for the first time in his life he became "popular." Three and a half years after the close of therapy, he was maintaining his gains and was reasonably unescapist and unhostile.

Rational therapists, then, are frank re-educators who believe in a rigorous application of the rules of logic, of straight thinking, and of scientific method to everyday life. They ruthlessly uncover the most important elements of irrational thinking in clients' experience and energetically direct them into more reasonable channels of behaving. In so doing, they do not ignore or eradicate the clients' emotions. On the contrary, they help change emotions, when they are disordered and self-defeating, through the same means by which they commonly arise in the first place—that is, by thinking and acting. Through exerting consistent interpretive and philosophic pressure on clients to change their thinking and actions, the rational therapist gives them a specific impetus toward achieving mental health without which it is not impossible, but quite unlikely, that they will move very far.

Man and woman are uniquely suggestible as well as uniquely rational animals. Other animals are to some degree suggestible and reasoning, but peoples' better-equipped cerebral cortex gives them unusual opportunities to talk themselves into *and* out of many difficulties.

The rational therapists hold that although humans' possession of a high degree of suggestibility and negative emotionality (such as anxiety, guilt, and hostility) may possibly have been adequate or advantageous for primitive survival, they can get along much better today when they become more rational and less suggestible. Perhaps it would be more realistic to say that since suggestibility seems to be an almost ineradicable human trait, we should not aim at destroying but at modifying it so that men and women become more *intelligently* suggestible.

In other words: people act in certain ways because they *believe* that they should or must act in these ways. If they are irrationally suggestible, they believe that they should act in intensely emotional, self-defeating ways; and if they are more rationally suggestible, they believe that they should act in less negatively emotional, less neurotic ways. In either event, the deeds in which they believe they tend to actualize. As Kelly (1955) has noted, an individual's difficulty frequently "arises out of the intrinsic meaning of his personal constructs rather than out of the general form which they have assumed. A person who believes that punishment expunges guilt is likely to punish himself."

The main problem of effective living then, would seem to be not that of eradicating people's beliefs, but of changing them so that they become more closely rooted to information and to reason. This can be done, says the rational therapist, by getting people to examine, to question, to think about their beliefs, and thereby to develop a more consistent, empirically based, and workable set of constructs than they now may possess. . . .

Aaron Beck

Aaron Beck, a psychiatrist with a psychoanalytic background, teaches at the University of Pennsylvania Medical School, where he also directs the Center for Cognitive Therapy. Beck and the center he heads have been pioneers in the development of cognitive therapy as a treatment for mood disorders, particularly for depression. Despite his analytic training, the cognitive therapy Beck evolved is closer to Ellis' "rational-emotive therapy" than to analysis.

Cognitive therapy focuses on a person's thoughts and feelings in the here and now; it does not try to trace the origins of a patient's problem into his past. The cognitive approach assumes that a person's emotional reactions, motives, and actions are guided by his habitual patterns of thought. Most often, notes Beck, we are not aware of these thoughts, nor of the great degree of control they exert over our inner life.

When a patient comes to a cognitive therapist for treatment, therapy immediately focuses on the maladaptive thoughts that are behind the problem. "In cognitive therapy," writes Beck, "the patient focuses on those thoughts or images that produce unnecessary discomfort or suffering or lead to self-defeating behavior." Such thoughts are often obvious to the patient with little introspection. For example, the patient who is morbidly depressed years after the death of his wife may be preoccupied with extreme thoughts such as "It's my fault she died," or "I can't live without her." Such maladaptive thoughts are recognized by their exaggerated and unrealistic nature.

Maladaptive thoughts typically are automatic and intrusive, occupying the patient's mind almost constantly, or exerting a subtle background influence on how he feels and acts. Once these thoughts are identified and highlighted, the patient is encouraged to take careful note of the day-to-day situations that activate them, as well as the consequences the thoughts have—e.g., fear or depression.

The very processing of objectively observing such maladaptive thoughts, says Beck, can begin a process of "distancing," whereby they lose their hold. Distancing allows the patient to sort out what aspects of these thoughts are realistic, which might be mistaken—he can question the validity of his thoughts. The therapist then works with the patient to pinpoint habitual distortions of reality in his thinking that have led to his present problem.

Cognitive therapists have a wide range of tactics at their disposal. The course of therapy, Beck advises, should be tailored to the particular needs of the patient. But, in general, cognitive therapy follows a specific framework. First, the patient's distorted thoughts and their maladaptive consequences are clarified, then the underlying mental habits that have led to them are revised. Demonstrating the fallacy a patient's erroneous ways of thinking can, according to Beck, clear the way for a change in maladaptive habits of thought—and so produce a cure.

From TECHNIQUES OF COGNITIVE THERAPY

by Aaron Beck

Emotional reactions, motivations, and overt behavior are guided by thinking. A person may not be fully aware of the automatic thoughts that influence to a large extent how he acts, what he feels, and how much he enjoys his experiences. With some training, however, he may increase his awareness of these thoughts and learn to pinpoint them with a high degree of regularity. It is possible to perceive a thought, focus on it, and evaluate it just as one can identify and reflect on a sensation (such as pain) or an external stimulus (such as a verbal statement).

The term "maladaptive thoughts" is applied to ideation that interferes with the ability to cope with life experiences, unnecessarily disrupts internal harmony, and produces inappropriate or excessive emotional reactions that are painful. In cognitive therapy, the patient focuses on those thoughts or images that produce unnecessary discomfort or suffering or lead to self-defeating behavior. In applying the term "maladaptive," it is important that the therapist be wary of imposing his own value system on the patient. The term is generally applicable if both the patient and the therapist are able to agree that these automatic thoughts interfere with the patient's well-being or with the attainment of his important objectives.

Possible exceptions to this definition immediately spring to mind. Is a disturbing thought considered maladaptive if it is consonant with reality? It would seem difficult to justify applying the label "maladaptive" to an accurate appraisal of danger (and its associated anxiety) or to the recognition of a real loss and the resulting arousal of grief. Yet, under some circumstances, even such reality-oriented ideation may be regarded as maladaptive because of its interference with functioning. For example, steeplejacks, bridge-workers and mountain climbers may not only suffer serious discomfort, but may be subjected to greatly increased risk by a stream of thoughts or images about falling. Such ideation not only distracts them from concentrating on their task, but the associated anxiety may lead to swaying, dizziness, and trembling that may disturb their balance. Similarly, a surgeon distracted by thoughts of making a slip with his scalpel may endanger his patient's life. People engaged in hazardous activities generally acquire the ability to disregard or extinguish such thoughts. With experience, they seem to form a psychological buffer that diminishes the force and frequency of the thoughts. The presence of this buffer separates the seasoned veteran from the novice.

In actual clinical practice, the therapist is rarely forced to make a fine distinction between maladaptive and realistic thoughts. The distortions or self-defeating characteristics are usually obvious enough to justify calling them maladaptive. A man, depressed for years after the death of his wife, went beyond the realistic consequences of the loss and was preoccupied with extreme ideas such as, "It's my fault she died," or "I can't exist without her," or "I will never find any satisfaction." Similarly, a student with pre-examination jitters thought, "It will be the end for me if I fail; I will never be able to face my friends," or "I will end up on skid row." After the examination, he easily realized the exaggerated, unrealistic nature of these thoughts.

Ellis (1962) refers to this kind of maladaptive thinking

as "internalized statements" or "self-statements" and he describes them to the patient as "things you tell yourself." Maultsby (1968) uses the term "self-talk" to label these thoughts. Such explanations are of practical value in that they imply to the patient that the maladaptive thoughts are voluntary, and therefore he can voluntarily switch them off or change them. While recognizing the practical usefulness of this terminology, I prefer the term "automatic thoughts," because it more accurately reflects the way the thoughts are experienced. The person perceives these thoughts as though they arise by reflex—without any prior reflection or reasoning; and they impress him as plausible and valid. They can be compared to statements made to a believing child by his parent. The patient can frequently be trained to terminate this kind of thinking, but in severe cases, especially phychoses, physiological interventions such as administration of drugs or electroconvulsive therapy may be required to stop the maladaptive thoughts.

The force and prominence of maladaptive thoughts appear to increase in measure with the severity of the patient's disturbance. In severe disorders, the thoughts are generally salient and may, in fact, occupy the center of the ideational field. This phenomenon may be observed in acute or severe cases of depression, anxiety, or paranoid states. In depression, the patient may have no voluntary control over ruminations such as "I'm no good . . . My insides are gone . . . Everything bad happens to me." Analogous types of preoccupations with danger occur in anxiety states and preoccupation with abuse in paranoid states.

On the other hand, obsessional patients who are not acutely or severely disturbed may be very conscious of certain types of repetitive statements. These incessant thoughts are diagnostic indications of this disorder. Moreover, people who are free of neurosis may experience similar preoccupations. A mother alarmed about her sick child or a student concerned about an imminent examination is apt to experience the relentless repetition of unpleasant thoughts about the particular problem. Any person who has such "worries" can attest to how involuntary they seem.

A person experiencing a mild disturbance in his feelings or behavior may not be aware of the automatic thoughts—even though they are accessible to consciousness. In such cases, the automatic thoughts do not attract his attention—although they can exert an influence on how he feels and acts. By concentrating on the thoughts, however, he can easily recognize them. We can observe this phenomenon in people who have recovered from the acute phase of a psychological disturbance or who are only mildly disturbed.

People who characteristically avoid situations that upset them, such as phobics, will not be conscious of their maladaptive ideation as long as they maintain a comfortable distance from the threatening situations. However, when they are forced into the situation or imagine themselves in the situation, these maladaptive thoughts become activated, and can readily be identified.

When a patient states he had never been aware of his automatic thoughts until after he had been trained to observe them, we are faced with a philosophical problem: How can a person be unaware of something in his field of consciousness? Yet, many of us have had the experience of having been exposed to a particular stimulus but having no conscious awareness of it until it was pointed out to us. At that point, we might remark, "I realize that it was there all the time, but I just did not notice it before." In such situations, it seems that the perception occurred but we did not pay any attention to it. Yet, this perception may have influenced our train of thought or feelings. A person having difficulty in falling asleep may not be aware that his restlessness is influenced by noxious sounds such as the loud ticking of a clock or heavy traffic. Similarly, automatic thoughts occur within the realm of consciousness, but, until he has been trained, the person may not observe them. By shifting his attention to these thoughts he becomes more aware of them and can specify their content.

FILLING IN THE BLANK

When the automatic thoughts are in the center of awareness, there is no problem in identifying them. In cases of mild to moderate neurosis, a program of instructions and practice sessions is generally necessary to train the patient to delineate those thoughts. Sometimes, by fantasizing the traumatic situation, the individual may stir up such thoughts.

A basic procedure for helping a patient identify his automatic thoughts is to train him to observe the sequence of external events and his reactions to them. The patient may report a number of circumstances in which he felt unaccountably upset. Usually, there is a gap between the stimulus and emotional response. The emotional upset becomes understandable if he can recollect the thoughts that occurred during this gap.

Ellis describes the following techniques for explaining this procedure to the patient. He calls the sequence: "A, B, C." "A" is the "Activating stimulus" and "C" is the excessive, inappropriate "Conditioned response." "B" is the Blank in the patient's mind, which, when he fills it in, serves as a bridge between "A" and "C." Filling in the blank, which derives from the patient's belief system, becomes the therapeutic task.

One patient outlined the sequence of A, seeing an old friend, and C, experiencing sadness. Another patient reported the sequence: A, he heard a report about somebody being killed in an automobile accident, and C, felt anxiety. In these instances the patients were able to replay the events in slow motion, as it were, and could then successfully recall the thoughts that had occurred in the gap. Seeing the old friend had elicited B, the following sequence of thoughts: "If I greet Bob, he may not remember me . . . He may snub me . . . It's been so long, we won't have anything in common. It won't be like old times." These thoughts evoked the sad feelings. The patient who felt anxious after witnessing the auto accident was able to fill in the blank when he recalled having had a fantasy image of himself as the victim.

The A B C sequence may be illustrated by the common fear of dogs. A person may assert that although he has no reason for fearing dogs, he experiences anxiety whenever he is exposed to them. One such patient was puzzled by the fact that he became frightened when near a dog even when there was no possibility of his being attacked. He would feel nervous when a dog was chained or fenced in, or when a dog was obviously too small to injure him. I recommended that he focus on whatever thoughts occurred to him the next time he saw a dog—any dog.

At the next interview, the patient reported having seen a number of dogs between appointments. He reported a phenomenon that he had not noticed previously—mainly, that each time he saw a dog he had a thought such as, "It's going to bite me." By focusing on the intervening thoughts, he was able to understand why he felt anxious: He automatically regarded every dog as dangerous. He commented that he experienced the fear of being bitten even when he saw a miniature poodle. He stated, "I realized how ridiculous it was to think that a small poodle could hurt me." He also recognized that when he saw a large dog on a leash he would think of the most deleterious eventualities: "The dog will jump up and bite out one of my eyes." "It will jump up and bite my neck and kill me." Within three weeks, the patient was able to overcome his long-standing fear by repeatedly recognizing his thoughts when exposed to dogs.

The technique of "filling in the blank" can be of great help to patients disturbed by excessive shame, anxiety, anger, or sadness in interpersonal situations, or handicapped by fears of specific locations or structures. A college student avoided public gatherings because of inexplicable feelings of shame, anxiety, and sadness in these situations. After having been trained to recognize and record his cognitions, he reported having had these thoughts in social situations: "Nobody will want to talk to me . . . They think I look pathetic . . . I'm just a misfit." After having these thoughts, he experienced feelings of humiliation, anxiety, and sadness and would have a strong desire to leave.

Another patient complained that he became almost uncontrollably angry whenever he had interchanges with strangers—when making purchases, asking for information, or just conversing. After two training sessions, he reported that he recognized intermediate thoughts such as, "He's pushing me around." "He thinks I'm a pushover," "She's trying to take advantage of me." Immediately after experiencing these thoughts, he would feel angry at the person toward whom they were directed. Until this time, he had not realized that he had a tendency to regard other people as adversaries. Another patient felt chronically irritated in the presence of other people without realizing it. After focusing on his thoughts, he realized he was having continuous critical ideas about these people.

Many times, maladaptive ideation occurs in a pictorial form instead of, or in addition to, the verbal form (Beck): A woman with a fear of walking alone had images of having a heart attack and being left helpless and dying on the street. Then she would feel acute anxiety. Another woman who experienced a surge of anxiety when driving across a bridge recognized that the anxiety was preceded by a pictorial image of her car breaking through the guard rail and her falling off the bridge. A student discovered that his anxiety at leaving his dormitory at night was triggered by visual fantasies of being attacked by gangsters.

DISTANCING AND DECENTERING

Some patients who have learned to identify their automatic
thoughts recognize their unreliable and maladaptive nature
spontaneously. With successive observations of their thoughts,
they became increasingly able to view these thoughts objectively. The process of regarding thoughts objectively is labeled *distancing.* The concept of distancing is derived from
its usage to denote the ability of patients who are adminis-
tered a projective test, such as Rorschach's ink-blot test, to
maintain the distinction between the ink-blot configurations
and the association or fantasy stimulated by the figure. Patients who are "carried away" by strong emotional reactions
to the perceptions aroused by the configuration are often
found to regard the ink blot as though it were the same as
the object or scenes it conjured up. The patient who is able to
withdraw his attention from this association and to perceive
this stimulus as simply an ink blot is said to be able to "take
distance" from the blot.

In an analogous way, a person who can examine his automatic thoughts as psychological phenomena rather than as
identical to reality is exercising the capacity for distancing.
Take, for example, a patient who, for no justifiable reason,
has the thought, "That man is my enemy." If he automatically equates the thought with reality, his distancing is poor.
If he can regard the idea as a hypothesis or inference, rather
than accept it as fact, he is distancing well.

Concepts such as distancing, reality testing, authenticating
observations, and validating conclusions, are related to epis-
temology. Distancing involves being able to make the distinction between "I believe" (an opinion that is subject to
validation) and "I know" (an "irrefutable" fact). The ability
to make this distinction is of critical importance in modifying
those sectors of the patient's reactions that are subject to distortion.

In various psychological disorders—anxiety, depression,
paranoid states—major distortion in thinking results from the
patient's proclivity to personalize events that have no casual
connection to him. A depressed man blames himself for the
fact that a family picnic he had scheduled had to be canceled
because of rain. An anxious woman sees a burned building
and thinks that *her* house may be on fire. A paranoid patient
sees a frown on the face of a passerby and concludes that
person wants to harm him. The technique of prying the pa-

tient loose from his pattern of regarding himself as the focal point of all events is called decentering. The successful application of this method is illustrated in the following case (Schuyler, 1973).

A graduate student had a good deal of anxiety prior to taking examinations. His anxiety was exacerbated because he interpreted the physiological symptoms (shortness of breath, tachycardia, etc.) as signs of an impending heart attack. According to his philosophy of predestination, he decided that fate had singled him out for a special hardship. He passed the written examination for an advanced degree but failed the oral examination. Although he realized that his anxiety had interfered with his oral examination, he interpreted the failure itself as evidence that fate was against him.

At the time he was to take his oral examination a second time, there was considerable snow on the ground. On the way to the examination, he slipped and fell. He then became quite anxious. He was able to identify the relevant thought: "The snow has been put there so that I would fall." Then he recalled what his therapist had told him about his tendency to personalize external events. He looked around and saw that other people were slipping, that automobiles were skidding on the ice, and that even a dog had slid and fallen. As he was struck by the realization that the snow was not a special hardship directed at him, his anxiety disappeared.

AUTHENTICATING CONCLUSIONS

It generally does not occur to a person to question the validity of his thoughts. He tends to regard ideas as though they were a microcosm of the outside world. He attaches the same truth value to his thought as he does to his perception of the external world.

Even after a patient is able to make a clear distinction between his internal mental processes and the outside world that stimulates them, it is still necessary to educate him regarding the procedures for acquiring accurate knowledge. People continually set up hypotheses and draw inferences. They tend to equate an inference with reality and to accept a hypothesis as though it were a fact. Under ordinary circumstances, they might be able to function adequately because their ideation may be sufficiently in phase with the real world so as not to substantially interfere with their adjustment.

In cases of neurosis, the distorted concepts can have a dis-

abling effect. These distorted concepts lead to faulty thinking
in certain circumscribed areas of experience. In these particular sectors they tend to make global undifferentiated judgments instead of the fine discriminations that are necessary to
keep in tune with reality. . . . The patient frequently detours
logic and leaps to arbitrary inferences, overgeneralizations,
and magnifications.

The psychotherapist can apply certain techniques to determine whether the patients' conclusions are inaccurate or
unjustified. Since the patient has been habitually making distortions, the therapeutic procedure consists essentially of exploring his conclusions and testing them against reality. The
therapist works with the patient to apply the rules of evidence
to his conclusions. This consists initially of checking his observations and then following the route to the conclusions.

CHANGING THE RULES

We have seen that people apply rules (formulas, equations,
premises) in regulating their own lives and in trying to modify the behavior of other people. Moreover, they label, interpret, and evaluate according to sets of rules. When these rules
are framed in absolute terms, are unrealistic, or are used
inappropriately or excessively, they frequently produce
maladjustment. The ultimate result is often some kind of disturbance: anxiety, depression, phobia, mania, paranoid state,
obsession. When the rules lead to difficulties, they are by definition maladaptive.

Ellis (1962) refers to such rules as "irrational ideas." His
term, while powerful, is not accurate. The ideas are generally
not irrational but are too absolute, broad, and extreme; too
highly personalized; and are used too arbitrarily to help the
patient to handle the exigencies of his life. To be of greater
use, the rules need to be remolded so that they are more precise and accurate, less egocentric, and more elastic. When
rules are discovered to be false, self-defeating, or unworkable,
they have to be dropped from the repertoire. In such cases,
the therapist and patient work together to substitute more realistic and adaptive rules.

Inasmuch as other writers have used terms such as attitudes, ideas, concepts, and constructs to refer to what we
have called rules, those terms will be used interchangeably in
the following discussion. Irrespective of terminology used,
many therapists have reported that helping the patient to

modify his maladaptive ideas or to substitute more realistic attitudes has led to the disappearance of crippling anxieties, phobias, and depressions. Therapists sometimes overlook the obvious truth that if a patient's incorrect assumptions or personal mythology are not related to his difficulties, it is not necessary to change them. The therapist's mandate does not require that he educate his patient to be a Renaissance man.

The content of the rules for coding experiences and steering behavior seems to revolve around two main axes: *danger versus safety* and *pain versus pleasure*. Patients' difficulties arise in their assessments of risk and safety or in their conceptions of pain and gratification.

The rules dealing with safety and danger include physical harm and psychological harm. The concerns about physical harm cover a broad range of "dangerous situations"; being assaulted or killed by other people or animals; being injured or killed by falling from high places, or by collisions (as in automobile accidents); suffocating or starving by being deprived of air or food; or being afflicted by a wide host of diseases and poisons. It is obvious that these noxious events occur in the real world. For purposes of survival, people use their mental rule books to interpret dangerous situations and to assess the degree of risk. The person who encounters difficulties either by being unnecessarily apprehensive or by behaving recklessly does not have the correct rules, or else does not apply them correctly.

Psychosocial harm covers the varieties of hurt feelings, humiliations, embarrassments, and sadness that occur after a person has been insulted, criticized, or rejected. It should be noted that these feelings can occur when a person simply *thinks* he has been insulted, criticized, or rejected—when indeed he has not been. Furthermore, unlike physical injury, which generally provides some reliable index of the degree of trauma (for example, bleeding, specific localized pain), rejection or criticism does not leave any telltale marks. The person simply feels bad but we cannot discern from this reaction whether the bad feeling is based on a real or on a fancied insult.

In order to minimize danger, people generally apply rules to estimate the probabilities and degree of harm and the likelihood of dealing successfully with the threat. The ratio between the potential harm and coping mechanisms may be labeled the risk. If a person overestimates the risk, he is unnecessarily anxious and may lead a constricted life. If he underestimates the risk, he is more prone to having accidents.

The complexities of interpersonal relations and the lack of a reliable index of another person's intentions to cause hurt add a fuzziness to the rules used in interpersonal situations. Some people regard themselves as highly vulnerable in all interpersonal contacts and thus feel constantly on the razor's edge. Conversely, those who are oblivious to signals from other people, of course, may regularly get into interpersonal difficulties.

Because most problems presented by patients seem to arise in the context of interpersonal relations, some of the common interpersonal attitudes will be considered first. Interpersonal dangers are epitomized by a rule such as the following: "It would be awful for someone to form a low opinion of me." The other person might be a close friend, a parent, a peer, remote acquaintance, or a stranger. In clinical practice, we find that our patients are generally most afraid of being devalued by members of their peer group—their classmates, fellow workers, colleagues, or friends. Many patients, however, are even more afraid of the prospect of appearing ridiculous to strangers. They are apprehensive of the reactions of clerks in stores, waiters, taxi drivers, passengers on a bus, or passersby on a street. It is possible that the strangers' reactions are more threatening because these patients have not learned from direct experience what to expect.

A person may dread a situation in which he considers himself vulnerable to other people's adverse criticisms of him (either overt or unexpressed). He is sensitized to situations in which some "weakness" or "fault" of his might be exposed. He might be afraid of disapproval for not expressing himself well, behaving too aggressively, appearing different from other people—or even seeming to be afraid of disapproval. In more extreme cases, he may be afraid of losing control: being too emotional, fainting, or acting insane.

All kinds of negative reactions may be envisioned, ranging from stony stares to denunciations. It is essential to understand that the person regards such reactions from other people as very bad. When patients are asked why it might be so bad to be criticized by a stranger, it becomes apparent that they simply regard this as bad *by definition*. They are usually at a loss to explain why it is so bad. They have a vague notion that a rejection or criticism will in some way permanently and irreversibly damage their social image and self-image.

* * * * *

THE OVER-ALL STRATEGY

There are so many different therapeutic tactics available to the cognitive therapist that unless he develops an over-all strategy for a given case, the therapy may follow an erratic course based on trial and error. The principles that form the framework for cognitive therapy have been outlined previously: clarifying the patient's distortions, self-injunctions, and self-reproaches that lead to his distress or disability, and helping him to revise the underlying rules that produce these faulty self-signals. Some of the methods used by the cognitive therapist are similar to those used previously by patients in their successful attempts at problem-solving. The therapist works with the patient in a more systematic way on psychological problems he has been unable to resolve independently. The specific mechanics consist of defining the problem area precisely, filling in the informational gaps, establishing relations among the data, and forming generalizations. The therapist then helps the patient to use his own problem-solving apparatus in making the necessary adjustments in his ways of interpreting his experiences and regulating his behavior.

The *techniques* of psychotherapy overlap considerably with the *process* of psychotherapy, so that it is difficult to draw a line between what the therapist does and the patient's responses. Furthermore, the therapist may be employing several procedures simultaneously, and the patient may be reacting to these with a series of therapeutic responses. For instance, in training the patient to recognize his automatic thoughts, the therapist directly or indirectly questions their validity. In turn, the process of extending the patient's awareness of this form of ideation is accompanied by greater objectivity (distancing). As the patient recognizes that these self-signals are maladaptive or discordant with reality, he has a tendency to correct them automatically. Moreover, this kind of self-scrutiny leads directly to the recognition of the underlying premises and equations—the rules that are responsible for the faulty responses. The following case illustrates the interaction of the therapist's procedures and the patient's psychological processes.

An attractive young mother of three children was seen in a

university psychiatric clinic because of episodes of anxiety lasting up to six or seven hours a day. These periods of anxiety had occurred practically daily for over four years. She had frequently consulted her family physician, who had prescribed a variety of sedatives and Thorazine, without any apparent improvement.

At the time of my first interview with her, the following facts were elicited. Her first anxiety episode occurred about two weeks after she had had a miscarriage. She was bending over to bathe her one-year-old son, when she suddenly began to feel faint. She then had her first anxiety attack, which lasted several hours. The patient could not find any explanation for her anxiety. When I asked whether she had had any thought at the time she felt dizzy, she recalled having had the idea, "Suppose I should pass out and injure the baby." It seemed plausible, as a working hypothesis, that her dizziness (which was probably the result of a postpartum anemia) led to the fear she might faint and drop the baby. This frightening notion produced anxiety, which she interpreted as a sign that she was "going to pieces."

Until the time of her miscarriage, the patient had been reasonably carefree and did not recall having experienced any episodes of anxiety. After her miscarriage, however, she periodically had the thought, "Bad things can happen to me." Subsequently, when she heard of someone becoming sick, she often would think, "This can happen to me," and she would begin to feel anxious.

The patient was instructed to try to pinpoint any thoughts that preceded further episodes of anxiety. At the next interview, she reported:

1. One evening, she heard that the husband of one of her friends had severe pneumonia. She immediately had an anxiety attack lasting several hours. In accordance with the instructions, she tried to recall the cognition preceding her anxiety. She remembered thinking, "Tom [her husband] could get sick like that and maybe die."

2. She had considerable anxiety just before leaving on a trip to her sister's house. She focused on her ideation and recognized that she had the repetitive thought, "I might get sick on the trip." She had had a serious episode of gastroenteritis during a previous trip to her sister's house and evidently believed that she was likely to get sick again.

3. On another occasion, she was feeling uncomfortable,

and objects seemed somewhat unreal to her. She then had the thought, "I might be losing my mind," and immediately experienced an anxiety attack lasting almost an hour.

4. She learned that one of her friends had been committed to a state mental hospital. This bit of information led to the thought, "This could happen to me. I could lose my mind." When questioned about the specific details of losing her mind, she stated that she was afraid that if she went crazy, she would do something that would harm either her children or herself.

It was evident that the patient's major fears revolved around the anticipation of loss of control, whether by fainting or by becoming psychotic, and consequently doing something harmful. I explained to the patient that there was no evidence that she was becoming psychotic. She was also provided with an explanation for the arousal of her anxiety and of her secondary elaboration of the meaning of these attacks: Her underlying formula was that the symptoms of anxiety indicated she was on the verge of psychosis. During the next few weeks, her anxiety attacks became less frequent and less intense and, by the end of four weeks, they disappeared completely.

The major therapeutic thrust in this case was coaching the patient to recall the thoughts that preceded an anxiety attack and to assess their validity. The recognition that these attacks were initiated by a cognition rather than by some vague mysterious force convinced her that her notion that she was totally vulnerable was incorrect. She also realized that her belief that she was unable to control her reactions was erroneous. By learning to pinpoint the anxiety-producing thoughts, she was able to gain some detachment and to subject them to reality testing. Consequently, she was able to nullify the effects of those thoughts.

The formulation of the progress of this patient can now be fitted into the therapeutic model: (1) *self-observations* that led directly to the ideation preceding the anxiety; (2) establishing the relation between the thoughts and anxiety attack; (3) learning to regard thoughts as hypotheses rather than facts; (4) testing the hypotheses; (5) piecing together the assumptions that underlay and generated these hypotheses; (6) demonstrating that these rules composing her belief system were incorrect. Her belief system consisted of equations regarding probable mental and physical illness, loss of control, and involuntarily hurting somebody. Furthermore, she had developed the superstition that if something bad hap-

pened to someone else, it was likely to happen to her or a
member of her family. Finally, she had developed the universal frightener, "Anything can happen to me." By demonstrating the fallacy of her equations and self-references, we were
able to revise the faulty belief system.

Milton H. Erickson

Milton H. Erickson (1901-1980) did more than anyone else to establish hypnosis as a respectable mode of therapy. A psychiatrist by training, Erickson became interested in hypnosis while an undergraduate at the University of Wisconsin. Erickson was himself a master of the craft, trained thousands of health professionals in its clinical applications, and wrote more than 140 articles on hypnosis, as well as several books.

The use of hypnosis in treating human suffering dates back centuries. Freud studied hypnotic techniques with Charcot in Paris early in his career, and later with Braid in Nancy. Although there seemed to be clinical improvement in the cases Freud observed and, indeed, in the cases he himself treated, he rejected the method in favor of the "talking cure"—free association. Meanwhile, although hypnosis never entirely disappeared from the psychotherapeutic domain, it fell into disrepute. Some hypothesized that hypnosis fostered dependence on the therapist or on the hypnotic technique itself, and although this idea was never substantiated, it remained a suspicion in the minds of many conventional therapists.

Traditionally, hypnosis has been understood as a heightened suggestibility fostered in susceptible people by a combination of relaxation, distraction, and one-pointed focus to the exclusion of other stimuli. In the altered state of consciousness thus induced the patient's attention is dissociated and regressed while being highly receptive to the hypnotherapist's suggestions. These suggestions can serve such clinical ends as uncovering repressed material, retrieving memories, examining alternatives, and erasing phobias.

Erickson's techniques, though, relied as much on psycholinguistic nuances as on relaxation and focus during hypnotic trance. Incapacitated by polio twice, he relearned walking through careful study of a toddler's every movement. Tone-deaf and almost completely color-blind, he became exquisitely sensitive to the nuances of light and sound. Confined to a wheelchair for more than a decade, Erickson nevertheless continued to teach and treat patients.

Dr. Erickson's unique approach to psychotherapy depended more on the subtleties of communication than on the induction of formal hypnotic trance. As a psychiatrist and family counselor he treated disorders of all sorts, from schizophrenic reactions to delinquency to marital discords. Erickson never formulated a precise theory to describe his therapeutic techniques. "Each person," he wrote, "is a unique individual. Hence, psychotherapy should be formulated to meet the uniqueness of the individual's needs, rather than tailoring the person to fit the Procrustean bed of a hypothetical theory of human behavior." Although he himself left no formal theoretical system, several students have analyzed his technique. His methods—both of hypnosis and of short-term therapy— have had considerable influence in the conduct of individual, group, and family therapy in the United States and abroad. The following article should be of particular interest to students, since it describes successful treatment of an extreme fear of examinations.

EXPERIENTIAL KNOWLEDGE OF HYPNOTIC PHENOMENA EMPLOYED FOR HYPNOTHERAPY

by Milton H. Erickson

INTRODUCTION

In the use of hypnosis for the therapeutic handling of psychogenic problems, there is often too ready a dependence upon hypnosis itself and the immediate use of some well-known structured form of hypnotic approach. For example, the author has seen many instances where hypnotherapy was attempted by a routine use of regression by various therapists with disappointing results, and sometimes with an antagonizing of the patient toward hypnosis. Although hypnotic regression, dissociation, abreaction and revivification may be useful in general, each patient's problem needs individual scrutiny and the structuring of the therapeutic approach to meet the individuality of the problem.

To illustrate this need, the following account is given in detail to portray the character of a problem that had to be met, the purposes that had to be served, the procedures that had to be considered and utilized in therapy, and the methods that had to be employed in devising a successful therapeutic handling of the problem.

The question of therapeutic procedure will be discussed first to present certain vital aspects of the therapeutic situation as a background for a general understanding of the total problem.

One of the considerations was that therapy would have to be successful on the first completed effort. If there were a failure, there could be no opportunity for any second effort by a revision of therapeutic measures nor any measure of "second guessing." One and only one opportunity existed for a successful outcome. Both the patient and the author were aware of this fact, a matter so much in evidence that no mention of it was needed.

The problem was one of long duration and it had many times been confirmed and accepted by respected authoritative persons. Additionally, the patient had been aided and abetted in circumventing his problem most successfully many times.

He was now confronted inescapably with the need to confront his problem in a situation vital to his whole future with no possibility of any circumvention as had always been done successfully in the past.

He approached the author with a request for help by means of hypnosis but with no adequate understanding that hypnosis could help him only by making more available to him his own potentials for self-help. Nor was he in any frame of mind to be given such understanding. He "knew" beyond all doubt that he was helpless and he simply surrendered himself to the author with complete dependence upon what the author could do. Hence, any therapeutic procedure would have to be patterned to permit an inclusion of this mistaken understanding by the patient but doing so without invalidating therapy.

The idea of circumvention had become a fixed idea, it was always by the same method, and it had always proved to be the "right and only" method. Now he was barred from circumvention, *hence he had to depend entirely upon the author.*

Since this was the patient's fixed belief, hypnotherapy would have to include circumvention which would not be so recognized by him at the time, since, in his own mind, he was rigidly convinced that circumvention was impossible. Therefore the structuring of the therapeutic procedure would have to be around something in which the patient fully believed but also fully believed to be impossible of utilization.

The patient himself unwittingly gave the author a rather full statement of how this circumvention could be achieved but which the author did not recognize at the time. Nor did the author recognize, at least consciously and probably not unconsciously, the meaningfulness of the patient's informative statement until after structuring and restructuring the complete plan, and to the author's chagrin, he realized he had not listened sufficiently carefully to the patient's own significant statement so vital to the final plan of therapeutic procedure.

Finally, in developing any therapeutic plan that must succeed upon the first effort, the author realized that he would have to do much speculative work and would have to follow the trail of many of his own thoughts on the matter that would turn out to be useless. In this presentation, the useless work done will not be reported. The fruitful work only will be reported and in brief form since the kind, not the extent of the work, is all that is important.

THE PROBLEM

A patient, a professional man, seeking certification in a medical specialty, sought the author's aid. His story was that, since high school days, oral examinations were nightmarish ordeals. Invariably he developed a multitude of psychosomatic symptoms ranging in kind from mild to severely disabling. He had always been an excellent student and none of his teachers and instructors, upon seeing the state of his physical collapse when attempting to meet the needs of an oral examination, had ever doubted the genuineness of his reactions.

With a feeling of shame and humiliation when confronted with the possibility of an oral examination, he usually secured a physician's statement affirming his inability to comply and recommending, as a medical necessity, that he be given a written examination. Such medical statements usually stated that there would be no objection to making the written examination much more rigorous and searching than the oral examination would ordinarily be. Invariably he received an excellent grade since he was a most brilliant and dedicated student.

This special disability had haunted him throughout high school, college and medical school. On several occasions, only his earnestness, brilliance, unassuming and modest behavior, and the actual breadth of his knowledge induced some of his instructors to make special allowance for his handicap, or to "humor" him, since a few resented the situation.

State board examinations were trying ordeals for him when both written and oral examinations were required. Only the unusual excellence of the written part of the examination and the documentation of his past experiences induced the two state boards of medical examiners which required an oral examination to accord him special consideration. The reason for examinations by several state boards was his desire to inform himself about the practice of medicine in various parts of the country.

In the actual practice of medicine this patient was well respected and his competence was readily recognized. He experienced no personal problems, and his home and marital adjustments were excellent. He had consulted several psychotherapists, all of whom had regarded his problem as a circumscribed manifestation that did not warrant therapy.

He finally decided to secure certification in a certain specialty. The examining board was considerate about substituting an additional written examination for the customary oral examination part. He received his certification without difficulty. Some years later he decided upon additional certification in an allied field and undertook extensive training for that purpose.

He applied for admission to the examination conducted by the specialty board in that field. He received a letter of acceptance accompanied by a letter from the president of the board of examiners and signed by him. This letter stated that all examinees, in accord with a newly established policy of examination, were required without exception to take an oral examination lasting a minimum of 4 hours. This would be conducted by the president of the board and 2 other examiners. The patient recognized the president's name at once as that of a classmate he had had in high school, college and

medical school. That man was fully aware of the patient's
oral examination problem; moreover, he had carried throughout the years an unreasoning, intense and bitter hatred for
the patient. With the passage of years, occasional encounters
at medical meetings had disclosed no abatement of that man's
hatred, for which the patient knew no basis and for which no
provocation was needed to elicit some unpleasant manifestation.

The patient consulted a colleague who also intended to
take the examination at the same time. This colleague had received a letter of acceptance containing the same information
but it was signed by the secretary of the board.

He wrote to two other friends with whom he had taken
specific postgraduate courses and who were also taking the
examination. Their letters were similar in content to his but
were signed by the board secretary.

The patient then said simply, "There you have it. The term
of office for that man is 4 years. I need to be certified this
year. I know for an absolute certainty that I cannot measure
up to an oral examination. I have no doubts about knowing
my stuff. I could pass any written examination with flying
colors. But I also know with absolute certainty that I cannot
take an oral examination, much less one conducted by a man
who hates me bitterly for no reason that I know of and who
knows my weakness. I regard my situation as hopeless unless
hypnosis can do something for me. That is why I have come
to you, and I place myself unreservedly in your hands. I am
your patient if you will accept me. If you do, you will have
my full cooperation in anything that you wish to do or anything that you may wish me to do." This placing of all responsibility upon the author was immediately apparent, as well as
his fixed limited understanding of his situation.

INITIAL PROCEDURES AND APPRAISAL OF PROBLEM

He was assured that he was accepted as a patient and he was
asked to give in full detail every item of symptomatology he
had ever developed in connection with oral examinations. He
was asked to execute this task as a simple recounting rather
than as a vivification of his symptoms as he recited them.

The patient thoughtfully, slowly, and in a most orderly systematic fashion detailed his symptoms fully. They were
many and included intense fear, uncontrollable tremors, ex-

cessive perspiration, nausea and vomiting, palpitation, bladder and bowel incontinence, severe vertigo, and a final physical collapse resembling shock. He added, with a reflective smile, that there seemed to be no direct correlation between the severity of his symptoms and the importance or unimportance of the examination. The only requisite was that the oral examination must be definitely recognized as being an examination. A recitation offered no difficulty. He explained further that, even in taking examinations for an automobile driver's license, he was forced to the measure of taking a pen and a pad of paper with him. When asked a question, he would simply write the answer on the paper pad and then "read it aloud." This behavior had occasioned some lifted eyebrows but it was a measure by which he "could avoid the oral examination situation." Even such questions as his age and the number of years he had been driving an automobile had first to be written and then "read" to the examining clerk.

The patient was then told that he would not be given any therapeutic or otherwise helpful hypnotic suggestions until he had been hypnotized a sufficient number of times to give him an adequate experiential background for therapy. To accomplish this, he might be used as an experimental subject in a current project. To this he readily agreed.

He proved to be an excellent somnambulistic subject but several hours were spent merely eliciting the various hypnotic phenomena repeatedly. He was then used as an experimental subject in special work in which the author was interested with intentional additions for him requiring wide use of deep trance phenomena. The reason for such use of him in this experimental work was to secure some measure of his competence for prolonged hypnotic work of any type.

In the meantime the problem of how to help him was being given consideration.

His initial account and all subsequent inquires indicated that his problem was of a limited, circumscribed character. After much thought it was reasoned that therapy would need to be similarly circumscribed. That the patient would have to take additional oral examinations other than the one impending was considered to be most unlikely. Hence, there would be no need to devise a therapeutic design to meet future contingencies.

Another consideration was that any measure that met the patient's needs would also have to include elements that were definitely not therapeutic but might even serve to enhance his own pattern of circumscribed neurotic structure by a utilization of it. This would be occasioned by the fact that a vital part of the situation to be met was of an unalterable character, namely, the man who hated him and who would be examining him. Any therapeutic or helpful plan would have to include this fact and have to be structured accordingly. Furthermore, there could be no clouding or falsification of this significant aspect of the situation to be met.

The patient, in the time spent with him, had shown himself to be of good strong character, readily able to face all ordinary challenges of life. His war record had been excellent in combat service. Apparently his Achilles heel was only the matter of oral examinations, compounded in this instance by an examiner's intense hatred.

That a simple direct or even indirect therapeutic approach be made was ruled out by several important factors. Foremost was the fact that he came for help in relationship to a specific impending examination, not for therapy. Also, there were his fixed and rigid "certainties" about his condition. These could not be immediately changed; help by the author as the patient understood matters was only to permit success in the examination. Other psychotherapists had assured him he did not need therapy. Also, the usual therapeutic methodologies would take too much time, much more time than was available for him. Then, too, ordinary psychotherapy by whatever school of thought could quite conceivably fail.

Therefore, some plan of procedure had to be devised whereby the patient's needs as he understood them had to be met. It could not include direct or even indirect suggestion since such suggestions would be in contradiction to the patient's fixed understandings. To attempt some direct procedure such as regression, direct, or indirect by dissociation, offered no promise of success. Nor could there be risked a failure of any sort with hypnosis, since failure would lessen greatly or actually destroy his remaining hope of achieving success.

Since the patient was so rigidly convinced that he had no means whatsoever of his own with which to meet his problem, it was finally decided to devise a "therapeutic" (as he would or might construe whatever the author did) procedure that would give to him various new ways and means of dealing successfully with the impending examination. That it would actually be therapeutic in the usual sense of the word was not of importance. What was important was that the patient would be given entirely new ways of reacting and responding of a sort that would preclude the development of his long-established pattern of behavior. Further thought suggested that the rigid limited circumscribed character of his problem be employed to structure the final procedure. To do so might enable him to enter the examination room with his medical knowledge readily available, this to be presented adequately as needed by wholly new and different methods of reacting and responding. All of this would be so structured that it could be achieved within a highly restricted circumscribed frame of reference.

Having reached these conclusions, a systematic plan of therapeutic work was devised. Previous hypnotic work which served primarily to enable the patient to develop a trance satisfactorily was repeated in large part and fitted into the following plan described in detail.

THE THERAPEUTIC PROCEDURE

A deep somnambulistic hypnotic trance was induced on repeated occasions in the patient and each time he was asked to experience fully in a fashion entirely unrelated to his problem all of the various phenomena of the deep trance. Some of this work fitted into a current experimental project, but the patient had no knowledge of what the experimental work was. Most of the work done with him was merely to insure adequate experiential learning by the patient. Thus, he learned to develop positive and negative visual and auditory hallucinations, superficial and deep anesthesia, regression, revivification, dissociation, selective amnesia, partial or total amnesia, hypermnesia, posthypnotic suggestion, depersonalization, automatism, and time distortion. The patient was given to understand that many of these learnings would be of no service to him and he was allowed to think that the author was meeting the needs of personal experimental work. In no way was he allowed to realize that this additional work might serve a definite purpose for him, namely, that of preventing him from attaching any of his anxiety and fears to any of those learnings or from distorting those learnings in any way by an over-eagerness to benefit from them. Also, the knowledge that the author was already engaged in an hypnotic experiment of which he knew nothing furthered this needed distraction of the patient from the author's work with him. It may be added that if the author had not already been engaged in some ex-

perimental work, he would have immediately devised some
that would have required the recording of data, this fact of
recording being unobtrusively disclosed to the patient without
revealing the data. This measure is often most effective in circumventing the hindrance caused by too intense an interest
by the patient in his own therapy.

When the author was fully satisfied that the patient was adequately trained, the plan of therapy that had been devised
was put into action. This plan was based upon (1) the ability
to hallucinate visually, (2) the ability to dissociate from the
self and to dissociate the self from objects, (3) the ability to
maintain a coherent train of thought while verbally expressing another or while attending auditorially to the utterances
of another person, (4) the ability to execute posthypnotic
suggestions, (5) the ability to develop amnesia, (6) the ability to behave like an automaton, (7) the ability to distort and
to transform realities, and (8) the ability to present an appearance of alert, attentive consciousness, however deep a
trance state might develop. Since all instructions given to the
patient were permissive in character, the patient was entirely
at liberty to utilize these various learnings as best befitted him
in the impending situation.

THE RESULTS

In essence, the patient utilized all of the instructions given
to him, not always in the order or manner intended by the
author but rather in accord with his own understandings of
what he was to do. What actually happened is best related in
the patient's own words.

"As soon as I got back home, I realized I had to see you
again. So I called for an appointment. I had a feeling it was
urgent and that you also wanted to see me right away. I literally didn't remember anything until my wife met me at the
airport. I read the good news on her face and then I remembered that I had telephoned the good news to both of you. I
was in a complete mental daze while going there. I knew I
was completely clear-headed and at ease during the examination. I knew I didn't miss a single question. I remembered
that they told me my diploma would arrive in about three
weeks. Then I telephoned you and my wife. But I forgot all
this. Then I must have come home in a daze. I don't remember even checking out of my hotel or catching my plane. I

knew where I was. I was just without any memories of what had occurred while I was away from home when my wife met me at the airport. When she said how glad she was I had passed, I could remember notifying her and you. That's all, though. So I told her that I had to go the the office right away on something urgent and as soon as I got there, I telephoned you and called a cab. Will you put me in a trance and help me to remember?"

The author replied, "The important thing is that you passed your examination. It really is not necessary to induce a trance for a systematic orderly account of what happened. *You can remember now while completely alert and wakeful.*"

In an astonished tone of voice, the patient began, "That's right. I was in a daze all the way there, I acted like a robot. I said and did all the right things. I got there, perfectly comfortable. I had my notice with me telling me where and at what hour to report. I was there about 20 minutes early. Sat like a robot. Walked in the examination room when the girl called me. My 'friend' showed all his teeth in his smile. They needed cleaning. He said, 'Glad to see you, Jack. Sorry we can't make any special arrangements for you.' But all the time he was speaking, I was looking at his face. It looked as young as when we were in high school. Then I saw it getting older and older, changing like the face of Dorian Grey in the movie. But I just said, 'It's all O.K. with me. I'm ready to go anytime.' Then he said, 'Just take a seat in that chair there.' I looked at it and wondered what a nice chair like that was doing there, but I sat down facing the three of them.

"Then he fired the first question. I heard every word of it, but I kept watching the way his mouth moved. It looked so interesting in such a peculiar way. Then when I told him the answer I knew he wanted but didn't think I knew, you should have seen the look on his face. I knew that he knew my answer was right. But he looked as if he just couldn't believe something about me. I couldn't figure out what it was. Then he asked me a great long question. I tipped my head a bit to hear him better and looked past him and he disappeared. Just his voice was there. Heard every word but as I heard the words, pages from text books appeared before my eyes. I could see the page numbers and certain paragraphs were in large print. I looked at them carefully while I listened to the words, and when the words stopped I just summarized what was in those paragraphs. I thought I gave a pretty good summary, but just then my 'friend' came back looking mad. Before I could figure out why, he picked up a sheet of paper and began reading a page-long typewritten question. As he began reading to me, a large sheet of white paper appeared before me and every word he read showed up in big black print and I kept reading right along with him about a word or two behind him. When he finished, I just looked that sheet of paper over carefully a few seconds and explained that there were three different possible interpretations. So I told him what they were. You should have seen the agony on his face. That man was in pain." Here the patient interrupted himself to say, "Now I know what really happened. I was in some kind of hypnotic state and you must have taught me how to use it in the examination situation. It's obvious that I was hallucinating and that I was behaving automatically some of the time. There's probably some things I did that I don't know the technical terms for."

He was assured that his interpretation was entirely correct, but that the author wanted him to continue with his account.

The patient resumed, "Well, then the next man introduced himself and I realized that my 'friend' hadn't done the proper thing. This man looked like an awful nice fellow and he spoke as if he really needed some help on a problem that was troubling him, so I told him what he needed to know."

Here the patient interrupted himself again, "That's exactly what happened with each of the other two examiners. They each looked like a person you would like to know and when either of them asked me a question, they looked like they needed help, and so I listened carefully and then I told them what they needed to know. Oh yes, at the end of an hour and a half they nodded to each other and then to my 'friend.' He looked madder than ever. Then those two stood up and both shook hands with me and congratulated me. Then my 'friend' stepped over and shook my hand and congratulated me and I wondered why, and why he didn't get a rug for his baldness and have the hair on his ears clipped. That was it."

To this the author replied, "Not entirely, tell me a bit more about what you did in relation to your so-called friend."

"In complete detail? I remember everything and can do it, or will a summary be sufficient?"

He was told that a summary would be satisfactory.

"Well, there was that question where I could see myself standing behind him looking over his shoulder and reading what he was reading and then reading the answer. Then once he seemed to be trying to sing a silly song so I recited some medical prose. Then he seemed to be beating time while I was talking to him and I would purposely rephrase what I was saying to get him off beat.

"Oh, yes! There are two especially interesting things, one that puzzled me and both that I enjoyed. Well, several that I enjoyed. The puzzler was where 'friend Henry' looked to be about a block away so I could barely see him. Couldn't recognize him, but I could hear his voice right in front of me. I tried to figure out whether he had moved away from me or if I had moved away from him, but how could his voice be right in front of me? So I replied to him and never did figure that one out till now. But the best ones were when Henry asked about some specific condition or some syndrome and I actually felt myself in white uniform on the ward examining a patient. Each time the patient was Henry and he was in terrible condition—looked awful—and I explained the condition very carefully so that the interns with me could understand fully. I was just one of the fellows taking postgraduate work making rounds with the interns and really enjoying myself.

"In fact, not once did I know what I was there in that examination room for. I just was interested in how I saw things, and I did and said all the right things. Did you teach me how to do all those things in those hypnotic sessions I had with you? And did you make me have amnesia so I just wouldn't worry and fret and get into a horrible stew?"

He was told that such was the case and that he had been taught various other things, all for the purpose of permitting an adequate examination performance with no neurotic distress. He was also told that he was at liberty to ask more questions of the author and also free to remember or to forget his examination experience. However, it was stressed that he retain any measure of learning that might be useful to him and that he could feel comfortably certain that he need never use his hypnotic learnings except appropriately and in times of special need.

The patient has been seen repeatedly many times since then in a casual way. He has referred patients to the author, and he would, if asked, do hypnotic work with the author. He is not interested in employing hypnosis himself, but he has stated that his approach to patients and their problems has been changed for the better. This he explained as, "Perhaps I am unconsciously using hypnotic techniques."

DISCUSSION

It is at once apparent that an unrecognizable (to him) circumvention of the examination situation had been effected. There had been also a bizarre distortion of it, fully as bizarre as his own neurotic behavior that disabled him. This distortion of the examination situation had been amusing, puzzling, even bewildering, but in no way distressful, nor did it interfere with the examination procedure. Posthypnotic suggestion had served to enable him to present an appearance of ordinary wakefulness, alertness and responsiveness. Well-learned forms of the various types of hypnotic behavior were posthypnotically employed by him in his own private personal manner of meeting the requirements of the examination.

Such an elaborate procedure, paradoxically, was not evolved for the patient's sake. A general explanation can be found in the question, "Why do neurotic and psychotic patients so frequently develop such elaborate psychological structures to give expression to their illness?" Undoubtedly because the expression they do give is so inadequate. As for the patient, why did he have such elaborate and so many and such intense symptoms? Nausea and vomiting alone were sufficient. Certainly bladder and bowel incontinence were more than adequate to prevent an oral examination. Then why were there all the other symptoms? Did they serve some other purposes or relate to unrecognized significances? As in the case with other patients, the author simply does not know. Nor does he know of anybody who has ever really understood the variety and purposes of any one patient's multiple symptoms despite the tendency of many psychiatrists to hypothecate, to their own satisfaction, towering structures of explanation often as elaborate and bizarre as the patient's symptomatology.

As for the therapy evolved for this patient, it was he who developed it, not the author. The patient was taught simply how to experience various hypnotic phenomena. Thus he learned how to develop a negative hallucination for the author, for a part of the author such as his hand, his head, or his torso. He was taught to alter visual stimuli by experiencing them as coming from near at hand or from a remote distance. He was taught to hallucinate printed pages and printed words and various other objects, as well as movements by the author or by objects in the office. He learned to change and to distort visual stimuli. He could see the author smiling and experience it as frowning and vice versa. He learned to see tears streaming down the face in a picture on the author's desk, he saw that face burst into a smile, and then he saw that face in the picture talking and he hallucinated the apparently spoken words. He saw a black and white picture in bright colors. He experienced visually a small oblong ashtray as square, as a circle, as tall, as flat, as transparent, as opaque, as of many different colors, as twisted into various shapes, as floating in midair, moving back and forth or up and down rapidly, slowly, in various rhythms. In each of these teachings, care was taken to make sure he understood the nature or kind of experience he was to learn; but, unless absolutely necessary, never the degree or extent of the suggested experience. Thus it was he who decided that a negative hallucination for a part of the author's body should be of the hand, the foot, the head, or the torso. The shapes in the twisting of the ashtray were determined entirely by him and no effort was made to inquire what those shapes were. The words hallucinated as spoken by the face in the picture remained unknown to the author. The *kind* of task was the author's responsibility in this hypnotic teaching of the subject. The *content* was the patient's. *All of the teachings that he had been given or that would be given to him by the author,* he was told, *he was to use profitably and well in any needful situation.*

In relation to the auditory field one precaution was emphasized, namely, that he would hear clearly and easily every verbal stimulus and that he would listen most understandingly to all utterances. If he wished, he might have the speaker standing up, sitting down or leaning on a chair, but always he was to hear clearly and understand thoroughly.

Each of the various hypnotic phenomena was developed in this same detailed fashion until the author was convinced of the patient's competence. Great care was taken to insure his appearance as a person alert, attentive, interested, understanding, responsive and fully wide awake regardless of what hypnotic phenomena he was experiencing.

Posthypnotic suggestion and amnesia, while taught with the same meticulous care, were used directly by the author to insure certain things. These were that the patient make the trip to the city where the examination was held with a generalized amnesia, but with a responsive alertness to meet every expected or unexpected development concerning the trip itself. Thus he made the trip and appeared in proper time for the examination but with an amnesia for and a total unconcern about the purpose of the trip. In his own words, "I just went comfortably. I read a novel that I had long wanted to read and I took it with me." His telephone calls to the author and to his wife were both the outcome of posthypnotic suggestion. He was told that he might forget telephoning his wife, but that he could "read" that fact upon seeing her and that this might make him realize the importance of seeing the author promptly who knew the hour of his return flight. The amnesia on the way there was to prevent any building up of tension, and on the way back it served to let him rest without sensing unduly his fatigue or building up an elated tension over his probable success.

The final interview with the author was to give the patient a full recollection of all that occurred, all or any part of which he was at liberty to remember or to forget. He has, since then, forgotten much that occurred but of noteworthy significance is the fact that he can speak of his past oral examination experiences casually and that he took his next examination for a renewal of his driver's license quite unconcernedly. As for his "friend Henry," the patient now speaks of him as a rather absurdly emotional man.

BACKGROUND OF EXPERIMENTATION

Since 1935, the author has many times induced hypnotic trances in normal college students to discover if they could take an examination successfully in a college course while in a posthypnotic trance state. The results were always equal to or better than might have been expected in relation to their class grades. Unless special understandings had been given to the students, they always developed persistent spontaneous amnesia for having taken the examination, which had to be removed by the author. In some instances, this amnesia was allowed to persist for as long a period as a year.

These experiences led the author to induce in professional persons the development of posthypnotic trance states during which they might give to students or colleagues (even psychiatrists) a prepared or impromptu lecture, present patients at a staff conference, discharge a day's duties on the ward, or spend a social evening or day with friends without the trance state being detected. They always succeeded, and similarly developed spontaneous amnesia which had to be removed by the author.

A third-year resident in psychiatry, who was an experimental subject of the author's but who was unaware of this special work, asked to be taught auto-hypnosis. Without inducing a hypnotic trance, the author casually and conversationally outlined various methods of auto-hypnosis, intending to give more adequate instruction later. About a month afterwards, before any further instruction had been given, the author received a telephone call from the resident who declared, "I must see you. It's four o'clock in the afternoon, and there's something I do not understand. May I come to your office?"

Upon arriving at the office, the resident stated very simply, "This morning I dressed to go to town (Detroit) for some shopping with a friend. I looked at the clock on the dresser and it was a few minutes of eight. I saw that I had just time to meet Dr. ———, have breakfast, and then catch the bus to town. I took a second look at the clock and it read four o'clock. Then I noticed that the sun was shining through the west window, and then I turned and looked at the rest of the room. There was my bed all made up, with a lot of packages on it. I looked at some of the wrappings. They were from stores in Detroit. I opened a couple of them. They were things I had promised myself to buy months ago, but had completely forgotten about. That's when I knew I ought to see you, and here I am. Put me in a trance and see if my unconscious knows anything at all about this, because I don't."

The author gave a cue used in experiments with this subject and a somnambulistic trance ensued. The subject, with open eyes, smiled and waited expectantly. The author then asked, "Do you know what happened?" The reply was, "I do now, but I don't when I'm awake." The author asked, "What do you want me to do?" "Ask me about everything, then wake me up and tell me." The author answered, "Would it be all right if I just awakened you and then let you remember everything sequentially?" "I think that would be better, so wake me up so I can start."

The subject aroused from the trance state, appeared astonished and said, "I'm sure you must know everything, but I'm just beginning to remember. Today I was off duty, and I had arranged to go to Detroit by bus with Dr. ———, who was also off duty, after we had breakfast together. But just after I looked at the clock I went into an auto-hypnotic trance. I had been thinking about auto-hypnosis since the day you discussed it with me. I had been impressed by your statements that, in developing auto-hypnosis, you cannot tell your unconscious mind all the things it should do and how it should do them, because that would be making it a conscious task. And it's also a useless task because your unconscious mind already knows what you know a lot better than you do. So I knew that I would have to go into auto-hypnosis unexpectedly. Now I have just remembered that this morning my unconscious mind simply took over, and there I was in an auto-hypnotic trance. Now I'll tell you what happened, because I am remembering things one by one just as they happened."

Then there followed a long, sequential detailed narrative of the day's events, with interspersed comments. The account included conversations with Dr. ——— (also a psychiatrist), and with other friends, an accidental meeting with two former high-school classmates who had not been seen for more than eight years, eating lunch with Dr. ——— and the two friends at a favorite restaurant, shopping in various stores, purchasing four items long wished for but always previously forgotten, returning on the bus with Dr. ———, putting the packages on the bed, and then turning to look at the clock as a self-determined cue for awaking.

This account was then related by both the resident and the author to various members of the hospital psychiatric staff. A few of them indignantly declared, with all the weight of their lack of knowledge, that a person in a hypnotic trance would necessarily act "like a zombi." This was disputed with equal indignation by Dr. ———.

A few weeks later, at a Staff Conference, the same resident presented several patients, discussed the clinical records, and answered questions adequately, even those asked by some unexpected visitors at the Staff Conference. The fact that the resident was in an auto-hypnotic trance throughout the Conference was recognized only by the author, although it was strongly suspected by another staff member (not Dr. ———). He later demanded confirmation of his suspicions from the author. This being given, he emphatically discredited to his colleagues the "zombi" misunderstandings which had been previously expressed. To substantiate his statements, he called upon the resident, who was found to have a total and seemingly unbreakable amnesia for that particular Staff Conference, even when confronted by the typewritten record.

Joseph Wolpe

Joseph Wolpe is a South African psychiatrist now living in America who originated "systematic desensitization," one of the first techniques in the behavior therapist's repertory. Wolpe originally studied the behavior of cats who had been shocked in a particular cage; the cats gradually lost their fear of the cage by being brought closer to it in small steps, with feedings at each step. He reasoned that in parallel fashion, a person can more easily overcome anxiety if he or she approaches a feared situation gradually. In systematic desensitization, the therapist teaches a state of deep relaxation to produce the physiological state that is incompatible with fear. Rather than using the actual feared object or situation, systematic desensitization is typically practiced with imagined scenes, in the expectation that losing anxiety over an imagined situation will transfer to real life. The therapist prepares a graded list, or hierarchy, of anxiety-provoking scenes. Finally the learned relaxation is paired with each step of the graded hierarchy in a series of sessions, until finally the feared situation can be approached without anxiety.

Systematic desensitization is tailored for use with phobias. But behavior therapists have developed many other techniques designed for use with the full range of psychological disorders.

Briefly, behavior therapy is the systematic application of principles of learning to the analysis and treatment of behavior disorders. Although reports of such applications began to appear sporadically in the 1920s, there was little effect upon the mainstream of psychotherapy until the last twenty-five years.

The approach to a clinical problem by a behavioral therapist involves describing, as objectively and quantitatively as possible, the maladaptive responses involved—a process called behavioral analysis. The behavioral analysis must not only define the patient's problematic responses, but also identify the factors in the environment that occasion the responses, and the consequences of the responses as well. From this analysis, a fitting treatment strategy is chosen.

In the following article Wolpe describes how behavior therapy can be used in treating neuroses. He acknowledges the objection that nonbehaviorists make, that behavior therapy can lead to changes in a symptom but don't change the underlying problem; Wolpe's reply is that there is no proof that supports this charge. Wolpe describes three cases where behavior-therapy techniques were used with neurotic problems. In each, the same approach was taken: translate the patient's behavior into stimulus-response relationships, and modify them accordingly.

BEHAVIOUR THERAPY IN COMPLEX NEUROTIC STATES

by Joseph Wolpe

In recent years it has become widely known that behaviour therapy (conditioning therapy) is effective in the treatment of neuroses. However, in many minds, this knowledge has come to be hedged by some erroneous qualifications, of which the commonest are: (*a*) that behaviour therapy leaves the "deep" cause of neurosis untouched, and (*b*) that it is successful with "monosymptomatic" and allegedly simple cases like phobias, but not with more complex neuroses, such as obsessions and "character neuroses".

Obviously, behaviour therapy, or, for that matter, any form of therapy, can influence the alleged "deep" neurotic process only if there really is such a process, as the psychoanalysts claim. But, as pointed out elsewhere (Wolpe, 1963a) because the psychoanalysts have misapprehended the requirements of scientific evidence they have adduced no acceptable support for their theory, beguiling themselves with surmises, analogies and extrapolations. Until now, whenever direct tests have been made of major tenets of the theory (e.g. the Oedipus theory [Valentine, 1946] or of major implications of it (e.g. the likelihood of relapse in unpsychoanalysed recovery [Wolpe, 1961a]), the facts have been contrary to psychoanalytic expectations. It would be futile to consider whether behaviour therapy has effects on processes whose causal relationship to neurosis we have no reason to credit and whose very existence may be doubted.

The belief that the efficacy of behaviour therapy is limited to phobias can scarcely be maintained by anybody who has followed the relevant literature (e.g. Wolpe, 1958; Eysenck, 1960; Bond and Hutchison, 1960). But it is a belief that has been encouraged by several factors. First, in the case material which behaviour therapists have used to illustrate their techniques phobias are prominent, precisely because they are well-defined. Second, a good deal of press publicity was given a few years ago to the successful treatment of a cat phobia (Freeman and Kendrick, 1960). Third, and perhaps most important, the behaviouristic analysis of a case frequently results in its acquiring a phobia-like appearance. The distinctive feature of a classical phobia is the presence of ostensible stimulus antecedents of anxiety. *A behaviouristic analysis aims at establishing the stimulus antecedents of all reactions in every variety of neurosis.* When subsequently the case is reported and the non-behaviouristic reader finds himself presented with cut-and-dried relationships between stimuli and anxiety-responses, he may be constrained to comment, "*My* cases are not as clear-cut as that!" The behaviour therapist might justly retort, "If *this* had been your case it would not have seemed clear-cut either, for your training does not lead you to analyse stimulus-response relationships."

The basic premise of behaviour therapy of neurosis is that neuroses are persistent unadaptive learned habits of reaction that have been acquired under conditions of emotional disturbance (anxiety) (Wolpe, 1958). Almost universally anxiety is prominent among the reactions learned; and since this learning is at a primitive (hypothalamic) level it can be reversed only through applying the learning process so as to involve this primitive level. That is why neuroses cannot be overcome by appealing solely to reason.

It was in the context of experimental neuroses that it first became clear that neuroses are learned, and can be unlearned by counteracting anxiety by feeding (Wolpe, 1952, 1958). This finding suggested the *reciprocal inhibition principle* of therapy of the neuroses—that *if a response inhibitory of anx-*

iety can be made to occur in the presence of anxiety-evoking stimuli it will weaken the bond between these stimuli and the anxiety. In human neuroses, not only feeding but also a considerable number of other responses each of which, empirically, appears to inhibit anxiety, have been successfully used to weaken neurotic anxiety-response habits as well as other neurotic habits. Many of the techniques have been described in detail (Wolpe, 1958), and at least one more has since emerged (Lazarus and Abramovitz, 1962). The most widely used techniques employ assertive responses, relaxation responses (systematic desensitization), and sexual responses.

While the reciprocal inhibition mechanism is central in the elimination of neurotic autonomic response habits, the usual extinction mechanism can sometimes be effectively used to remove neurotic motor habits (e.g. Yates, 1958; Walton, 1961).

VARIETIES OF COMPLEXITY IN NEUROSIS

Starting from the clinical fact that neuroses generally present themselves as unadaptive, obstinate habits of behaviour (with anxiety most often to the forefront), a patient may be regarded as having a *simple* neurosis if he has only one such habit and if it consists of responses to a single and obvious family of stimuli. For example, he may be afraid only of heights, or only of dogs, or only of asserting himself.

There are several kinds of features that can give complexity to a neurosis and they are often found in combination:

1. Multiple families of hierarchies may be conditioned to neurotic reactions.

2. The reactions may involve unadaptiveness in important areas of social behavior ("character neuroses").

3. The neurosis may involve obsessional behaviour.

4. The neurosis may have somatic consequences.

5. There may be continuous anxiety in addition to that which is associated with specific stimuli.

6. Essential stimulus antecedents of the neurotic reactions may be obscured by conditioned inhibition of associations.

1. *Multiple Families of Stimuli Conditioned to Neurotic Reactions*

While neurotic reactions confined to single families of stimuli are undoubtedly widespread in the general population, many of them, consisting of fears such as of mice, harmless snakes, the sight of much blood, or the appearance of "madness", do not intrude into the individual's life sufficiently to motivate him to seek treatment, especially if the reactions are relatively mild. In people who come for treatment several families of stimuli-producing neurotic reactions are usually to be found. Of the 88 cases upon whom I reported in 1958, anxiety was aroused by direct interpersonal interchanges of various kinds in 57, and in 51 of these there were also other families of stimuli that evoked neurotic anxiety. Sometimes there are many such families. For example, one patient had fears of self-assertion, criticism from others, rejection, silences, social occasions, people in authority, his mother, dirt and disorder, being heard in a toilet or seen emerging from one. When neurotic reactions are producible by a great many situations the patient may be said to have a *disseminated neurosis*.

2. *Reactions Involving Unadaptiveness in Social Behaviour (Character Neuroses)*

The unadaptive social behaviour that is observed in some patients takes various forms—e.g. inability to get on with people, inefficiency at work, constant changing of jobs, kleptomania, sexual promiscuity, homosexuality, and exhibitionism. In the great majority of such cases the deviant behaviour is secondary to anxiety, whose sources need to be carefully ferreted out. If this is not done, therapeutic failure can almost be guaranteed. It is perhaps because psychoanalysts do not concern themselves with anxiety-arousing stimuli that they find such cases especially difficult to treat. An example is afforded by Case 2.

3. *Obsessional Neuroses*

In certain cases of neurosis, in addition to the usual autonomic discharges, there may be prominent ideational, motor or sensory responses. The term obsessional is applied to such responses when they are "complex and variable in detail, consisting of well-defined and often elaborate thought-sequences or relatively intricate acts . . ." (Wolpe, 1958, p. 89). As I have pointed out, some obsessional behaviour elevates the level of anxiety; other obsessional behaviour reduces it. In either case the deconditioning of neurotic anxiety is usually the crux of therapy. (Case 3 provides an interesting example.) It is sometimes found that obsessional behaviour continues even when there is no longer any apparent basis for it in terms of anxiety. Such autonomous habits have been effectively treated by aversive conditioning (Wolpe, 1958). (In some cases, e.g. transvestism [e.g. Glynn and Harper, 1961] or fetishism [Raymond, 1956], aversive conditioning has been the sole treatment used, with beneficial effects that appear to have been durable.)

4. *Neuroses with Somatic Consequences*

Somatic disorders are of course central in classical hysteria; but somatic effects also frequently accompany the much more common anxiety-dominated neuroses. These effects have, as is well known, been "explained" by the psychoanalysts as due to the operation of unconscious agencies that purposively select the malfunctioning of one organ system rather than another.

However, in every case a physiological explanation is possible. In different individuals different combinations of reactive elements make up an anxiety reaction; and even in the same individual variously constituted disturbed reactions may be conditioned. It is postulated that, because of peculiarities of physiological development, or because of special features either of earlier conditioning or of the conditioning of the neurosis itself, the anxiety reaction may be characterized by especially strong autonomic discharges in a particular organ system. It is because of this that in one patient emotional disturbance is accompanied by migraine, in another by asthma, in a third by dermatitis, in a fourth by the development of peptic ulceration. In yet other persons anxiety leads to interference with the speech mechanism (stammering). It has been found (Wolpe, 1958) that such concomitants of neurosis can be abolished by eliminating neurotic anxiety and without treating the somatic symptom itself or paying the least attention to the supposed "significance" that "dynamic" theories allege symptoms to have.

5. Reactions That Include Continuous Anxiety

There are some psychiatrists who say that while they can understand how anxiety reactions triggered by specific stimuli may be subject to deconditioning, they do not see how conditioning can be relevant to anxiety that is present all the time and in all situations. They seem to suggest that there is a variety of neurotic anxiety that has no stimulus antecedents.

If the word "stimulus" is employed according to Lundberg's (1937) excellent definition—"that to which response is made"—it is obvious that every response must have stimulus antecedents, for no response can be causeless. It is true that under certain conditions, e.g. beri-beri, there is continuous anxiety that does not depend on any *particular* neural inputs, because, apparently, thresholds in the autonomic nervous system are so greatly lowered that practically all stimulation has anxiety-like consequents. The remedy here is, of course, biochemical.

But if neuroses are due to learning, continuous anxiety that is actually neurotic must also be due to learning. Observations upon patients reveal three conditioned sources of continuous anxiety.

1. The patient may be continuously anxious in all situations except when a specific "security-object" is present. For example, there are cases of agoraphobia in which the patient is free from anxiety only when an intimate person is near him.

2. There may be a conditioned habit of dwelling upon contents of thought that would evoke anxiety in almost everybody. One finds, most often, continual imaginings of scenes of the patient's death or that of loved ones.

3. There may be true "free-floating anxiety", which I have suggested should be re-named *pervasive anxiety*. This anxiety is not attributable to any clear-cut stimulus configuration either in thought or in the outer world, but appears to be conditioned to various more or less pervasive aspects of stimulation in general. The most pervasive aspects of experience are the awareness of space, time, and one's own body (Kant, 1781). Any or all of these may be conditioned to anxiety. Less pervasive concomitants of experience, such as light, verticality, and light-and-shade contrasts may also be conditioned. A wide range of further possibilities for pervasive conditioning may be found in Taylor's important book on perception (1962). When closely questioned, many pa-

tients can clearly identify the pervasive stimulus-elements that are connected with their continuous anxiety.* The mechanisms of pervasive anxiety and the conditions under which it occurs are matters that urgently call for research.

A fourth kind of continuous anxiety is not due to conditioning but occurs with exposure to an ongoing conflict situation, such as an undesired marriage. Here we have *unconditioned* anxiety, that is automatically generated when the organism has simultaneous impulses to opposing actions (Fonberg, 1956).

6. Reactions in Which Crucial Stimulus Antecedents Are Obscure

Obscurity of central stimulus antecedents may be due to lack of skill or care on the part of the therapist or to concealment on the part of the patient. Such concealment might be deliberate, but occasionally the patient may simply be unaware of certain of his reactions. This may be due to conditioned inhibition of awareness of particular responses. For example, a recent case presented herself as an acute fear of scrutiny of 8 years' duration. Attempts at desensitization failed, because on the face of it no viable dimension of generalization could be found. When (after about 25 sessions) I was about to abandon the case, a clue emerged of unacknowledged rebellion at her domination by her husband. The complete exposure of this set of attitudes within her led to the possibility of expressing these attitudes and to therapeutic change.

This kind of phenomenon, of course, gave rise to the repression theory of neurosis, but it is an infrequent incident without causal significance (Wolpe, 1958, 1961a).

ILLUSTRATIVE CASES

Case 1

Mrs. Y., aged 56, had suffered much anxiety since early childhood. She had been very timid and inadequate in interpersonal situations, but had improved considerably in these

---

*In most cases the level of pervasive anxiety can be sharply reduced by 1–4 full capacity inhalations of a mixture of 65 per cent carbon dioxide and 35 per cent oxygen and remains at the lower level until the patient is again exposed to *specific* anxiety-evoking stimuli (see Wolpe, 1958).

during the past ten years. Her general level of anxiety had
fluctuated a good deal over the years, being at its worst in association with periods of special stress, when it tended to be
displaced by a particularly unpleasant sort of depression. Numerous "phobic" constellations were also present.

There was a good deal in her history to account for her
disturbed reactions. She was the only child of a father who
was rarely at home, and a harsh, brutal mother who beat her
frequently and often confined her alone in an upstairs room.
Later experiences compounded the anxious conditioning that
these unhappy circumstances began.

She had had a good deal of therapy intermittently. Between 1950 and 1956, she had had a sustained course of
psychoanalysis, averaging about three times a week to an
estimated total of about 1,000 sessions. She did not feel that
the psychoanalytic procedures had produced any beneficial
change, but the analyst, who was a down-to-earth person, had
instigated a good deal of assertive behaviour, which was instrumental in overcoming to a considerable extent the interpersonal inadequacies. However, her general level of anxiety
remained very high, with no improvement at all in the phobias
and phobia-like sources of disturbance.

When Mrs. Y. was first seen in May, 1960, she was extremely anxious all day, but gradually improved towards evening, though the measure of this improvement was affected
by exposure to a variety of possible situations to which anxiety
had been conditioned. Especially important among these situations were rejection and aloneness, which had recently become an increasing problem because her children, growing
up, were often away from home.

A great deal of effort was expended upon determining the
stimulus antecedents of the patient's reactions. Some of these
were quite obvious, but others required a considerable
amount of probing.

Treatment consisted partly of extending the assertive training begun during the psychoanalysis, to remove such anxieties
as persisted in interpersonal situations. Much the greater part
of the sessions was spent on the systematic desensitization of
a large number of anxiety hierarchies. The more important of
these were: (1) aloneness; (2) rejection; (3) heights; (4)
aeroplanes; (5) her mother; (6) waking times; (7) her own
early morning depression; (8) prospects of journeys; (9)
being lied to; (10) saying goodbye to dear ones; (11) urinating while people waited outside.

In some of these hierarchies sensitivity was extreme so that the amount of work required was very great indeed. For example, in the case of fear of aloneness, Mrs. Y. was initially so sensitive that if she were at home accompanied only by her daughter, anxiety would be evoked if the daughter closed herself up in a room for five minutes in order to make a phone call. Desensitization began with the use of this particular situation, and separation in time and distance was then progressively increased until the patient was able without anxiety, to imagine being quite alone at home for periods of ten days, separated from the nearest person of consequence to her by 300 miles. She could then also endure without anxiety this situation in reality. Her neurotic fear of aeroplanes was also initially very great, so that even the sound of a plane overhead, or the sight of a stationary one in a distant airfield produced very substantial anxiety. For purposes of desensitization it was found necessary to commence with getting her to imagine that she was looking at a toy plane with a six-inch wing span. At subsequent presentations the size of the plane was gradually increased, and a succession of increasingly large model planes were presented standing on a large lawn, and then real planes which she was gradually made to "board", at first silent and, later, with engines running. Eventually an air liner at an exhibition was made a stepping stone to the boarding of commercial air-liners which first made short hops and then ever longer flights. This patient has recently been able to fly wherever she needs to in the United States with equanimity and indeed with pleasure.

Similar systematic deconditioning led to the elimination of all the other reactions. It is not unlikely that if the case and its treatment had first come to the attention of the same analyst after the conditioning therapy, he would have judged it to be different from *his* usual run of cases!

Case 2

Mrs. Z. was a 36-year-old divorced social worker with a lifelong history of emotional disturbance that had become much worse when she had developed tuberculosis at the age of 23 and her husband, who could not bear illness, had kept away from her. She had subsequently manifested general fecklessness, shiftlessness at work, and considerable sexual promiscuity. In the course of the years she was thrice divorced and attempted suicide very many times. For 9 years she had undergone psychoanalysis with only brief interruptions but without any benefit. She had felt better only when she was running a particularly exciting love affair. Each of her five analysts had regarded her as having a severe character neurosis and had spent countless hours endeavouring to get at its "unconscious roots".

When I first saw Mrs. Z. she was engrossed in a fairly recent love affair with a man she wanted to marry but who was much less enthusiastic about her. She usually entered my consulting room tearful and distrait, and during our first few weeks made several further attempts at suicide.

A behaviouristic analysis of the case revealed interpersonal fear of disapproval that inhibited almost any kind of assertiveness and thus made her largely incapable of withstanding the demands of others or of making known her own. The therapist strongly urged her to express her legitimate demands; and soon grasping the reasonableness of this she made efforts to comply. An early success occurred when her supervisor criticized her on the ground that she was allowing a client's problems to activate her own emotions. Mrs. Z. disagreed.

Mrs. Z.: "That is not so. You have no justification for that statement and it's unfair of you to say it."

Supervisor: "That's your reaction because you have unconscious expectations of unfairness and interpret remarks accordingly."

Mrs. Z.: "Why not? You *are* often unfair."

She proceeded to give instances of his unfairness and had the best of the interchange. There was great satisfaction in this, for in the past this kind of criticism from him "would have left me helpless, and I would have curled up and cried".

Within the general framework of her fear of disapproval were two areas of acute sensitivity that lent themselves to systematic desensitization—fears of rejection and ridicule. Hierarchies were constructed on each of these two themes. (Examples of low intensity items from the rejection hierarchy were: (1) an acquaintance not reciprocating her invitations; (2) a teacher does not see the merit of her viewpoint; and high level examples were: (1) a respected friend behaves condescendingly; (2) her foster mother is angry with her.)

Mrs. Z.'s treatment was a combination of sustained encouragement of self-expression and desensitization of the hierarchies. After 31 sessions she felt well and "really calm", more so than she could ever remember. She was mastering situations with people and was no longer upset by the neurotic range of "disapprovals". She worked well and handled her lover with new confidence and was shortly able to give him up. At a 9-month follow-up she had married somebody else and her gains had been maintained, both emotionally and socially.

Case 3

Mr. T. was an 18-year-old youth with a very severe washing compulsion. The basis of this was a fear of contamination by urine, and most especially his own urine, mainly because he dreaded to contaminate others with it. When the treatment to be described began, the patient was almost completely impotentiated by his neurosis. After urinating, he would spend up to 45 minutes in an elaborate ritual of cleaning up his genitalia, followed by about two hours of hand-washing. When he woke in the morning, his first need was to shower, which took him about four hours to do. To these "basic requirements" of his neurosis were added many others occasioned by the incidental contaminations inevitable on any day. It is scarcely surprising that Mr. T. had come to conclude that getting up was not worth the effort, and for two months had spent most of his time in bed.

The neurosis evidently originated in an unusual situation at home. Until the age of 15 Mr. T. had been made to share a bed with his sister, two years older, because she had a fear of being alone. Having sexual responses to his sister had made him feel very guilty and ashamed. He had become angry with his parents for imposing this on him and had hostile and at times destructive phantasies about them. He had been horrified at these, and had begun to regard himself as a despicable individual.

Treatment in the first place consisted of the usual form of desensitization, employing imaginary scenes against a background of relaxation. Since he was also disturbed at the idea of anybody else's independent contamination with urine, the first scene he was asked to imagine was the sight of an unknown person dipping his hand into a forty-cubic-foot trough of water into which one drop of urine had been deposited. Even this scene produced some disturbance in Mr. T. at first, but this waned and disappeared in the course of a few presentations. The concentration of urine was then "in-

creased" until the man was imagined to be inserting his hand
into pure urine. At each stage a particular scene was repeated until it no longer evoked any anxiety.

In the next series of imaginary situations Mr. T. himself
was inserting his hand into increasingly concentrated solutions of urine.

During the course of these procedures, which occupied
about five months of sessions taking place about five times a
week and lasting, as a rule, about twenty minutes, there was
considerable improvement in Mr. T.'s clinical condition. For
example, his hand-washing time went down to about 30
minutes, his shower time to just over an hour, and he no
longer found it necessary to interpose the *New York Times*
between himself and his chair during interviews. However, at
about this time it also became evident that there was an increasing lack of transfer between what he could imagine himself doing and what he actually could do. Whereas he could
imagine himself immersing his hand in pure urine, to do so in
actuality was out of the question.

It was therefore decided to try desensitization *in vivo*. This
means that relaxation was opposed to increasingly strong *real*
stimuli evoking anxiety. Accordingly, he was, to begin with,
exposed to the word "urine" printed in big block letters. This
evoked a little anxiety which he was asked to relax away.
The next step was to put him at one end of a long room and
a closed bottle of urine at the other end. Again, he had to
relax away the anxiety; and then step by step the bottle of
urine was moved closer until eventually he was handling it
with only minimal anxiety which again he was able to relax
away. When the bottle of urine was no longer capable of
evoking anxiety, the next series of manœuvres was started.
First of all, a very dilute solution of urine (1 drop to a gallon) was smeared on the back of his hand and he was made
to relax until all anxiety disappeared; and then, from session
to session the concentration was gradually increased. When
he was able to endure pure urine his own urine began to be
used; and finally, he was made to "contaminate" all kinds of
objects with his uriniferous hands—magazines, doorknobs,
and people's hands.

The numerous acts of desensitization outlined were completed at the end of June, 1961. By then Mr. T. had achieved
greatly increased freedom of movement; he was dressing
daily, his hand-washing time had gone down to 7 minutes

and his shower time to 40 minutes, and his cleaning-up ritual was almost eliminated. In September, 1961, he went back to school and was seen only occasionally until March, 1962. During this time, without active treatment, he made virtually no further progress. In March, 1962, he began weekly sessions and improvement was resumed. When last seen in June, 1962, his hand-washing time was 3 minutes and his shower time 20 minutes. He said that he was coming to think of urine as "sticky and smelly and nothing else". During the later stages measures were also applied to overcome sexual and social anxieties.

RESULTS OF BEHAVIOUR THERAPY IN COMPLEX NEUROSES

In respect of the whole range of neurotic cases presenting for treatment, I have reported (1958) that 89 per cent of 210 patients in 3 series treated by behaviour therapy were either apparently recovered or at least four-fifths improved on Knight's (1941) criteria (symptomatic improvement, increased stress tolerance, and improved function at work, sex and socially). In the last series, comprising 88 patients, the median number of interviews was 23 and the mean 45.6. *All* neurotic patients were accepted for treatment but no psychotics. (More recently Hussain [1963] has claimed 95 per cent of favourable results on Knight's criteria in 105 patients; and Lazarus [1963] states that of 408 neurotic patients who consulted him, including even those who came only once or twice, 321 [78 per cent] "derived marked benefit on very stringent criteria".)

In reviewing the 88 cases I have found that 65 were *complex* in one or more of the senses defined in this paper, 21 were non-complex, and 2 turned out to be schizophrenic. Fifty-eight of the 65 (89 per cent) were judged either apparently cured or much improved. This percentage is the same as that obtained for the whole group. However, the median number of sessions for the complex group is 29 and the mean 54.8, in contrast to a median for the non-complex remainder of 11.5 and a mean of 14.9 (see Table I).

Thus, complex cases respond to behaviour therapy as often as simple ones do, but therapy takes longer, presumably because there is more to be done. The principles are the same.

TABLE I

Comparison of Numbers of Sessions in Complex and Single Neuroses. The Total is only 86 because 2 Cases that turned out to be Schizophrenic are Excluded

	Number	Median Number of Sessions	Mean Number of Sessions
Complex neuroses	65	29	54.8
Simple neuroses	21	11.5	14.9
Whole group ..	86	23	45.4

There is a constant need to find new methods that utilize these principles as well as to improve our skills in the methods we have.

Meanwhile it must be stressed that the unravelling of the stimulus-response relations of neurotic reactions is usually no simple matter and quite often very difficult. In general, a high level of knowledge and skill is required for the adequate practice of behaviour therapy. A presumption has arisen that "anyone can do it", and assessments of it have been made (e.g. Cooper, 1963) on the results obtained by untrained and inexperienced therapists—a practice that obscures the realities (Wolpe, 1963b).

SUMMARY

This paper seeks to examine the allegation that behaviour therapy is of value only for "simple" neuroses. One of the major experimental bases of behaviour therapy is described and its main techniques are outlined. Six types of features that give complexity to a neurosis are defined.

A previously published series of 88 cases treated by behaviour therapy is re-examined to see what differences of outcome there were between "simple" cases and those that were complex in one or more of the ways defined. The recovery rate (apparently cured, or much improved) was the same in both groups, but the median number of sessions used for the complex group was two and a half times that for the noncomplex group, and the mean was almost quadruple.

REFERENCES

BOND, I. K., and HUTCHISON, H. C. (1960). "Application of reciprocal inhibition therapy to exhibitionism." *Canad. Med. Assoc. J.*, 83, 23–25.

COOPER, J. E. (1963). "A study of behaviour therapy." *Lancet, i,* 411.

EYSENCK, H. J. (1960). *Behaviour Therapy and the Neuroses.* Oxford: Pergamon Press.

FONBERG, E. (1956). "On the manifestation of conditioned defensive reactions in stress." *Bull. Soc. Sci. Letter.* 7, 1–12. Lodz. Class III.

FREEMAN, H. L., and KENDRICK, D. C. (1960). "A case of cat phobia." *Brit. med. J., ii,* 497–502.

GLYNN, J. D., and HARPER, P. (1961). "Behaviour therapy in transvestism." *Lancet, i,* 619.

HUSSAIN, A. (1963). "Behaviour therapy in 105 cases." In *The Challenge in Psychotherapy.* (Ed.: Wolpe, J., Salter, A., and Reyna, L. J.) New York: Holt, Rinehart & Winston.

KANT, I. (1781). *Critique of Pure Reason.*

KNIGHT, R. P. (1941). "Evaluation of the results of psychotherapy." *Amer. J. Psychiat.*, 98, 434–438.

LAZARUS, A. A. (1959). "The elimination of children's phobias by deconditioning." *Med. Proc.*, 5, 261–264.

——— (1963). "An evaluation of behaviour therapy." *Behavior Research and Therapy*, I, 69–79.

——— and ABRAMOVITZ, A. (1962). "The use of emotive imagery in the treatment of children's phobias." *J. Ment. Sci.*, 108, 191–195.

LUNDBERG, G. A. (1937). *Foundations of Sociology.* New York: Macmillan.

RAYMOND, M. J. (1956). "Case of fetishism treated by aversion therapy." *Brit. med. J., ii,* 854–857.

TAYLOR, J. G. (1962). *The Behavioural Basis of Perception.* New Haven: Yale University Press.

VALENTINE, C. W. (1946). *The Psychology of Early Childhood.* London: Methuen.

WALTON, D. (1961). "Experimental psychology and the treatment of a tiqueur." *J. Child Psychol. Psychiat.*, 2, 148–155.

WOLPE, J. (1952). "Experimental neuroses as learned behaviour." *Brit. J. Psychol.*, 43, 243–268.

——— (1958). *Psychotherapy by Reciprocal Inhibition.* Stanford: Stanford University Press.

——— (1961a). "The prognosis in unpsychoanalysed recovery from neuroses." *Amer. J. Psychiat.*, 117, 35–39.

——— (1961b). "The systematic densensitization treatment of neuroses." *J. Nerv. Ment. Dis.*, 132, 189–203.

—— (1962). "Isolation of a conditioning procedure as the crucial psychotherapeutic factor." *Ibid.*, 134, 316–329.

—— (1963a). "Psychotherapy: the nonscientific heritage and the new science." *Behav. Res. Ther.*, I, 23–28.

—— (1963b). "Behaviour Therapy." *Lancet, i,* 886.

YATES, A. J. (1958). "The application of learning theory to the treatment of tics." *J. Abn. Soc. Psychol.*, 56, 175–182.

Helen Singer Kaplan

Helen Singer Kaplan, a psychoanalyst by training, holds both a Ph.D. in psychology and an M.D. Kaplan teaches psychiatry and heads the sex-therapy program at the Cornell Medical School. Sex therapy, as Kaplan describes it, combines standard techniques of psychotherapy with the technical insights into sexual dysfunction that derive from such sex research as that of Masters and Johnson.

Sex therapy has evolved as a hybrid, borrowing standard techniques from such diverse sources as family therapy, behavior therapy, and psychodynamic approaches. Because this is a field defined by a problem-focus rather than a specific psychological orientation, sex therapists have been pragmatic in developing their methods, using whatever approaches have proven effective for a given problem.

As Kaplan describes it, when a patient comes for treatment of a sexual problem, the therapy is twofold. One part of treatment deals with the mechanical aspects of the problem, such as a man's inability to get an erection, or a woman's inability to have orgasm. The other focus of treatment is the psychological issues that underlie the problem.

Often sexual problems embody a difficulty a couple has in communicating; if so, therapy will aim to help the couple be more free and open with each other. Other sexual disorders may be due in the main to psychological problems of only one member of the couple—for example, vaginismus (in which a woman's vaginal muscles tighten and prevent intercourse) is typically due to the woman's fear of vaginal penetration. In such cases the woman's phobia must be treated apart from the couple's attempts to have normal intercourse.

Kaplan's methods of sex therapy represent the mainstream of treatments that combine mechanical with psychodynamic interventions: "We deal first and foremost with immediate sexual problems, so that women and men can enjoy sex to its fullest. . . . We also attack the conflicts and defenses that are obstacles to sexual functioning." Treatment includes a psychiatric examination of both partners, a detailed history of their sex life, and an assessment of their relationship. The specifics of treatment will depend on which of these areas is most problematic. If, for example, one or the other partner's guilt and anxiety about sex is a major problem, then therapy will focus on relieving his or her negative feelings. If the couple are having sexual problems because of a poor overall relationship, then marital therapy is emphasized as well.

If the mechanics of sex are also at cause—e.g., with premature ejaculation—then the couple will be taught techniques like the "stop-start" method of controlling orgasm, and given a program of "homework" to practice the method during lovemaking. As Kaplan describes it, then, what sets sex therapy apart from the standard techniques it borrows as needed are the unique symptom-specific methods that have evolved from the laboratories of sex research.

THERAPY FOR SEXUAL MALFUNCTIONS

by Helen Singer Kaplan

Since William H. Masters and Virginia E. Johnson published their research on the physiology of sexual intercourse, and talk about sex has become respectable, a growing number of men and women know they are being cheated. They are seeking help at new sex therapy clinics throughout the nation.

In our clinic at Cornell University Medical School, we see couples who have one or more of the six basic sexual problems:

1. Male impotence: inability to produce or maintain an erection.
2. Premature ejaculation: inability to control orgasm.
3. Retarded ejaculation: inability to trigger orgasm.
4. General female sexual dysfunction: lack of erotic response to sexual stimulation, commonly called frigidity.
5. Female orgasmic dysfunction: difficulty in reaching orgasm.

6. Vaginismus; spasm of muscles at the entrance of the vagina, preventing penetration.

As sex therapists we deal first and foremost with immediate sexual problems, so that women and men can enjoy sex to its fullest. However, we also attack the conflicts and defenses that are obstacles to sexual functioning. We are, of course, concerned with *why* a man persists in wilting his erection by obsessively monitoring his own behavior, or why he is so worried about performing sexually, or what experiences and fantasies make a woman so insecure that she cannot ask her lover to stimulate her clitoris. But we are primarily interested in teaching individuals to abandon themselves completely to the erotic experience of sexual intercourse.

To do this, we teach patients sexual exercises to remove the immediate anxieties and defenses that create and maintain their anti-erotic environment. We employ psychotherapy when deep anxieties or underlying pathologies impede our progress.

We begin treatment of all sexual dysfunctions with a psychiatric examination of both partners, a detailed history and assessment of their sexual functioning, and an evaluation of the marital relationship. We give the couple a clear picture of what to expect during treatment, and we make a therapeutic contract with them that clearly establishes their responsibility for treatment.

Sex is composed of friction and fantasy; deficiencies in either can produce problems. A pleasurable sexual response depends both on receiving the proper sexual stimulation and responding freely to it. Most couples with sexual problems practice poor, insensitive and ineffectual sexual techniques.

Some inadequate lovemaking results merely from a couple's misinformation or ignorance about sex. Frequently, for instance, neither spouse knows where the clitoris is or recognizes its potential for eliciting erotic pleasure. They have intercourse as soon as the husband has an erection, and he ejaculates without considering whether his partner is ready. Such couples genuinely wonder why the wife does not reach orgasm. Both partners contribute to this sexual ineffectiveness. She will not ask for the kind of stimulation she wants because she is unaware of her own needs; he doesn't know that he's not a very effective lover. So, in silence, they continue their unsatisfactory sexual habits.

In other couples, feelings of guilt or anxiety about erotic

needs prevent one or both partners from enjoying sex. They may actively discourage their partners from stimulating them effectively. Careful questioning often reveals that such persons respond to sexual excitement by immediately stopping the activity which produces it. The man who is excited by an actively seductive woman may literally forbid his wife to be aggressive. The woman who is responsive only to slow tender caresses may push her husband away when he tries to kiss her breasts or to caress her buttocks. Patients who avoid effective sexual expression tend to focus on genital stimulation and an orgasm, and are apt to neglect the sensual potential of the rest of their bodies and of nonorgasmic eroticism.

Some persons have as much difficulty giving pleasure as others do in receiving it. These individuals don't provide their partners with enough sexual stimulation because they lack either the knowledge and sensitivity to know what to do, or they are anxious about doing it. Others are consciously or unconsciously hostile towards their mates and don't really want to please them.

Therapists have overlooked immediate sources of anxiety until the advent of the new sex therapy. Traditional approaches to sexual dysfunction looked for subtle and profound anxiety sources, such as oedipal conflicts and marital power struggles. We find there are also more obvious reasons for sexual anxiety, such as fear of sexual failure, fear that the partner expects too much, or fear that the partner will reject sexual advances. These fears create various sexual defenses and introduce conscious control into lovemaking, which in turn prevents persons from abandoning themselves to the experience.

We have found that the three male dysfunctions, impotence, retarded ejaculation, and premature ejaculation all seem to be associated with some form of sexual conflict, but there are different symptoms for each dysfunction, and each of them responds to different therapeutic strategies and tactics.

Premature ejaculation is one of the most common and easily relieved male complaints. Men with this malady are unable to control voluntarily their ejaculatory reflex. Once they become sexually aroused, they reach orgasm very quickly. Some ejaculate after several minutes of foreplay, others just prior to or immediately upon entering their partner's vagina, and others after only a few pelvic thrusts. The essential problem, however, is not how quickly the man ejaculates, but his inability to control the reflex. In contrast to a premature ejaculator, an effective lover continues to engage in sex play while he is in a highly aroused state. He is able to forestall climax until his partner, who is slower to respond, can reach orgasm. At the least, prematurity restricts the couple's sexuality; at worse, it destroys it.

Most men who suffer this distress are unhappy about their condition, and often employ a variety of common-sense techniques to relieve the difficulty. They shift their attention to nonsexual thoughts during intercourse, tense their anal muscles, bite their lips or dig their fingernails into their palms. In this manner they can delay the onset of intense erotic arousal, but once aroused, they still can't control ejaculation. They feel sexually inadequate, and guilty that they have not satisfied their partners.

The term "primary prematurity" refers to a man who has never been able to control orgasm. If he is otherwise healthy, there is little reason to suspect his difficulty arises from a physical cause. On the other hand, a physician should conduct thorough urological and neurological exams on the secondary ejaculator, a man who has developed the problem after a history of good control. Diseases of the posterior urethra or pathology along the nerve pathways serving the orgasmic reflex mechanisms may cause secondary prematurity. Sex therapy should begin only after a physician rules out any physical basis for the condition.

Different therapeutic schools emphasize various psychological explanations for premature ejaculation. Psychoanalysts say it is the result of a neurosis, marriage counselors believe it comes from hostilities between the partners, common-sense theorists blame it on excessive sensitivity to erotic sensation. Masters and Johnson contend that stressful conditions during a young man's initial sex experiences bring on premature ejaculation, while Wardell Pomeroy, co-author of the Kinsey reports, says that anxiety is the culprit. All these speculations may be theoretically interesting, but they are of little comfort to the patient.

In 1956, James Semans, a urologist, demonstrated a simple manipulative technique to help cure premature ejaculation. Semans realized that the distinguishing feature of premature ejaculation was the rapidity of the orgasmic reflex. Consequently, his treatment goal was to prolong the reflex. To do this, he directed the patient's wife to stimulate her husband's erect penis until he felt he was just about to have orgasm, and signal her to stop. When he could recapture control, the patient would tell her to resume stimulation until he again felt the sensations that signaled ejaculation. Again she would stop. Over a period of several weeks the couple practiced this stop-start method until the patient could tolerate stimulation without ordering a halt. At this point, his prematurity was permanently cured.

Semans reported on eight men who were premature ejaculators, and in every case the symptoms disappeared. Other clinicians have used his method with the same success. I believe the technique works because it focuses a man's attention on the sensations preceding orgasm. Apparently he has previously failed to acquire control because he has not received, or let himself receive, the sensory feedback necessary to bring the reflex under control.

In our treatment program at Cornell we teach the patient to clearly identify his intensely erotic preorgasmic sensations and, initially, to avoid being distracted by his wife's needs. We advise the couple that, provided they adhere to the prescribed therapeutic exercises, we can cure the symptom in most cases.

We use a variation of the Semans "stop-start" method in our treatment. The couple carries out their exercise assignments in their home. After three or four of these noncoital sessions, the patient usually feels he has attained some improvement in orgasmic control. We then suggest that the couple attempt intercourse using the same stop-start method. They first have coitus with the woman in the superior position, then while both lie on their sides, and finally with the man on top. Since this is usually the most stimulating position for the male, he has conquered his problem when he can maintain control in this position.

This procedure can be quite unexciting and frustrating for the wife. Therefore, we suggest that the couple work out an agreement previous to treatment where the husband stimulates his wife to orgasm before or after the stop-start treatment. If the wife is unable to have an orgasm, we tell her that our first goal is to cure her husband's prematurity, then we can shift treatment to her.

If either partner resists any part of the treatment procedures, we root out the cause and intervene with appropriate psychotherapy. This might involve marriage counseling, psychoanalysis, or anxiety-reduction techniques. During therapy we continue to reinforce the couple's progress by reminding them that in a relatively short time, most, if not all, premature ejaculators respond to treatment.

Whereas the man suffering from prematurity cannot control orgasm, the retarded ejaculator cannot trigger it. Men with a mild form of this disorder can ejaculate by employing fantasy or distracting themselves from their sexual worries, or by additional stimulation. A few others have never experienced orgasm. At one time clinicians thought retarded ejaculation was a relatively rare phenomenon. Now it appears it may be highly prevalent, at least in its mild forms. At Cornell, we are seeing an increasing number of patients with this difficulty.

In its mildest form, a man's ejaculatory inhibition is confined to specific anxiety-provoking situations, such as when he is with a new partner, or when he feels guilty about the sexual encounter. The patient who seeks help, however, usually is more severely restricted in his sexuality. The man who suffers from primary ejaculatory retardation has had the difficulty since his first attempt at sexual intercourse, has never achieved orgasm during coitus, but may be able to achieve it by masturbation, manipulation or oral stimulation. Secondary retarded ejaculators enjoyed a period of good sexual functioning before the onset of retarded ejaculation; commonly, a specific trauma brought on their difficulty. Like the premature ejaculator, the retarded ejaculator often anticipates failure and frustration, which can eventually impair his ability to sustain an erection.

Few physical illnesses play a role in retarded ejaculation. Clinical evidence suggests that a strict religious upbringing, sexual conflict from an unresolved oedipal complex, strongly suppressed anger, ambivalence toward one's partner, fear of abandonment, or a specific sexual calamity are causes of retarded ejaculation.

Our treatment goal is to overcome the mechanism that inhibits ejaculation and resolve the underlying problems that impede sexual functioning. We use a series of progressive sexual exercises to relieve the patient of his anxieties and fears about the sexual act. We start with the couple performing the sexual practices that can elicit any existing ejaculatory capacity. As the patient is successful in one situation, he moves on to a more threatening or difficult one. Concurrently, the psychotherapy sessions at the clinic foster the patient's insight into any of his irrational fears, traumatic memories or destructive interactions with his partner that inhibit ejaculation.

Masters and Johnson cured 14 out of 17 retarded ejaculators using a similar method. Our preliminary results are similar to theirs. One of our successful cases was Mr. J., who had been in psychoanalysis for some time when he came to our clinic.

We traced Mr. J.'s difficulty to the traumatic termination of a sexual relationship. He had left his wife and four children for another woman, who subsequently left him. He became deeply depressed and sought psychoanalytic treatment. Although his depression subsided during analysis, he continued to have ejaculatory problems.

The patient had remarried, and his new wife agreed to cooperate in our sex therapy program. Before entering treatment, they had worked out a way to have frequent and enjoyable sex, except for the limits imposed by his inability to ejaculate during intercourse. They would engage in imaginative sex play and have intercourse until she reached orgasm. Then she would stimulate him manually or orally until he achieved orgasm.

Treatment in this case was brief and effective. First we instructed the couple to participate in sex play without intercourse or orgasm. Then she stimulated him to orgasm with his penis near the mouth of her vagina. Finally, we told the wife to stimulate her husband almost to orgasm, at which point he was to enter the vagina with strong pelvic thrusting. In order to ejaculate during coitus, Mr. J. initially needed to fantasize that his wife was stimulating him orally, but gradually he could ejaculate without distracting himself from lovemaking with fantasy.

At the same time that Mr. and Mrs. J. practiced the sexual desensitization exercises at home, we conducted psychotherapy with them at the clinic. Their relationship had many immature elements in it. He was infantile, jealous and demanding, and haunted by the fear that his wife would leave him. At times, she acted like a stubborn, irresponsible and provocative child. In the therapeutic sessions we discussed the quality of their relationship from this perspective. Two years after we terminated therapy, we were pleased to learn that the patient had retained his ejaculatory competence, felt well, and seemed more assertive and less anxious.

A man who suffers from impotence is often almost unbearably anxious, frustrated and humiliated by his inability to produce or maintain an erection. Although he may become aroused in a sexual encounter and want to make love, he can't. He feels his masculinity is on the line. Clinicians and researchers estimate that half the male population has experienced at least transient impotence. Men seek help only when the problem becomes chronic.

Primary impotence is the rarest and most severe form of the disorder; men who suffer from it have never been potent with a woman, although they may be able to attain good erections in other situations. Secondary impotence is less severe, but still debilitating. These patients functioned well for some time prior to their erectile difficulties. The prognosis for treating impotence depends on how long the patient has suffered from it and how severe it is. Here again, the prospective candidate should have a thorough physical checkup before he goes into therapy. Stress, fatigue, undiagnosed diabetes, hepatitis, narcotics use, low androgen levels and other physical factors may cause impotence.

Although some traditional therapists believe impotence is always a sign of a deep underlying pathology, we believe there are often more obvious and immediate causes. Fear of sexual failure, pressures created by an excessively demanding wife, and guilt or conflict may prevent a man from producing or maintaining an erection. Therefore, we feel our brief, symptom-focused form of treatment is preferable to lengthy, reconstructive insight therapy that essentially ignores the immediate antecedents of impotence. Masters and Johnson report they cured 70 percent of their secondary impotent patients using treatment very similar to ours.

Because depression or marital discord can accompany or cause impotence, we must often relieve these symptoms before we can treat the man's impotence. Therefore, we always combine sexual tasks at home with therapeutic sessions in the clinic. The following case history demonstrates the variability and flexibility of this combined approach.

A 26-year-old Jewish law student applied for treatment. Although he and his 29-year-old West-Indian wife reported they had enjoyed a good sexual relationship during the year and a half they lived together, he began to have erectile difficulty after they were married, and she admitted that even while they lived together, intercourse was often hurried and more infrequent than she wished. Most recently, the patient had been unable to achieve an erection under any circumstances, and had lost all interest in sex. In the course of our initial evaluation and interview, the patient admitted that he had experienced potency problems with girls of his own ethnic background before he met his wife. But he emphasized that he had functioned well with her at first.

The wife had no sexual problems. She had orgasm during coitus, but only if intercourse lasted for 10 minutes or more. She could climax through clitoral stimulation, but was reluctant to allow him to engage in this activity.

Although there were many elements in the patient's psychiatric and family history that could indicate underlying psychological reasons for his impotence, we did not raise those issues in therapy. They had no immediate relevance to our belief that the cause of the patient's impotence was his wife's demands for frequent intercourse of long duration, and his progressive fear of failure.

We saw the couple in our office once a week. We also instructed them to gently caress each other during sexual play at home, but not to engage in coitus. We encouraged the wife to accept clitoral stimulation to orgasm if her sexual tension became excessive. These exercises produced intense excitement in both partners. He experienced a spontaneous erection, and, "against our advice," their passion led them to try coitus. The wife did not reach orgasm, but the patient felt sufficiently encouraged by his success to attempt intercourse again the following night. This time, he lost his erection when he became afraid he would be unable to sustain it long enough to bring his wife to orgasm.

We talked about their experience in the next therapeutic session. When the wife understood the destructive effect of her sexual demands, she admitted for the first time that her husband was not very skilled at clitoral stimulation. Moreover, she said she felt this form of stimulation was "homosexual." We corrected her misconception and encouraged the couple to communicate more freely with each other about their sexual responses.

This couple developed a good sexual partnership, free of the pressures and demands which had caused his impotence. Without making her husband feel deficient the wife achieved postcoital orgasm by clitoral stimulation when she did not climax during intercourse. He learned to abandon himself to his erotic sensations. We terminated treatments after four therapeutic sessions, conducted over a three-week period, and the couple reported no difficulty in sexual functioning a year later.

This case was relatively simple. Others are more difficult. Impotence can be tenacious, and we often have to employ extensive psychotherapy to relieve the anxieties produced by deep-seated pathology or by marital discord.

In contrast to male dysfunctions, the female sexual dysfunctions are not as clearly understood. For example, the term "frigidity" is confusing on two counts. Because it has traditionally referred to all forms of female sexual inhibition, covering both total lack of erotic feeling and the inability to have orgasm, it fails to convey the fact that these are two separate components of the female sexual response. It also implies that women who suffer from inhibitions are cold and hostile to men, which is both inaccurate and pejorative.

Confusion also centers on the relationship between female orgasm and coitus. Some clinicians believe that if a woman cannot achieve orgasm during coitus, she suffers from sexual dysfunction. Others do not attach any particular importance to how a woman reaches a climax. Our clinical experience supports the second viewpoint. A woman who is otherwise orgasmic, but who does not reach orgasm during coitus, is neither frigid nor sick. This pattern seems to be a normal variant of female sexuality for some women. Our impression is that eight to 10 percent of the female population has never experienced orgasm, and of the 90 percent who have, only about half do so regularly during intercourse.

We also believe no one can yet resolve the debate about whether there are one or two female orgasms. But physiological data do give us an idea of how women experience climax. Apparently, the stimulation of the clitoris or the surrounding area triggers orgasm, but women respond to and perceive the climax primarily in the vagina.

Women are slower than men to become aroused, and their arousal signs are much less obvious than the male's erect penis. Because men cannot easily discern whether or not a woman is ready for intercourse, and because women are culturally conditioned to put their husbands' needs first, couples often proceed to coitus before the woman is sufficiently aroused to reach orgasm during intercourse.

A woman's reluctance to express her needs, however, is not always based on cultural paranoia. Women may run a real risk of displeasing their husbands if they become sexually assertive. Such behavior repels some men, who regard women who assume active roles in sex as aggressive, castrating females. Other men feel threatened when their wives express sexual needs. They think their partners are challenging their sexual adequacy. Too often men fail to realize that they can become good lovers if they simply supply their partners with gentle, sensitive stimulation instead of perpetual erection.

The inability of some women to become aroused even though they receive adequate stimulation probably indicates some underlying sexual conflict. A restrictive upbringing; a hostile marital relationship; severe psychopathology; conflicts about the female role in lovemaking; fear of men, of losing control, of rejection and abandonment can cause female sexual dysfunctions.

General sexual dysfunction, usually referred to as frigidity, is the most severe of the female inhibitions. Women plagued with it derive little, if any, erotic pleasure from sexual stimulation. They are essentially devoid of sexual feelings. Many nonresponsive women consider sex an ordeal. Those who suffer from primary frigidity have never experienced erotic pleasure, and those who have secondary general sexual dysfunctions responded at one time to sexual stimulation, but no longer do so. Typically, these patients were aroused by petting before marriage, but loss the ability to respond when intercourse became the exclusive objective of all sexual encounters.

To help these nonresponsive women, we create a relaxed, sensuous ambience to permit the natural unfolding of sexual responses during lovemaking. To help foster such an environment, we encourage the couple to communicate openly about their sexual feelings and wishes, and we prescribe systematic sensuous and erotic experiences for the couple to perform at home.

Masters and Johnson developed a technique called sensate focus which is an ingenious and invaluable tool in treating general female sexual dysfunction. This exercise consists of having the couple forgo sexual intercourse and orgasm while the wife caresses her husband's body, after which he stimulates her in like manner. By telling the wife to act first, we help counteract her guilt about receiving something for herself, and her fear that her husband will reject her. When we free women from the pressure to produce orgasm, they often experience erotic and sensuous sensations for the first time.

When the patient reports that she feels sensuous and erotic during the sensate focus exercises, we expand the caressing to include light, teasing genital play. After the husband caresses his wife's body he gently touches her nipples, clitoral area, and vaginal entrance. The woman guides his actions verbally and nonverbally. If, during these sessions, he becomes too sexually aroused, we tell the patient to bring him to orgasm manually or orally after she has had a chance to experience nonpressured, reassuring genital play.

Genital stimulation typically produces a definite increase in the patient's sexual responsiveness. When she reaches a high level of erotic feeling during these exercises, the couple moves on to intercourse. On top of her husband, she initiates coitus with slow and exploratory thrusts at first, while she focuses her attention on the physical sensations emanating from her vagina. If her partner's urge to ejaculate becomes too intense during her thrusting, we tell the couple to separate. The husband manually stimulates his wife until his premonitory orgasmic sensations disappear and they can resume intercourse. They repeat this cycle several times until she feels like driving for orgasm. If she does not want to try to reach climax, the couple proceeds with coitus until the husband reaches orgasm.

Frequently these sexual experiences evoke highly emotional responses and resistance in the patient. We use these feelings to help identify the specific obstacles which impede her eroticism. We deal with these obstacles on both an experiential level and in psychotherapy.

There is a good chance that women who suffer from general sexual dysfunction will improve. To a great extent the outcome of treatment seems to depend on the quality of the patient's relationship with her husband. If he does not reject her and she has no deep-seated psychopathology, the great majority of these women learn to enjoy sex and to reach orgasm.

Problems in reaching orgasm are probably the most prevalent sexual complaint of women. A woman suffers from primary orgasmic dysfunction if she has never experienced an orgasm, and from secondary orgasmic dysfunction if the disorder developed after a period of being able to reach orgasm. An inorgasmic woman has an absolute problem if she can't achieve orgasm under any circumstances, and a situational one if she can reach a climax only under specific circumstances. Women who suffer solely from orgasmic problems frequently have strong sex drives. They fall in love, enjoy sex play, lubricate copiously, and love the sensation of phallic penetration. They simply get stuck at or near the plateau phase of the sexual response.

Women who can achieve orgasm only by masturbation when they are alone, or those who must use vibrators for half an hour to reach orgasm obviously have a problem. But when a clinician sees a woman who can climax during masturbation, or when her husband stimulates her either manually or orally, but she cannot reach orgasm during coitus, he often faces a dilemma. It is difficult for a therapist to decide whether she is suffering from a pathological inhibition or whether she merely exhibits a normal variation of female sexuality. If the clinician cannot uncover any sexual anxieties, conflicts or fears during his initial interview with the couple, he should probably reassure them that she functions within the normal sexual range, and encourage them to work out lovemaking patterns that satisfy them both. However, if they still want to achieve coital orgasm, we will accept them, and try to increase her sexual responsiveness. Some of these women learn to climax during coitus, and others do not.

The first goal of therapy with a woman who has never experienced orgasm is to eliminate as many inhibiting factors as possible from the sexual environment so she can have her first climax. Because it is the rising tide of clitoral sensations which triggers the female climax, and because women are least threatened when they are alone, we first instruct the inorgasmic woman to masturbate at home alone in an environment free from possible interruption. If several attempts at this fail to produce orgasm, we tell her to use an electric vibrator to stimulate her clitoris. Some sexologists feel the vibrator is the only significant advance in sexual technique since the days of Pompeii. Because the patient may become "hooked" on this device, however, we transfer her to manual stimulation as soon as she has had a few orgasms using the vibrator.

When she can stimulate herself to orgasm regularly, we bring her husband into the treatment program. First we instruct them to make love in the usual way, telling her not to make any special effort to achieve orgasm during coitus. After he has ejaculated, and there is no pressure on her to perform quickly, he uses the vibrator or stimulates her manually to orgasm. We tell her to be utterly "selfish," and to focus on her own sensations. After a few of these sessions some women climax during intercourse without the manual stimulation.

One of our patients was a 28-year-old social worker who had never experienced orgasm. Her husband was a 34-year-old physician. They were very much in love, and were frequent and passionate lovers. During the early years of their marriage, Mrs. E. had simulated orgasm because she was afraid her husband would feel hurt and guilty if he knew she could not climax. A year before they sought treatment, she admitted to Dr. E. that she could not reach orgasm, and since then he had tried to bring her to orgasm by clitoral stimulation.

Mrs. E. arrived for the initial interview alone. She explained she had been reluctant to ask her husband to come because of his busy schedule. This was typical of her overprotectiveness of him. We explained that he would have to participate in treatment, and scheduled the first therapy session for two weeks later. In the meantime we instructed her to try to reach orgasm with an electric vibrator.

At our next meeting, Mrs. E. told us she had easily achieved orgasm with a vibrator in solitude. But she was afraid to ask her husband to use the vibrator to stimulate her clitoris. She thought it would repel him and make him feel inadequate. He reassured her that this was not true, and said he was eager to try to bring her to orgasm.

We also learned that Mrs. E. never abandoned herself completely to her sexual feelings, because, like many other women, she was overly concerned with satisfying and pleasing her husband. This meant that the couple's lovemaking was never governed by her needs. This was not Dr. E.'s fault. Often he aroused her to a high level of sexual tension, but at this point she would think, "That's enough, he must be getting tired." And she would signal him to begin coitus. Not surprisingly, he misinterpreted her signal to mean that she was ready to commence coitus because she too was ready to have an orgasm.

It became clear that the patient's orgasmic inhibition was not associated with severe psychopathology or marital difficulties. It was her great need to please her husband, motivated by her own insecurity.

We treated this couple by enhancing the communication between them, prescribing sexual experiences to sensitize Mrs. E. to her own feelings, and by helping develop a sense of responsibility for obtaining her husband's adequate stimulation to bring her to orgasm. Both the therapist and her husband reassured her that her sexually assertive behavior would not diminish her husband's sexual enjoyment or jeopardize their relationship.

We encouraged Mrs. E. to develop sexual autonomy during lovemaking, and to assume responsibility for obtaining pleasure, first during foreplay and then during coitus. We instructed her to ask her husband to stimulate her, and tell him where to kiss and caress her. If he ejaculatd during intercourse, she was to ask him to stimulate her to orgasm. We also helped her stop monitoring her own progress toward orgasm, which distracted her from her sexual sensations.

Dr. E.'s acceptance of Mrs. E.'s growing sexual maturity and activity helped her progress. After 12 sessions, she easily reached orgasm via clitoral stimulation and was beginning to experience coital orgasm. Both enjoyed sex tremendously, and after therapy Mrs. E. became more assertive and happier in general.

More common than the woman who has never had an orgasm is the patient who is orgastic in low tension situations, but cannot reach a climax under circumstances that make her even slightly anxious. She may be able to climax during solitary masturbation, but not when she is with a partner. We treat these patients by uncovering and resolving the specific conflicts which inhibit the patient.

With a woman who cannot have orgasm during intercourse, our goals are to identify and remove any psychic blocks to marital problems that inhibit her during coitus, to have her perform erotic tasks to heighten her sexual arousal, enhance her awareness of and pleasure in her vaginal sensations and to maximize clitoral stimulation. We find that techniques that combine coitus with clitoral stimulation are very helpful. These are called "bridge" maneuvers.

A great majority of women, including those who suffer from absolute primary orgasmic inhibition, are able to achieve orgasm after a relatively brief period of therapy. Indeed, orgasmic inhibition is virtually 100 percent curable if the sole criterion for cure is the ability to reach orgasm. But, as mentioned before, some women never reach orgasm during intercourse, which suggests that the phenomenon is a normal variant of female sexual response.

The third, and relatively rare, female sexual dysfunction is vaginismus. Anatomically, a vaginismic woman is normal, but whenever a man tries to penetrate her vagina, the vaginal muscles literally snap the entrance shut so that intercourse is impossible. Physicians often must conduct vaginal examinations on these women under anesthesia. This disorder is due to an involuntary spasm of the muscles surrounding the vaginal entrance. These patients are usually afraid of vaginal penetration, and intercourse. They often suffer from general sexual dysfunction or orgasmic inhibition. However, many women who seek treatment for vaginismus are sexually responsive and highly orgastic.

Vaginismus results from a woman's association of pain or fear with vaginal penetration. The precipitating event may be physical pain or psychological stress. A rigid hymen, inflammatory pelvic diseases and tumors, childbirth pathologies, and hemorrhoids may cause it. Strict religious upbringing, a husband's impotence, or the psychological effects of rape also may bring on vaginismus, or it may result from ignorance and misinformation about sex, or guilt caused by deep sexual conflicts.

Our basic strategy for treating vaginismus is simple, provided all physical pain-producing conditions have been corrected. Our first goal is to uncover the basis for the patient's phobic avoidance of vaginal entry. Then, with progessive sexual exercises, we try to decondition the involuntary spasm of the muscles that guard the entrance to the vagina.

First we have both the patient and her husband examine her genitals in the privacy of their well-lit bedroom. We tell them to find and examine the exact location of the vaginal opening. In the first sexual assignment, we tell the woman to gently insert her own or her husband's finger into her vagina. When her usual discomfort disappears we tell her to move her finger back and forth inside her vagina until she can tolerate the motion without discomfort. We always allow the woman to control the situation to reduce her fears and apprehensions. Next, the husband or wife inserts two fingers in the vagina, and then rotates them gently, stretching the walls of the vagina. When she can tolerate this, the couple proceeds to intercourse. First they lie still with the man's penis inserted in his wife, then the husband begins gently thrusting at his wife's signal and withdraws if she wishes him to. Finally the couple thrusts to orgasm. Concurrently we conduct therapy sessions with the couple to work on the patient's phobia about vaginal penetration.

We have achieved excellent and permanent results with

women who suffer from vaginismus. Masters and Johnson report they achieved a 100 percent cure rate. We find that the length of treatment is more variable than that for the other sexual dysfunctions because of the tenacity of the phobia. But we have been able to resolve the phobic avoidance in 10 psychotherapy sessions. Within three to 14 weeks, we can go on to cure the vaginal spasm with four to eight home exercise sessions.

Sex therapy promises, and experience suggests it delivers, rapid and permanent relief of distressing sexual problems for many. But we have not scientifically substantiated its merits in a controlled study.

There can be no doubt, however, in light of the clinical evidence and the compelling conceptual considerations which underlie this approach, that the new methods merit further trial and development. We need to know which kinds of problems we can best treat with sex therapy, and under what conditions. We must learn precisely what components of these complex methods are actually responsible for the observed changes. At the present stage in its development, however, sex therapy appears to have great value. Indeed, it may close the door on sexual boredom and agony in America.

Salvador Minuchin

Salvador Minuchin is a psychiatrist who has been at the forefront in developing family therapy. Not a single treatment method, family therapy is rather a clinical orientation that includes many therapeutic approaches. It has been developed independently by many therapists; each family-therapy school views the methods of treating a family differently. Some merely extend standard techniques of individual therapy to include more people in the room, whereas others institute radically different methods.

Many family therapists do not treat a patient alone at all, but require that the entire family come to each interview. Indeed, the person with symptoms is called the "identified patient," implying that his problem is a sign of broader difficulties in the whole family. Others are willing to see a patient alone at times, and other family members alone as well, in conjunction with whole-family sessions. But whatever the treatment pattern, the difference between a family therapist and a one-to-one therapist is in how the patient's problems are viewed: a family therapist would be far more interested in the dynamics of a patient's place and function in his family. He would be more likely to look for clues as to how the patient's symptoms may actually help the family—e.g., by keeping his parents' marriage intact—and far less likely to offer any interpretations about the symptom's inner meaning for the patient. Because most family therapists were originally trained to treat patients singly, early family therapists adapted and expanded the methods they applied.

In the early days of family therapy, therapists would interpret the transference and help the family understand their unconscious dynamics. As they gained more experience, however, family therapists began to do therapy based on entirely new premises. Salvador Minuchin is one such innovator.

Minuchin takes the hierarchy of a family's organization into account. Pathology occurs, according to Minuchin, when there is a confusion in the hierarchy or when its rules are broken. Minuchin knows that adding a therapist to the family structure itself intervenes in the hierarchy. Coalitions formed between the therapist and any member of group within the family can be used to "unbalance" the family and pave the way for change. The therapist transforms strategic coalitions by expressing approval, siding with parents, or a child, or children against parents, or sometimes even blaming a family member. Such coalitions offer the therapist a chance to redefine the structure of the family.

For example, in a family in which the teenage anorectic daughter had starved herself to the point of malnutrition, Minuchin insisted that the mother was to force the girl to eat and the father was required to observe quietly. When the mother could not manage her daughter, Minuchin blamed her entirely for the problem and, siding with the father, let him have a chance to insist that his daughter eat. When both parents had failed, Minuchin pointed out that the girl had successfully controlled the family and she could therefore eat. She recovered.

In the following article, Minuchin reviews the case for family therapy.

FAMILY THERAPY: TECHNIQUE
OR THEORY?

by Salvador Minuchin

The past few years have seen a tremendous upsurge in the development of new forms of the delivery of mental health services. While some of these are old products in new packages, there has also been a drive for experimentation and innovation.

The innovations, most of which are still in the trial-and-error stage, have come under heavy attack by proponents of more established schools of thought. The major criticism most often leveled against them is that in the attempt to make mental health services more available to all, the innovators are dismissing established forms of treatment (dynamic individual therapy), accepted concepts of pathology and the exploration of deep psychodynamic and intrapsychic conflict, while venturing into areas of social intervention for which traditional psychotherapeutic methods were never intended. Consequently, the dangers of diffusion and superficiality threaten their professional identity.

However, the newer models for the delivery of mental health services have gained powerful supporters in Washington, with apparent consequences for the disbursement of funds for research and training; as a result, the polarization of the field is increasing. This is the visible part of the current struggle. Under the surface, painfully, haltingly, a new language of explanation of normal development and the phenomena of change is being wrought. Because the fluidity of certain processes is more visible on the frontiers, and because family therapy is one of the latest additions to our armamentarium, the influence of the interchanges of theory and technique is more evident in this area than in many. While we talk about "family therapy" (usually as opposed to "individual therapy") as a distinct technique, a simple overview of the work of a few of the major proponents of this form of intervention shows a wide diversity of techniques and explanations in this field.

The unit of intervention varies widely. Speck[12] in operating with the "social net" of schizophrenic patients, works with as many as 40 relatives, significant others and professionals. Laqueur et al[9] deal simultaneously with several families. Framo[4] deploys "all those immediate and extended family members as well as extrafamilial persons who exert a demonstrable influence on the total family system." Minuchin and Montalvo[11] work with significant subsystems of a family, such as the sibling group or the spouses; Bowen,[2] with individual members of a family as a pathway to total family change.

The length of interviews also varies. The traditional weekly 50-minute interview, borrowed from individual psychotherapy, is adhered to by some family therapists. MacGregor et al.[10] have developed a single discontinuous 2-day interview as part of their scheme of Multiple Impact Therapy. An intensive 3- or 4-hour intake interview is sometimes used.[1] And even longer periods of family interviews, or the Marathon Family Interview, are the subject of some experimentation.*

The interview may be held in the therapist's office or clinic.

---

*Dr. William Moore of Akron, Ohio (personal communication).

Bowen[2] has found it helpful to require the hospitalization of a schizophrenic's entire household. Donald A. Bloch is working on the idea of a "Family House" in which multi-problem families would live in an apartment under the supervision of an interdisciplinary professional team. Some therapists use interviews with the family in its home.[5] Others have held weekend "live-ins" of the patients and their families and the therapists and their families.[8]

The form of the family interviews varies through a wide range of possibilities. Some therapists use played-back interviews,* discussing the interactions while the families watch themselves performing. Others[11] use the one-way mirror to enable subsystems of the family to watch other members. A mother may observe her children, or a father watch his wife working with their children. Various instruments for diagnosis of family interaction have been developed for use in family interviews, such as Kwiatkowska's family art therapy.[7] Bowen has intervened in a family's system via letters to individual members of the family.[8]

Although all these techniques are included under the label of family therapy, conceptualizations of the family and the process of change can be organized under two main groupings.

Some family therapists remain in the theoretical framework of individual dynamic psychiatry. Family therapy is used as a technique, but change is conceptualized as occurring primarily in the intrapsychic spheres of the individual family members. Individual intrapsychic change is the goal of the manipulation of the family system. Other clinicians see the family as the significant unit, the individual being conceptualized as an interacting member of the system. The polarization is not between individual or family techniques of intervention, but between two theoretical points of view.

Techniques developed within a theoretical framework have often affected the theory itself. Dynamic psychiatry was built upon a philosophy of intrapsychic dynamics and the use of individual interviewing. Family psychiatry developed accompanied by a systems and communications theory and an emphasis on interviewing the total family.

We are now in a rather chaotic period which may prove to be transitional. Some family therapists, having used the tech-

---

*Virginia Satir is working with the use of played-back filmed interviews in California; Nathan Ackerman, in New York (personal communications).

niques of interviewing family subsystems (spouses, siblings and other dynamically significant family subgroups) have begun to be concerned with the degree of interaction and autonomy (the coupling) among subsystems and to study the dynamics of these interfaces. At this point, it has proved relatively easy to conceptualize the individual family member as a subsystem and return to individual therapy within a framework of family therapy. At the same time, many "individual dynamic psychiatrists" are using family therapy techniques and painstakingly conceptualizing multiple transferences, countertransferences and a family ego.

The efforts to explain and translate that are being made as a result of such explorations may well produce far-reaching effects on the theoretical frameworks themselves. Therefore, it may be useful at this point to consider briefly the growth from technique of both psychoanalysis and family therapy.

In the field of psychoanalysis,* theorizing grew from data gathered in a well-structured context, a controlled interaction between two people, hierarchically related, meeting to explore the life context of one of them. In this context, in which activity is curtailed to the minimum, the therapist remains by design a less defined person. The content is verbal; the material explored is in the past (or in the future). The relationship between the members of the dyad is paradoxical; the most active but less powerful member, the patient, talks and tells about his life to the less active but more powerful member, the therapist who, while relatively untouched by the present experience, exerts powerful influence by cognitive manipulation or interpretation of the patient's behavior outside of this interaction. (This is, of course, a simplistic model, requiring qualification. The use of corrective emotional experience by some psychoanalytic schools is an affective operation in the present which has to do with the interaction of therapist and patient. Transference also is an affective operation in the interaction between therapist and patient. Nevertheless, transference is conceptualized as having to do with

---

*I am here limiting this discussion to the methods of individual therapy which evolved under the influence of psychoanalytic theory. The contributions from other sources, such as the important impact of behavioral theory, are not at issue.

Also, I am of course talking about individual therapy methods as they are presented in the literature of the field. The fact that the practice of therapy may be quite different is, of course, acknowledged.

the patient's past; in that sense, this model stands.) In the context of this technique a theory emphasizing intrapsychic operations regardless of the interpersonal context, the prevalance of past over present experience, and the power of understanding as a tool for change, developed and grew.

The family therapist gathers his data in quite a different context. A natural social group, a family, whose interacting members follow rules established over years of mutual accommodation, meets with a therapist who sees himself as forming a new social system in which he is a controlling participant. Communications, both verbal and nonverbal, are multiple. They tend for the most part to move along established pathways. Though past experiences may often activate the material, the content of the session is almost always the here-and-now, and its actuality almost guarantees a wide range of affective components which can be very intense. The therapist finds his freedom of intervention curtailed by the patterns available; to maximize his therapeutic effectiveness and be able to make use of the total range of human experience and behavior, he must become a clearly defined member of the system.

The theory influenced by this technique emphasizes the power of the social system upon its participant members, the prevalence of the present transactions in their context over past experiences (that is, the accommodation of the memory of past experiences to the present context) and puts less emphasis on the understanding of intrapsychic operations as a significant tool for change and more on systemic manipulations of the interpersonal context.

The theory of human development and change which is emerging from the context of the family interview technique might be called an ecological theory. It is based on the truism that no man stands alone. Each human being is interdependent with the human beings who interact with him. Furthermore, the quality which makes man uniquely human—his communicating in symbolic formulation—depends upon his interaction with other humans.

> Let us consider an example of data-gathering. John is a 14-year-old only son being seen by a therapist in individual sessions. During these sessions he describes a relationship with his mother which is ambivalent, but with a strong element of attraction, and his hatred of his father. The therapist unravels the history of this process and its

repetitive nature throughout the development of the child. He is aware of the boy's anxiety and of his defensive patterns. He interprets the material as an oedipal conflict with paratactic distortion of the present situation.

In another data-gathering session John, a 14-year-old only son, is seen in family interviews by a therapist. In the interviews, the therapist sees that the relationship of John and Jocasta is characterized by intermingled closeness and hostility. During the sessions most of the communications John sends are directed towards his mother, and even when he does talk to Laius, his father, he seems to do so through his mother, who translates and explains her son to her husband.

The relationship between the spouses is characterized by a lack of intimacy and by very poor communication. There is an absence of marital conflict; disagreements usually are side-tracked into the father's attacking his son for his misbehavior outside the family.

We have presented two ways of describing an oedipal conflict. The therapist who gathers his data in individual sessions will build up an explanation of John's behavior which includes his internalization of his parent figures, the historical development of his conflict with them and the apparently compulsive intrusion of this conflict into extrafamilial and seemingly unrelated situations in John's life. The therapist who gathers his data in family sessions will necessarily be impressed with the actuality of the phenomena and their transactional nature. He will note the repetitive quality of the transactions, and be impressed with the differences between extrafamilial behavior (as it is described to him) and the intrafamilial transactions he has observed. In developing an explanation of John's behavior he will not have to postulate introjection of the other characters; the other characters will be present, showing him behavior which can be operationally described. He will attend not to the inner dialogue, but to the ways in which communication among the members of this group is expressed—both the content and pathways of messages. He will develop a transactional theory to explain the phenomena he is observing.

Now, if we took either of the parents into individual sessions, we would see how each member of the triad has "internalized" the other two. Each member of the triad forms part of the other members' "symbolic reference group." At the same time, they are all influenced by the current familial interactions.

A combination of both sets of data would explain the systemic organization of the family as a natural group and the functioning of each individual within his ecological system.

What are the factors in John's development which the "individual" therapist does not take into account? He is acquainted with extensive observations of John as an infant. He knows something about John's discovery of the world around him and about his processes of assimilation and accommodation to that world. He knows about his language development, and he knows something about John's interactions with his mother. But he has considerably less knowledge of John's relationship to his father, and only a vague understanding of the influence of John's birth on the interactions of the parents. He has no acquaintance with the systemic characteristics of the family—its styles of communicating, styles of solving conflicts, styles of approaching cognitive and affective problems, its myths, the mutually regulatory effects of the interactions of the three members and the differences between dyadic and triadic relationships in the family. If John has siblings, the individual therapist may make use of the vague formulation of "sibling rivalry," concerning interactions between the siblings in relation to their mother (or maybe their father), but he may have no knowledge of the characteristics of sibling interaction and the processes of mutual learning developing in the sibling subgroup. He will not know about the structure of the sibling subsystem, or about the difference between the way the children function when they are with their parents and the way they function without them or in general about the socializing function of the sibling group. He will have an understanding of the child's development of a concept of self via his reflective appraisal of his parents' labeling, but not of the also significant process of development via his siblings.

The family therapist will be aware of many of these factors, but if he works only with the nuclear family, his knowledge also will be incomplete. He may know something about the workings of the extended family—of the relationship of the mother's and father's in-laws to them and how this affects their behavior as spouses and parents; and he may know something of the continuous processes required in the disembedding from the family of origin and the formation of a new family organization. But John, you remember, is 14. What does the family therapist know about the extrafamilial institutions which influence him? What is his school, where for at least 9 years he has been spending more than a third of his waking life, like? The family has relinquished much of the task of socialization to an agency which usually conceives of its task mostly as an input in the cognitive area, and carries on other socializing functions casually, almost inattentively. The family therapist knows little about John's significant relationship with his teacher and less about his relationship to his classroom peers and the influence of class organization as a social context for learning how to learn. He knows little about the development of a sense of competence and effectance in school via mastery of cognitive and affective problems. He also knows little or nothing about the significance of John's peer group outside of school. The need for peer acknowledgment and acceptance has been variously described, but the "hows" of group organization, the systemic characteristics of natural peer groups, and the ways of belonging to and conforming to extrafamilial systems (which may conflict with the family's systems) remain to be studied.

The therapist also knows little or nothing about the influence of the community on John. With the formation of comprehensive mental health centers in disadvantaged areas we are beginning to learn more about the influence of formal and informal agencies on slum children, and sociologists have been interested for a long time now in the slum peer group—the gang. But John is a middle-class child. He may soon come in contact with a peer group which demands that he "drop out" of the adult community and reject its "old morality." If he does so, he will come in conflict with his family: and the family therapist will find himself in a *terra incognita* which requires charting.

These are all significant extrafamiliar influences which the family therapist's scope does not include; furthermore, what we have said about the need to study John's significant ecological contexts also applies to his father and mother.

An ecological theory in psychiatry has to take into account the functioning of the individual in all his social systems and the interrelationships of these systems. Within an ecological concept, with its expanded view of man embedded in his contexts, strategies of intervention that transcend present techniques and disciplines would be developed, drawing from both the behavioral and the social sciences.

I think family therapy as a technique has paved the way for a "psychiatry of context" (both social context and broader environmental contexts). But among all the questions raised, two very important ones remain unanswered.

First, how do we account for man's maintaining a sense of identity while moving through a diversity of ecological contexts in his life? How do we explain his belonging to and responding to the rules of different social systems while maintaining continuity?

Individuals must survive as social beings by conforming to the significant social systems to which they belong. But what happens to the individual who has learned his individual place in a primary group (the family) and incorporated its values, styles and so on, when this group must expand or change? What happens when he affiliates with a new group? How are his previous allegiances and ways of adapting carried over through his contact with new social systems? What happens in the conflict of continuation with circumstance?

Second, just how do the systems with which an individual is involved link with each other? Grinker[6] indicates a direction when he states that:

> Transaction . . . is the relationship of two or more systems within a specified environment which includes both, not as specific entities, but only as they are in relatedness with each other within a specific space-time field. It is a reciprocal and reverberating process. Using such a conceptual scheme we may view relationships of structures, functions, scientific disciplines, methodologies, etc. We may subject each system in the field to inquiry concerning a variety of processes of communication. From these processes we can extrapolate principles which are clearly present in biology, psychology, and sociology. Common to all, however, are relationships which exist independent of source of energy and transmission or power structures; all systems within themselves and among each other are involved in coding, transmitting, decoding, and rearranging information. (p. 33)

The exploration of this (or other) theoretical model to discover its assets and restraints, and the transformation of its general assumptions into empirical questions that can be useful in our clinical work, is an arduous task ahead.

In conclusion let me point out the dangers for the clinician inherent in the confusion of technique and theory. When techniques of intervention become crystallized, a body of theory develops that tends to defend the techniques as derivatives of processes. Classical psychoanalysis, with its emphasis on the individual and on intrapsychic phenomena as separate from their context, has encouraged the development of a diagnostic system and models of delivery of services which do not take into account the complexity of peoples' lives. I think that family therapy, also, will be in danger of ossification if it fails to move towards an ecological theory of man.

REFERENCES

1. BARCAI, A.: From the individual to the family and a step beyond. Paper presented at the 1967 meeting of the American Orthopsychiatric Association, Washington, D.C.
2. BOWEN, M.: Family psychotherapy with schizophrenia in the hospital and in private practice. *In:* Boszormenyi-Nagy, I., and Framo, J. L. (eds.): Intensive Family Therapy. New York, Harper & Row, 1965, pp. 213–243.
3. BOWEN, M.: Presentation of a family experience. Paper presented at the Conference on Systemic Research in Family Interaction, Philadelphia, 1967.
4. FRAMO, J. L.: Rationale and techniques of intensive family therapy. *In:* Boszoremenyi-Nagy, I., and Framo, J. L. (eds.): Intensive Family Therapy. New York, Harper & Row, 1965, pp. 143–212.
5. FRIEDMAN, A. S., ET AL.: Family Treatment of Schizophrenics in the Home. New York, Springer Publishing Company, 1965.
6. GRINKER, ROY S., SR.: Conceptual progress in psychoanalysis. *In:* Marmor, Judd (ed.): Modern Psychoanalysis. New York, Basic Books, Inc., 1968, pp. 19–43.
7. KWIATKOWSKA, H. Y.: Family art therapy. Family Process 6:37–55, 1967.
8. LANDES, J., AND WINTER, W.: A new strategy for treating disintegrating families. Family Process 5:1–20, 1966.
9. LAQUEUR, H. P., LaBURT, H. A., AND MORONG, E.: Multiple family therapy: Further developments. Int. J. Soc. Psychiat. Special Edition 2:70–80, 1964.
10. MacGREGOR, R., ET AL.: Multiple Impact Therapy with Families. New York, McGraw-Hill, Inc., 1964.
11. MINUCHIN, S., ET AL.: Families of the Slums. New York, Basic Books, Inc., 1967.
12. SPECK, R. V.: Psychotherapy of the social network of a schizophrenic family. Paper presented at the 1966 meetings of the American Psychological Association, New York.

John Weakland
Richard Fisch
Paul Watzlawick
Arthur Bodin

Anthropologist-turned-therapist John Weakland, psychiatrist Richard Fisch, and psychologists Paul Watzlawick and Arthur Bodin are all staff members at the Mental Research Institute (MRI) in Palo Alto, California. MRI was one of the earliest centers of family therapy; several of its staff members had a role in formulating the "double-bind" theory of schizophrenia, one of the first models of psychopathology that focused on the role of communications within the family.

Starting in the late 1960s, a group of therapists at MRI began to develop and test "brief therapy," a technique that draws on any useful therapy methods to achieve a positive change in the patient within ten once-a-week sessions. To accomplish this radical goal (many psychoanalytic therapies, for example, require that a patient stay in treatment for years), brief therapy starts from its own set of premises about the nature of psychological problems and of therapy.

One premise is that, no matter what caused it originally, psychological problems will persist "only if they are maintained by ongoing current behavior of the patient and others with whom he interacts." It follows that if the interactions that perpetuate the problem are changed, the problem will be resolved. Therapy can begin a cure by bringing about seemingly minor changes that will initiate a more widespread recovery.

The main practical inspiration for this therapeutic approach was the work of Milton Erickson (see pp. 188–205), both in hypnotherapy and in therapy where he used no hypnosis. Erickson utilized indirect means of influence, often getting a patient to take some action that was symbolic of his cure, but never explicitly mentioning its meaning to the patient. Apart from these covert techniques, Erickson would often simply redefine the situation in a way that allowed the

252

patient to see it differently, and so take steps to alter his behavior for the better.

Eclectic in spirit, the brief-therapy group has borrowed its methods widely. From family therapists, they take techniques of active intervention, juggling families to speed up finding solutions. They also have taken the tactics of assigning "homework" in real life, outside the therapy session.

Brief therapy follows a standard progression. At the first meeting, the therapist tells the patient that therapy will last no more than ten sessions, which sets up the expectation of rapid change. Then the patient is asked to explain why he has come; the therapist keeps questioning the patient until they agree on a concrete behavior that exemplifies the problem. Following this, the therapist is alert for those interactions in the patient's life that allow him to persist with his problem behavior. After this initial analysis of the problem, the therapist and patient set a specific goal that will show the problem is improving. All of this should be done by the second session.

The therapeutic intervention proper takes up most of the remaining sessions. The brief-therapy group sees "insight" as a waste of time in therapy; their focus is on producing the specific change agreed on with the patient. They draw on a wide gamut of techniques, including some that are highly unorthodox. The therapist, for example, may try to defeat a patient's resistance by taking the patient's own line and exaggerating it to the point where the patient himself objects to it; in some cases, the therapist may actually "prescribe" the patient's symptoms. The patient's family or friends may be called upon to create special situations that will get the patient to change.

Finally, at the point of termination, the therapist reviews whatever progress the patient has made, giving the patient full credit for any gains. About three months later, the therapist contacts the patient to see how he is doing, to offer encouragement, and in most cases, to remind him that therapy did not aim for a total cure, but an initial breakthrough.

BRIEF THERAPY: FOCUSED PROBLEM RESOLUTION

by John H. Weakland, Richard Fisch, Paul Watzlawick, and Arthur M. Bodin

In the last few years, brief treatment has been proliferating—both growing and dividing. As Barten's (2) recent collection of papers illustrates, "brief therapy" means many different things to many different therapists. The brief therapy we wish to present here is an outgrowth of our earlier work in that it is based on two ideas central to family therapy: (a) focusing on observable behavioral interaction in the present and (b) deliberate intervention to alter the going system. In pursuing these themes further, however, we have arrived at a particular conceptualization of the nature of human problems and their effective resolution, and of related procedures, that is different from much current family therapy.

We have been developing and testing this approach at the Brief Therapy Center over the past six years. During this period the Center, operating one day a week has treated 97 cases, in which 236 individuals were seen. (We have also had extensive experience using the same approach with private patients, but these cases have not been systematically followed up and evaluated.) These 97 cases reached us through a considerable variety of referral sources, and no deliberate selection was exercised. As a result, although probably a majority of our cases involve rather common marital and family problems, the sample covers a wide range overall. We have dealt with white, black, and oriental patients from 5 to over 60 years old, from welfare recipients to the very wealthy and with a variety of both acute and chronic problems. These included school and work difficulties; identity crises; marital, family, and sexual problems; delinquency, alcohol, and eating problems; anxiety, depression, and schizophrenia. Regardless of the nature or severity of the problem, each case has been limited to a maximum of ten one-hour sessions, usually at weekly intervals. Under these circumstances, our treatment has been successful—in terms of achieving limited but significant goals related to the patients' main complaints—in about three-fourths of these cases. We have also demonstrated and taught our approach to a number of other therapists in our area.

We present our approach here for wider consideration. Any form of treatment, however, is difficult to convey adequately by a purely verbal account, without demonstration and direct observation. We will, therefore, begin by discussing the significance and nature of our basic premises in comparison with other forms of treatment. Hopefully, this will provide an orienting context for the subsequent description—supplemented with illustrative case material—of our interrelated concepts, plan of treatment, specific techniques, and results.

PSYCHOTHERAPY—PREMISES AND PRACTICES

In characterizing treatment approaches, although some over-simplification may result, outlining basic premises may make their nature—and especially, their implications—more plain. Often, attention is concentrated on what is explicit and detailed, while what is common and general is neglected. Yet, the more general an idea, the more determinative of behavior it is—especially if its existence is not explicitly recognized. This holds for interpersonal influence as well as individual thinking and behavior; Robert Rosenthal's (21) experiments demonstrate how the beliefs, assumptions, expectations, and biases of an experimenter or interviewer have a profound effect on his subjects. Similarly, the beliefs and theories held by a therapist may strongly influence not only his technique but also the length and outcome of his treatments—by affecting his patient's behavior, his evaluation of that behavior, or both.

For instance, if schizophrenia is conceptualized as a gradual, irreversible mental deterioration involving loss of contact with reality, then attempts at psychotherapeutic contact make little sense, and the only reasonable course of action is long-term hospitalization. The hospitalized patient is then likely to react in a way that clearly justifies this initial "preventive" action. Alternatively, if schizophrenia is seen as a manifestation of a dysfunctional structure of family relationships, the outlook is different and more hopeful, although basic restructuring of the family system is now likely to be seen as necessary.

Again, in terms of the postulates of classical psychoanalytic theory, symptom removal must perforce lead to symptom displacement and exacerbation of the patient's condition, since it deals only with manifestations of deeper problems. The premises of the theory permit no other conclusion, except the alternative of claiming that the problem must not have been a "real" one (22). On the other hand, in therapies based on learning or deconditioning theories, symptom manipulation is consistent with the theoretical premises. This enables the therapist to try very different interventions—and, to some extent, constrains him to do so.

That is, all theories of psychotherapy (including our own) have limitations, of practice as well as conception, that are logically inherent in their own nature. Equally important, these limitations are often attributed to *human* nature, rather than to the nature of the theory. It is all too easy to overlook this and become enmeshed in unrecognized, circular explanations. Stating the basic premises of any psychotherapeutic theory as clearly and explicitly as possible at least helps toward perceiving also its implications, limitations, and possible alternatives.

OUR BRIEF THERAPY—BASES AND COMPARISONS

Much of the shorter-term treatment that has recently developed in response to the pressure of patient needs and situational limitations consists essentially of briefer versions of conventional forms of individual or family therapy. The same basic assumptions are involved, and, correspondingly, the methods used are similar, except for limited adaptations to the realities of fewer sessions (3, 5, 20). This is expectable, as the usual frameworks naturally offer more restraints to innovation than encouragement and guidance. Within their terms, new methods are apt to appear strange and unreliable (15). Consequently, "brief therapy" ordinarily connotes an expedient that may be necessary when a preferred treatment is not available or is considered not feasible—since the "best" therapies often require patients equipped with rather exceptional resources of time, money, intelligence, persistence, and verbal sophistication. The goals of such brief therapy correspondingly are conceived as limited "first aid"—such as relief of some pressing but not fundamental aspect of the patient's problems, or a supportive holding action until really thorough treatment becomes possible.

We recognize and value the practical and economic advantages for patients and society of shortening treatment. We do not, however, see our own kind of brief treatment as an expedient, nor is brevity in itself a goal to us, except that we believe setting time limits on treatment has some positive influence on both therapists and patients. Rather the nature of our therapy, including its brevity, is primarily a consequence of our premises about the nature and handling of psychiatric problems.

Our fundamental premise is that regardless of their basic origins and etiology—if, indeed, these can ever be reliably determined—the kinds of problems people bring to psychotherapists *persist* only if they are maintained by ongoing current behavior of the patient and others with whom he interacts. Correspondingly, if such problem-maintaining behavior is appropriately changed or eliminated, the problem will be resolved or vanish, regardless of its nature, origin, or duration (24, 26). Our general principles and specific practices of treatment all relate closely to these two assumptions.

This view, like any other, must be judged by its fruits rather than by its seeds. Yet, a brief consideration of two areas of shared prior experience and interest that appear to have had major implications for our present joint position may clarify it and give some due acknowledgment.

Our present brief therapy is visible first as pursuing further two main aspects of family therapy, in which we have all been extensively involved. A decade and a half ago family therapy began to focus attention on observable behavioral interaction and its influence, both among family members and between them and the therapist, rather than on long-past events or inferred mental processes of individuals (10). In line with this, we now see disturbed, deviant, or difficult behavior in an individual (like behavior generally) as essentially a social phenomenon, occurring as one aspect of a system, reflecting some dysfunction in that system, and best treated by some appropriate modification of that system. We differ, however, with those family therapists who consider the dysfunction involved to be necessarily a fundamental aspect of the system's organization and requiring correspondingly fundamental changes in the system. Instead, we now believe that apparently minor changes in overt behavior or its verbal labeling often are sufficient to initiate progressive developments. Further, while we recognize that along with its obvious disadvantages symptomatic behavior usually has some recognizable advantages or "pay-offs"—such as providing leverage in controlling relationships—we no longer consider these especially significant as causes of problems or obstacles to change.

Family therapy also has prompted greater activity by therapists. Once family interaction was seen as significant for problems, it followed that the therapist should aim to change the going system. Extending this, we now see the therapist's primary task as one of taking deliberate action to alter poorly functioning patterns of interaction as powerfully, effectively, and efficiently as possible.

On the matter of *how* the therapist can actively influence behavior effectively—the strategy and techniques of change—we are especially indebted to the hypnotic work of Milton Erickson and his closely related psychotherapy. Two points have been particularly influential. First, although Erickson is much concerned with how overt behavior affects feelings or states of mind, his moves to change existing behavior usually depend upon implicit or indirect means of influence. Even when behavior is explicitly discussed, his aim often is not to clarify the "reality" of a situation but to alter and ameliorate it by some redefinition. Second, both as hypnotist and therapist, Erickson has emphasized the importance of "accepting what the client offers," and turning this to positive use—in ways we will illustrate later—even if what is "offered" might ordinarily appear as resistance or pathology.

While our present approach thus derives directly from basic family therapy, in part, and from Erickson's work, in part, it also differs from both. For example, many family therapists attempt to bring about change largely by explicit clarification of the nature of family behavior and interaction. Such an attempt now seems to us like a family version of promoting "insight," in which one tries to make clear to families the covert rules that have guided them; we ordinarily avoid this. Meanwhile, our conceptualization of problems and treatment appears at least more general and explicit than Erickson's and probably different in various specific respects.

On the other hand, similarities as well as differences are observable between our treatment approach and other approaches with which we have had little interaction. For example, within the general field of family therapy, we share with the crisis-intervention therapy of Pittman, Langsley, and their co-workers (18) beliefs in the importance of situational change for the onset of problems and of both directive measures and negotiation of conflicts in promoting better functioning in family systems. Minuchin and Montalvo (16), together with a number of their colleagues at the Philadelphia Child Guidance Clinic, have increasingly emphasized active intervention aimed at particular reorderings of family relationship structure to achieve rapid problem resolution; we often pursue similar aims. Other family therapists than ourselves, notably Bowen, assign patients homework as part of treatment. Work with families similar to our own is also being developed abroad, for instance, at the Athenian Institute of Anthropos under Dr. George Vassilou and at the Istituo per lo Studio della Famiglia in Milan, under Prof. Dr. Mara Selvini Palazzoli. In addition, the behavior modification school of therapy involves a number of ideas and interventions rather parallel to ours, although that field still appears to give little attention to systems of interacton. Furthermore, as noted later, a number of the techniques of intervention we utilize have also been used and described, though usually in a different conceptual context, by other therapists.

In sum, many particular conceptual and technical elements of our approach are not uniquely ours. We do, however, see as distinctive the overall system of explicitly stated and integated ideas and practices that constitute our approach.

MAIN PRINCIPLES OF OUR WORK

1. We are frankly symptom-oriented, in a broad sense. Patients or their family members come with certain complaints and accepting them for treatment involves a responsibility for relieving these complaints. Also, since deviant symptomatic behavior and its accompanying vicious circles of reaction and counter-reaction can themselves be so disruptive of system functioning, we believe that one should not hasten to seek other and deeper roots of pathology. The presenting problem offers, in one package, what the patient is ready to work on, a concentrated manifestation of whatever is wrong, and a concrete index of any progress made.

2. We view the problems that people bring to psychotherapists (except, of course, clearly organic psychiatric syndromes) as situational difficulties between people—problems of interaction. Most often this involves the identified patient and his family; however, other systems such as a patient's

involvement with others in a work situation may be important at times.

3. We regard such problems as primarily an outcome of everyday difficulties, usually involving adaptation to some life change, that have been mishandled by the parties involved. When ordinary life difficulties are handled badly, unresolved problems tend increasingly to involve other life activities and relationships in impasses or crises, and symptom formation results.

4. While fortuitous life difficulties, such as illness, accidents, or loss of a job, sometimes appear to initiate the development of a problem, we see normal transitional steps in family living as the most common and important "everyday difficulties" that may lead to problems. These transitions include: the change from the voluntary relationship of courtship to the commitment of marriage, and from this to the less reversible commitment when the first child is born; the sharing of influence with other authorities required when a child enters school, and with the child himself and his peers in the adolescent period; the shift from a child-oriented marital relationship back to a two-party system when the children leave the home, and its intensification at retirement; and return to single life at the death of one spouse. Although most people manage to handle these transitions at least passably well, they all require major changes in personal relationships that may readily be mishandled. This view is similar to that of Erickson and Haley(12).

5. We see two main ways by which "problems" are likely to develop: if people treat an ordinary difficulty as a "problem" or if they treat an ordinary (or worse) difficulty as no problem at all—that is, by either overemphasis or underemphasis of difficulties in living.

The first appears related to utopian expectations of life. There are countless difficulties which are part and parcel of the everyday business of living for which no known ideal or ultimate solutions exist. Even when relatively severe, these are manageable in themselves but can readily become "problems" as a result of a belief that there should or must be an ideal, ultimate solution for them. For instance, there apparently has been a "generation gap" for the past 5000 years that we know of, but its difficulties only became greatly exacerbated into a "problem" when many people became convinced that it should be closed.

Inversely, but equally, "problems" can arise out of the

denial of manifest difficulties—which could be seen as uto-pian assertions. For instance, the husband and wife who insist their marriage was made in heaven, or the parents who deny the existence of any conflicts with their children—and who may contend that any one seeing any difficulty must be either bad or mad—are likely to be laying the foundation for some outbreak of symptomatic behavior.

Two other aspects of this matter need mention. First, over-or under-emphasis of life difficulties is not entirely a matter of personal or family characteristics; this depends also on more general cultural attitudes and conceptions. While these often may be helpful in defining and dealing with the com-mon vicissitudes of social life, they can also be unrealistic and provoke problems. For example, except for the death of a spouse, our own culture characterizes most of the transi-tions listed earlier as wonderful steps forward along life's path. Since all of these steps ordinarily involve significant and inescapable difficulties, such over-optimistic characterization increases the likelihood of problems developing—especially for people who take what they are told seriously. Second, inappropriate evaluation and handling of difficult situations is often multiplied by interaction between various parties in-volved. If two persons have similar inappropriate views, they may reciprocally reinforce their common error, while if one over-emphasizes a difficulty and another under-emphasizes it, interacton may lead to increasing polarization and an even more inappropriate stance by each.

6. We assume that once a difficulty begins to be seen as a "problem," the continuation, and often the exacerbation, of this problem results from the creation of a positive feedback loop, most often centering around those very behaviors of the individuals in the system that are intended to resolve the diffi-culty: The original difficulty is met with an attempted "solu-tion" that intensifies the original difficulty, and so on and on (26).

Consider, for instance, a common pattern between a depressed patient and his family. The more they try to cheer him up and make him see the positive side of life, the more depressed the patient is likely to get: "They don't even under-stand me." The action meant to *alleviate* the behavior of the other party *aggravates* it; the "cure" becomes worse than the original "disease." Unfortunately, this usually remains un-noted by those involved and even is disbelieved if any one else tries to point it out.

7. We view long-standing problems or symptoms not as "chronicity" in the usual implication of some basic defect in the individual or family, nor even that a problem has become "set" over time, but as the persistence of a *repetitively* poorly handled difficulty. People with chronic problems have just been struggling inappropriately for longer periods of time. We, therefore, assume that chronic problems offer as great an opportunity for change as acute problems and that the principal difference lies in the usually pessimistic expectations of therapists facing a chronic situation.

8. We see the resolution of problems as primarily requiring a substitution of behavior patterns so as to interrupt the vicious, positive feedback circles. Other less destructive and less distressing behaviors are potentially open to the patient and involved family members at all times. It is usually impossible, however, for them to change from their rigidly patterned, traditional unsuccessful problem-solving behavior to more appropriate behavior on their own initiative. This is especially likely when such usual behavior is culturally supported, as is often the case: Everyone *knows* that people should do their best to encourage and cheer up a loved one who is sad and depressed. Such behavior is both "right" and "logical"—but often it just doesn't work.

9. In contrast, we seek means of promoting beneficial change that works, even if our remedies appear illogical. For instance, we would be likely to comment on how sad a depressed patient looks and to suggest that there must be some real and important reason for this. Once given some information on the situation, we might say it is rather strange that he is not even *more* depressed. The usual result, paradoxical as it may seem, is that the patient begins to look and sound better.

10. In addition to accepting what the patient offers, and reversing the usual "treatment" that has served to make matters worse, this simple example also illustrates our concept of "thinking small" by focusing on the symptom presented and working in a limited way towards its relief.

We contend generally that change can be effected most easily if the goal of change is reasonably small and clearly stated. Once the patient has experienced a small but definite change in the seemingly monolithic nature of the problem most real to him, the experience leads to further, self-induced changes in this, and often also, in other areas of his life. That is, beneficent circles are initiated.

This view may seem insensitive to the "real," "big," or "basic," problems that many therapists and patients expect to be changed by therapy. Such goals are often vague or unrealistic, however, so that therapy which is very optimistic in concept easily becomes lengthy and disappointing in actual practice. Views of human problems that are either pessimistic about change or grandiose about the degree of change needed undermine the therapist's potentially powerful influence for limited but significant change.

11. Our approach is fundamentally pragmatic. We try to base our conceptions and our interventions on direct observation in the treatment situation of *what* is going on in systems of human interaction, *how* they continue to function in such ways, and *how* they may be altered most effectively.

Correspondingly, we avoid the question *"Why?"* From our standpoint, this question is not relevant and involvement with it commonly heads toward concerns about "deeper" underlying causes—historical, mental, familial—of problem behavior and about "insight" into these.

That is, the question "Why?" tends to promote an individualistic, voluntaristic, and rationalistic conception of human behavior, rather than one focused on systems of interaction and influence. Moreover, since underlying causes inherently are inferential rather than observable, concern about them distracts a therapist from close observation of the present problem and what behavior may be perpetuating it.

On the basis of this general conception of problems and their resolution, which is discussed more fully in Watzlawick, Weakland, and Fisch (25), we can now describe the overall practical approach and specific techniques that we utilize.

OPERATION OF THE BRIEF THERAPY CENTER

Our handling of all cases follows a six-stage schema, although in practice there may be some overlap among these:
1. Introduction to our treatment set-up.
2. Inquiry and definition of the problem.
3. Estimation of behavior maintaining the problem.
4. Setting goals of treatment.
5. Selecting and making behavioral interventions.
6. Termination.

Each of these will now be considered in order.

Introduction to Our Treatment Set-up

Patients intentionally are accepted with no screening. A first appointment is set by the project secretary whenever an applicant calls and there is a vacancy in our schedule. No waiting lists are kept; when we have no vacancy, people are referred elsewhere.

At the first meeting, our secretary has the patient or family fill out a form covering basic demographic data and brings him or them to the treatment room. The therapist begins by explaining the physical and organizational arrangements, mentioning the potential advantages for treatment of the recording and observation, and requests written consent to this. Only two patients have ever declined to proceed on this basis. The therapist also tells the patient at once that we work on a maximum of ten sessions per case; this helps to set a positive expectation of rapid change.

Definition of the Problem

Since our treatment focus is symptomatic, we want first to get a clear and explicit statement of the presenting complaint. Therefore, as soon as the therapist has taken a brief record of the referral source and any previous treatment, he asks what problem has brought the patient to see us. If a patient states a number of complaints, we will ask which is the most important. In marital or family cases, since viewpoints may differ, although they often are plainly interrelated, we ask each of the parties involved to state his own main complaint. From the beginning, then, we are following a form of the general principle, "Start where the patient is at."

Fairly often, the patient will give an adequate answer—by which we mean a clear statement referring to concrete behavior. In many cases, however, the response will leave the presenting problem still in doubt. Further inquiry is then needed to define more clearly this point of departure for the entire treatment. For example, patients with previous treatment experience or psychological sophistication are likely, after only the briefest mention of any present behavioral difficulty, to launch into discussion of presumed underlying matters, especially intrapsychic factors and family history, presenting these as the "real problem." We then press the question of what particular difficulties in living have brought them to see us *now*. To make things more specific, we often ask such questions as "What do you now do because of your problem that you want to stop doing, or do differently?" and "What would you like to do that your problem interferes with doing now?" Such inquiries also begin to raise the related question of treatment goals.

Other patients, especially younger ones, may state their complaints in vague terms that lack reference to any concrete behavior or life situation: "I don't know who I really am"; "We just can't communicate." Such patients can be particularly difficult initially. We find it important not to accept such statements as appropriate and informative but to continue inquiry until at least the therapist, if not the patient, can formulate a concrete, behavioral picture of the problem—of which such attachment to vague and often grandiose thinking and talking may itself be a major aspect.

Estimation of Behavior Maintaining the Problem

Our view, as mentioned earlier, is that problem behavior persists only when it is repeatedly reinforced in the course of social interaction between the patient and other significant people. Usually, moreover, it is just what the patient and these others are doing in their efforts to deal with the problem—often those attempts at help that appear most "logical" or unquestionably right—that is most important in maintaining or exacerbating it.

Once behavior is observed and considered in this light, the way this occurs is often rather obvious: The wife who nags her husband and hides his bottle in her efforts to save him from his alcohol problem and succeeds only in continually keeping drinking uppermost in his mind; the forgiving husband who never criticizes his wife until she feels he doesn't care anything about her, whatever she does, and becomes depressed—and he is forgiving of that too; the parents of a child dissatisfied with school who "encourage" him by talking all the more about how important and great education is—instead of it being a necessary drag. In other instances, of course, the reinforcements may be more difficult to perceive, either because they are subtle or complex—nonverbal behaviors, contradictions between statements and actions, different behaviors by several persons—or because even therapists are conditioned to accept cultural standards of logic and rightness without examining whether things really work that way.

In practice, the therapist first simply asks the patient and any family members present how they have been trying to deal with the problem. This alone may lead rapidly to a view of what keeps things going badly. If not, the inquiry, aiming always at concrete behavior, can be pursued at more length and in more detail, but sympathetically—the therapist's aim is to get enough information to understand what is happening, for which he needs cooperation, not to confront people with their mistakes. In addition to what the patient or others state explicitly, it is important to note *how* they discuss the problem and its handling, including their interaction. Such inquiry is likely to disclose a number of things that play some part in maintaining the problem, but working briefly demands choosing priorities. On the basis of observation and experience, one must judge which behavior seems most crucial.

Setting Goals of Treatment

Setting a goal both acts as a positive suggestion that change is feasible in the time allotted and provides a criterion of therapeutic accomplishment for therapist and patient. We, therefore, want goals stated clearly in terms of observable, concrete behavior to minimize any possibility of uncertainty or denial later. If parents bring us a child because he is failing in school, we ask for an explicit criterion of satisfactory progress—because we want to avoid subsequent equivocations such as "He is getting B's now instead of F's, but he isn't really learning enough." Also, we steer toward "thinking small" for reasons already discussed. Therefore, our usual inquiry is something like "At a minimum, what (change in) behavior would indicate to you that a definite step forward has been made on your problem?"

Concerning goals especially, however, patients often talk in vague or sweeping terms, despite our efforts to frame the question in terms of specific behavior. We then try to get more concrete answers by further discussion, clarification, and presentation of examples of possible goals for consideration. With vague, grandiose, or utopian patients, we have found it helpful to reverse our field, bringing them down to earth by suggesting goals that are too far out even for them. This again involves accepting what the patient offers, and even enlarging on this, in order to change it. For example, a student who was already in his mid-20's and was still being supported by a working mother told us he was studying "philosophical anthropology" in order to bring the light of India and China to bear on the West. He also, however, mentioned some interest in attending a well-known school of Indian music. It was then pointed out to him that this represented a rather limited aim compared to his concern to unite the spirituality of India with the practical communism of China and use both to reconstruct Western society. He then said that, since he was not doing well in his studies and was short of money, if he could secure a scholarship and really learn Indian music, this would be quite enough accomplishment for the present.

We usually are able, directly or indirectly, to obtain a stated goal that appears sufficiently explicit and appropriate to the problem. In some cases, however, we have not been able to do so. Either the patient persisted in stating only vague, untestable goals, or, rarely, the patient stated and stuck to an explicit goal which we judged inappropriate to his problem. Then we do not dispute what the patient insists on but privately set our own goal for the case by joint staff discussion of what sort of behavior would best exemplify positive change for the particular patient and problem. In fact, some such discussion occurs for all cases; at the least, the staff must always judge whether the patient's statement of his goal is adequate. Also, there is always staff discussion of intermediate behavioral goals; how does the patient—or his family members—need to behave so that the specific goal of treatment will follow?

Our aim is to have a definite goal established by the second session, but gathering and digesting the information needed for this sometimes takes longer. Occasionally, we may revise the original goal in the course of treatment or add a secondary goal.

Selecting and Making Interventions

Once we have formed a picture of current behavior central to the problem and estimated what different behavior would lead to the specific goal selected, the task is one of intervening to promote such change. This stage must be discussed at some length, since it ordinarily constitutes the largest, most varied, and probably most unusual part of our treatment.

Change and "insight." We have already stated that our aim is to produce behavior change and that we do not see working toward insight, at either an individual or a family level, as of much use in this. In fact, working toward insight can even be counter-productive. Simple, practical-minded patients are often put off by this, since they want action and results, while more intellectually minded patients are likely to welcome such an approach but use it to delay or defeat any change in actual behavior. However, in addition to suggesting or prescribing changes in overt behavior, we do utilize interpretations. Our aim, though, is simply the useful relabeling of behavior. Patients often interpret their own behavior, or that of others, in ways that make for continuing difficulties. If we can only redefine the meaning or implications attributed to the behavior, this itself may have a powerful effect on attitudes, responses and relationships. Such interpretation might look like an attempt to impart insight, but it is not. Using interpretation to promote insight implies that truth can helpfully be disclosed and recognized. This is not our aim or our belief. Rather, our view is that redefining behavior labeled "hostile" as "concerned interest," for example, may be therapeutically useful whether or not *either* label is "true," and that such truth can never be firmly established. All that is observable is that some labels provoke difficulties, while others, achievable by redefinition, promote adjustment and harmony—but this is enough.

Such relabeling may be especially important with rigid patients. It does not require overt behavior change, and it may even be accomplished without the need for *any* active cooperation by the patient or any family member. If the therapist's redefinition of an action or situation is not openly challenged—which can usually be arranged—then the meaning and effects of that behavior have already been altered.

Use of idiosyncratic characteristics and motivation. We attempt early in treatment to determine what approach would appeal most to the particular patient—to observe "where he lives" and meet this need, whether it is to believe in the magical, to defeat the expert, to be a caretaker of someone, to face a challenge, or whatever. Since the consequences of any such characteristic depend greatly on the situation in which it operates and how this is defined, we see these characteristics of different individuals not as obstacles or deficiencies, but as potential levers for useful intervention by the therapist.

For example, certain patients appear inclined toward defeating therapists, despite their request for help. This may be indicated by a history of unsuccessful treatment, repeated failure to understand explanations or carry out instructions, and so on. In such cases, the easiest and most effective course may be for the therapist to insist that the patient cannot possibly resolve his problem and that treatment can at most help him to endure it better. The patient is then likely to defeat *this* stance by improving.

A middle-aged widow first came to us with a complaint about the behavior of her 18-year-old son: delinquency, school failures, anger, and threatened violence toward her. She stated this was her only problem, although she also mentioned that she was an epileptic and was unable to use her right arm as a result of a work injury. Both mother and son had had about two years of previous therapy. We first suggested directly that her son was acting like a difficult, provoking, overgrown kid and, accordingly, she might gain by handling him more firmly in a few simple ways. She quickly thwarted such suggestions by increasing claims of helplessness: Now the epilepsy was emphasized; there was trouble with the other arm, too; a hysterectomy and appendectomy were also reported, along with childhood rheumatic fever, bleeding gums, troubles with her former husband and with her mother-in-law, constant worsening financial crises, and much more. In short, she was already a woman carrying on bravely amidst a sea of troubles that would have totally swamped anyone else; how could we ask her to do more yet? We then changed our approach to utilize this characteristic opposition. We began to insist to her that she was being unduly optimistic, was minimizing her troubles in an unrealistic way, and was not recognizing that the future very probably held even greater disasters for her, both individually and in terms of her son's behavior. It took some doing to surpass her own pessimistic line, but once we were able to do so, she began to improve. She started to oppose our pessimism—which she could only do by claiming and proving that she was not *that* sick and helpless—and to take a much more assertive attitude with her son, to which he responded well.

Directed behavior change. One of our main stated aims is to change overt behavior—to get people to stop doing things that maintain the problem and to do others that will lead toward the goal of treatment. While we are willing to issue authoritative directions, we find compliant patients rather rare. After all, most patients have already been exposed to lots of advice. If it was good, they must have some difficulty about profiting from advice; if it was bad, some preparation is needed for them to respond to quite different advice. Moreover, again, it is often just that behavior that seems most logical to people that is perpetuating their problems. They then need special help to do what will seem illogical and mistaken. When sitting on a nervous horse, it is not easy to follow the instructor's orders to let go of the reins. One *knows* the horse will run away, even though it is really the pull on the reins that is making him jump.

Behavioral instructions therefore are more effective when carefully framed and made indirect, implicit, or apparently insignificant. When requesting changes, it is helpful to minimize either the matter or the manner of the request. We will suggest a change rather than order it. If the patient still appears reluctant, we will back off further. We may then suggest it is too early to do that thing; the patient might think about it but be sure not to take any action yet. When we do request particular actions, we may ask that they be done once or twice at most before we meet again. We may request only actions that will appear minor to the patient, although in our view they represent the first in a series of steps, or involve a microcosm of the central difficulty. For example, a patient who avoids making any demands of others in his personal relationships may be assigned the task of asking for one gallon of gasoline at a service station, specifically requesting each of the usual free services, and offering a twenty-dollar bill in payment [sic].

This example also illustrates our use of "homework" assignments to be carried out between sessions. Homework of various kinds is regularly employed, both to utilize time more fully and to promote positive change where it counts most, in real life outside the treatment room.

Paradoxical instructions. Most generally, paradoxical instruction involves prescribing behavior that appears in opposition to the goals being sought, in order actually to move toward them. This may be seen as an inverse to pursuing "logical" courses that lead only to more trouble. Such instructions probably constitute the most important single class of interventions in our treatment. This technique is not new; aspects and examples of it have been described by Frankl (8, 9), Haley (11), Newton (17) and Watzlawick, *et al.* (24). We have simply related this technique to our overall approach and elaborated on its use.

Paradoxical instruction is used most frequently in the form of case-specific "symptom prescription," the apparent encouragement of symptomatic or other undesirable behavior in order to lessen such behavior or bring it under control. For example, a patient who complains of a circumscribed, physical symptom—headache, insomnia, nervous mannerisms, or whatever—may be told that during the coming week, usually for specified periods, he should make every effort to increase the symptom. A motivating explanation usually is given e.g., that if he can succeed in making it worse, he will at least suffer less from a feeling of helpless lack of control. Acting on such a prescription usually results in a *decrease* of the symptom—which is desirable. But even if the patient makes the symptom increase, this too is good. He has followed the therapist's instruction, and the result has shown that the apparently unchangeable problem can change. Patients often present therapists with impossible-looking problems, to which every possible response seems a poor one. It is comforting, in turn, to be able to offer the patient a "therapeutic double bind" (4), which promotes progress no matter which alternative response he makes.

The same approach applies equally to problems of interaction. When a schizophrenic son used bizarre, verbal behavior to paralyze appropriate action by his parents, we suggested that when he needed to defend himself against the parents' demands, he could intimidate them by acting crazy. Since this instruction was given in the parents' presence, there were two paradoxical positive effects: the son decreased his bizarreness and the parents became less anxious and paralyzed by any such behavior.

Not infrequently, colleagues find it hard to believe that patients will really accept such outlandish prescriptions, but they usually do so readily. In the first place, the therapist occupies a position of advice-giving expert. Second, he takes care to frame his prescriptions in a way most likely to be accepted, from giving a rationale appropriate to the particular patient to refusing any rationale on the grounds that the patient needs to discover some things quite unanticipated. Third, we often are really just asking the patient to do things they already are doing, only on a different basis.

We may also encourage patients to use similar paradoxes themselves, particularly with spouses or children. Thus, a parent concerned about her child's poor school homework (but who probably was covertly discouraging him) was asked to teach the child more self-reliance by offering incorrect answers to the problems he was asking help in solving.

Paradoxical instructions at a more general level are often used also. For example, in direct contrast to our name and ten-session limit, we almost routinely stress "going slow" to our patients at the outset of treatment and, later, by greeting a patient's report of improvement with a worried look and the statement, "I think things are moving a bit too fast." We also do the same thing more implicitly, by our emphasis on minimal goals, or by pointing out possible disadvantages of improvement to patients, "You would like to do much better at work, but are you prepared to handle the problem of envy by your colleagues?" Such warnings paradoxically promote rapid improvement, apparently by reducing any anxiety about change and increasing the patient's desire to get on with things to counteract the therapist's apparent overcautiousness.

On the same principle, when a patient shows unusually rapid or dramatic improvement, after acknowledging this change we may prescribe a relapse, on the rationale that it further increases control: "Now you have managed to turn the symptom off. If you can manage to turn it back on during this next week, you will have achieved even more control over it." This intervention, similar to Rosen's "re-enacting the psychosis" (18) and related techniques of Erickson, anticipates that in some patients improvement may increase apprehension about change and meets this danger by paradoxically redefining any relapse that might occur as a step forward rather than backward.

Since we as therapists are by definition experts, giving authoritative instructions on both thinking and acting, another pervasive element of paradox is created by the fact that ordinarily we do so only tentatively, by suggestions or questions rather than direct orders, and often adopt a "one-down" position of apparent ignorance or confusion. We find that patients, like other people, accept and follow advice more readily when we avoid "coming on strong."

Utilization of interpersonal influence. Although many of our treatment sessions include directly only one therapist and one patient, we consider and utilize more extended interpersonal relationships constantly in our work. First, even when we see only the "identified patient," we conceive the problem in terms of some system of relationships and problem-maintaining behavior involving his family, his friends, or his work situation. Therefore, we believe that any interventions made with the patient must also take their probable consequences for others into account. Equally, however, useful interventions may be made at any point in the system, and frequently it appears more effective to focus our efforts on someone other than the identified patient. Where a child is the locus of the presenting problem, we very commonly see the whole family only once or twice. After this we see the parents only and work with them on modifying their handling of the child or their own interaction. With couples also, we may see the spouses separately for the most part, often spending more time with the one seen by them as "normal." Our point is that effective intervention anywhere in a system produces changes throughout, but according to what the situation offers, one person or another may be more accessible to us, more open to influence, or a better lever for change in the system.

Second, the therapist and the observers also constitute a system of relationships that is frequently used to facilitate treatment. With patients who find it difficult to accept advice directly from a real live person, an observer may make comments to the therapist over the intercom phone to be relayed to the patient from this unseen and presumably objective authority. When a patient tends to disagree constantly, an observer may enter and criticize the therapist for his "poor understanding" of the case, forming an apparent alliance with the patient. The observer can then often successfully convey rephrased versions of what the therapist was offering originally. With patients who alternate between two different stances, two members of the treatment team may agree, separately, with the two positions. Then, whatever course the patient takes next he is going along with a therapist's interpretation, and further suggestions can be given and accepted more successfully. Such therapist-observer interaction strategies can bring about change rapidly even with supposedly "difficult" patients.*

As may be evident, all of these techniques of intervention are means toward maximizing the range and power of the therapist's influence. Some will certainly see, and perhaps reject, such interventions as manipulative. Rather than arguing over this, we will simply state our basic view. First, influence is an inherent element in all human contact. Second, the therapist's functioning necessarily includes this fact of life, but goes much further; professionally he is a specialist at influence. People come to a therapist because they are not satisfied with some aspect of their living, have been unable to change it, and are seeking help in this. In taking any case, therefore, the therapist accepts the assignment of influencing people's behavior, feelings, or ideas toward desirable ends.

---

*Team work facilitates such interventions but actually is seldom essential. A single therapist who is flexible and not unduly concerned about being correct and consistent can also utilize similar techniques—for example, by stating two different positions himself.

Accordingly, third, the primary responsibility of the therapist
is to seek out and apply appropriate and effective means of
influence. Of course, this includes taking full account of the
patient's stated and observed situation and aims. Given these,
though, the therapist still must make choices of what to say
and do, and equally what not to say and do. This inherent responsibility cannot be escaped by following some standard
method of treatment regardless of its results, by simply following the patient's lead, or even by following a moral ideal
of always being straightforward and open with the patient.
Such courses, even if possible, themselves represent strategic
choices. To us, the most fundamental point is whether the
therapist attempts to deny the necessity of such choices to
himself, not what he tells the patient about them. We believe
the better course is to recognize this necessity, to try whatever
means of influence are judged most promising in the circumstances, and to accept responsibility for the consequences.

Termination. Whether cases run the limit of ten sessions or
goals are achieved sooner, we usually briefly review the
course of treatment with the patient, pointing out any apparent gains—giving the patient maximum credit for this
achievement—and noting any matters unresolved. We also remark on the probable future beyond termination, ordinarily
in connection with reminding patients that we will be contact-
ing them, for a follow-up interview in about three months.
This discussion usually embodies positive suggestions about
further improvement. We may remind patients that our treatment was not intended to achieve final solutions, but an initial breakthrough on which they themselves can build further.
In a minority of cases, however—particularly with nega-
tivistic patients, ones who have difficulty acknowledging help
from anyone, or those fond of challenges—we may take an
opposite tack, minimizing any positive results of treatment
and expressing skepticism about any progress in the future. In
both instances, our aim is the same, to extend our therapeutic
influence beyond the period of actual contact.

In some cases, we encounter patients who make progress
but seem unsure of this and concerned about termination. We
often meet this problem by means of terminating without termination. That is, we say we think enough has been accomplished to terminate, but this is not certain; it can really be
judged only by how actual life experience goes over a period
of time. Therefore, we propose to halt treatment, but to keep
any remainder of the ten sessions "in the bank," available to

draw on if the patient should encounter some special difficulty later. Usually, the patient then departs more at ease and
does not call upon us further.

CONCLUSION: IMPLICATIONS

In this paper we have set forth a particular conception of
the nature of psychiatric problems, described a corresponding
brief treatment approach and techniques, and presented some
results of their application. Clearly, further clinical-research
should be done, as important problems obviously remain;
goals are still difficult to set in certain types of cases, the
choice of interventions has not been systematized, evaluation
is not perfected. Concurrently, though, there should also be
more thinking about the broader significance of these ideas
and methods. Our results already give considerable evidence
for the usefulness of our general conception of human problems and their practical handling. Since this is both quite different from more common views and potentially widely
relevant, we will conclude with a tentative consideration of
some broad implications of our work.

The most immediate and evident potential of our work is
for more effective use of existing psychiatric facilities and
personnel. This could include reduction in the usual length of
treatment and a corresponding increase in the number of patients treated, with no sacrifice of effectiveness. In fact, our
approach gives promise of more than ordinary effectiveness
with a variety of common but refractory problems, such as
character disorders, marital difficulties, psychoses, and
chronic problems generally. Further, it is not restricted to
highly educated and articulate middle-class patients but is applicable to patients of whatever class and educational background.

In addition, our approach is relatively clear and simple. It
might therefore be feasible to teach its effective use to considerable numbers of lay therapists. Even if some continuing
supervision from professionals should be necessary, the combination of brief treatment and many therapists thus made
possible could help greatly in meeting present needs for psychological help. Although this kind of development would
have little to offer private practice, it could be significant for
the work of overburdened social agencies.

Taking a wider view, it is also important that our model
sees behavioral difficulties "all under one roof" in two re-

spects. First, our model interrelates individual behavior and its social context instead of dividing them—not only within the family, but potentially at all levels of social organization. Second, this framework helps to identify continuities, similarities, and interrelations between normal everyday problems, psychiatric problems of deviant individual behavior, and many sorts of socially problematic behavior, such as crime, social isolation and anomie, and certain aspects of failure and poverty. At present, social agencies attempting to deal with such problems at the individual or family level are characterized by marked conceptual and organizational divisions—between psychological vs. sociological, supportive vs. disciplinary orientations, and more specifically, in the division of problems into many categories that are presumed to be distinct and discrete—reminiscent of the "syndromes" of conventional psychiatry. At best, this results in discontinuity; ineffective, partial approaches; or reduplication of efforts. At worst, it appears increasingly likely that such divisions themselves may function to reinforce inappropriate attempts at solution of many kinds of problems, as suggested by Auerswald (1) and Hoffman and Long (14). Our work thus suggests a need and a potential basis for a more unified and effective organization of social services.

Finally, our work has still broader implications that deserve explicit recognition, even though any implementation necessarily would be a very long-range and difficult problem. Our theoretical viewpoint is focused on the ways in which problems of behavior and their resolution are related to social interaction. Such problems occur not only with individuals and families, but also at every wider level of social organization and functioning. We can already discern two kinds of parallels between problems met in our clinical work and larger social problems. Problems may be reduplicated widely, as when concern about differences between parents and children becomes, in the large, "the generation gap problem." And conflicts between groups—whether these groups are economic, racial, or political—may parallel those seen between individuals. Our work, like much recent social history, suggests very strongly that ordinary, "common-sense" ways of dealing with such problems often fail, and, indeed, often exacerbate the difficulty. Correspondingly, some of our uncommon ideas and techniques for problem-resolution might eventually be adapted for application to such wider spheres of human behavior.

REFERENCES

1. AUERSWALD, E., "Interdisciplinary vs. Ecological Approach," *Fam. Proc.*, 7: 202–215, 1968.
2. BARTEN, H. (ed.), *Brief Therapies*, New York, Behavioral Publications, 1971.
3. BARTEN, H., and BARTEN, S. (eds.), *Children and Their Parents in Brief Therapy*, New York, Behavioral Publications, 1972.
4. BATESON, G., JACKSON, D., HALEY, J., and WEAKLAND, J., "Towards a Theory of Schizophrenia," *Behav. Sci.*, 1: 251–264, 1956.
5. BELLAK, I., and SMALL, L., *Emergency Psychotherapy and Brief Psychotherapy*, New York, Grune and Stratton, 1965.
6. FISKE, D., HUNT, H., LUBORSKY, L., ORNE, M., PARLOFF, M., REISER, M., and TUMA, A., "Planning of Research on Effectiveness of Psychotherapy," *Arch. Gen. Psychiat.*, 22: 22–32, 1970.
7. FRANK, J., *Persuasian and Healing*, Baltimore, Johns Hopkins Press, 1961.
8. FRANKL, V., *The Doctor and the Soul*, New York, Alfred A. Knopf, 1957.
9. FRANKL, V., "Paradoxical Interventions," *Amer. J. Psychother.*, 14: 520–535, 1960.
10. JACKSON, D., and WEAKLAND, J., "Conjoint Family Therapy: Some Considerations on Theory, Technique, and Results," *Psychiatry*, Supplement to 24:2: 30–45, 1961.
11. HALEY, J., *Strategies of Psychotherapy*, New York, Grune and Stratton, 1963.
12. HALEY, J., *Uncommon Therapy: The Psychiatric Techniques of Milton H. Erickson, M.D.*, New York, W. W. Norton, 1973.
13. HALEY, J. (ed.), *Advanced Techniques of Hypnosis and Therapy: Selected Papers of Milton H. Erickson, M.D.*, New York, Grune and Stratton, 1969.
14. HOFFMAN, L., and LONG, L., "A Systems Dilemma," *Fam. Proc.*, 8: 211–234, 1969.
15. KROHN, A., "Beyond Interpretation," (A review of M.D. Nelson, *et al.*, *Roles and Paradigms in Psychotherapy*). *Contemporary Psychology*, 16: 380–382, 1971.
16. MINUCHIN, S., and MONTALVO, B., "Techniques for Working with Disorganized Low Socioeconomic Families," *Amer. J. Orthopsychiat.*, 37: 880–887, 1967.
17. NEWTON, J., "Considerations for the Psychotherapeutic Technique of Symptom Scheduling," *Psychotherapy: Theory, Research and Practice*, 5: 95–103, 1968.
18. PITTMAN, F. S., LANGSLEY, D. G., FLOMENHAFT, K., DE YOUNG, C.D., MACHOTKA, P., and KAPLAN, D.M., "Therapy Techniques of the Family Treatment Unit." pp. 259–

271 in Haley, J. (ed.), *Changing Families: A Family Therapy Reader,* New York, Grune and Stratton, 1971.

19. ROSEN, J., *Direct Analysis,* New York, Grune and Stratton, 1953.

20. ROSENTHAL, A., Report on brief therapy research to the Clinical Symposium, Department of Psychiatry, Stanford University Medical Center, November 25, 1970.

21. ROSENTHAL, R., *Experimenter Effects in Behavioral Research,* New York, Appleton-Century-Crofts, 1966.

22. SAIZMAN, L., "Reply to the Critics," *Int. J. Psychiat.,* 6: 473–478, 1968.

23. SPIEGEL, H., "Is Symptom Removal Dangerous?" *Amer. J. Psychiat.* 123: 1279–1283, 1967.

24. WATZLAWICK, P., BEAVIN, J., and JACKSON, D., *Pragmatics of Human Communication,* New York, W. W. Norton, 1967.

25. WATZLAWICK, P., WEAKLAND, J., FISCH, R., *Change: Principles of Problem Formation and Problem Resolution,* New York, W. W. Norton, 1974.

26. WENDER, H., "The Role of Deviation-Amplifying Feedback in the Origin and Perpetuation of Behavior," *Psychiatry,* 31: 317–324, 1968.

CARL ROGERS

Client-centered therapy is the creation of Carl Rogers, Ph.D., a clinical psychologist. As his research, theory-building, and experience broadened, Rogers coined the term "non-directive," and then "client-centered," therapy to describe his approach. Rogers chose the term "client" to replace "patient," to underscore his new orientation toward the person in therapy, whom he saw as self-responsible and valuable. During the 1950s and 60s, Rogers broaded his approach to include an orientation toward all human relationships. His methods were used not only with the disturbed, but also with business executives and other professionals who wished to enhance their interpersonal contacts through participation in small client-centered encounter groups.

The evolution of client-centered therapy differs from most other therapies in the degree to which it was based on research. Rogers and his associates taped and studied thousands of hours of psychotherapeutic interaction, evaluating the effectiveness of various interventions. This research led Rogers to see the relationship between therapist and client as crucially important. Research findings by Rogers and others suggest that the most important conditions for success in psychotherapy are the therapist's genuineness, sensitive understanding, and unconditional positive regard in accepting what the client expresses.

As Rogers sees it, therapy is needed when the client feels unable to express his real self to himself or others. At the same time he must be able to perceive the therapist as having a warm, cherishing attitude toward him and an accurate sensitivity. These conditions, according to Rogers, are essential if therapeutic change is to ensue. During the course of therapeutic change the client should become increasingly free and genuine in expressing his feelings.

As he begins to experience himself more fully, he will discover feelings and meanings that he has previously denied to awareness. As this process continues, the client will feel more congruency between his true feelings and his ability to express them to his therapist and others.

In the article that follows, Rogers describes what is required of a therapist to develop a "helping relationship" with his client. The therapist must first let the client know he is trustworthy—that he himself has the capacity for "congruence," where what he says and does accurately reflects what he feels and means. Congruence in the therapist, Rogers contends, is experienced by the client as dependability. Rogers, in advocating that the therapist be open, warm, and real to his clients, stands in opposition to the formal distance that other schools of therapy (such as psychoanalysis) encourage.

Rogers sees the therapist's full unconditional acceptance of the client as essential; the therapist must be willing to "accompany a person wherever his feelings lead him—no matter how strong, deep, destructive, or abnormal they seem." The therapist should let the client feel he is accepted just as he is, without judgment. Finally, Rogers borrows, from the existentialist philosopher Martin Buber, the concept of seeing a person as "becoming." "If I accept him as a process of becoming," says Rogers, "then I am doing what I can to confirm or make real his potentialities." In taking this stance, Rogers and his followers negate the value of the standard therapeutic practice of diagnosis, and of the view that a person is shaped and determined by his past experience. In its stead, they offer a technique that sees as the goal of therapy not a conventional cure, but rather growth. For this reason Rogers sees the therapist-client interaction as one instance of a broad range of human relationships that foster growth.

From THE CHARACTERISTICS OF A HELPING RELATIONSHIP

by Carl R. Rogers

My interest in psychotherapy has brought about in me an interest in every kind of helping relationship. By this term I mean a relationship in which at least one of the parties has the intent of promoting the growth, development, maturity, improved functioning, and improved coping with life of the other. The other, in this sense, may be one individual or a group. To put it in another way, a helping relationship might be defined as one in which one of the participants intends that there should come about, in one or both parties, more appreciation of, more expression of, more functional use of the latent inner resources of the individual.

Now it is obvious that such a definition covers a wide range of relationships which usually are intended to facilitate growth. It would certainly include the relationship between mother and child, and father and child. It would include the relationship between the physician and his patient. The relationship between teacher and pupil would often come under this definition, though some teachers would not have the promotion of growth as their intent. It includes almost all counselor-client relationships, whether we are speaking of educational counseling, vocational counseling, or personal counseling. In this last-mentioned area it would include the wide range of relationships between the psychotherapist and the hospitalized psychotic, the therapist and the troubled or neurotic individual, and the relationship between the therapist and the increasing number of so-called "normal" individuals who enter therapy to improve their own functioning or accelerate their personal growth.

These are largely one-to-one relationships. But we should also think of the large number of individual-group interactions which are intended as helping relationships. Some administrators intend that their relationship to their staff groups shall be of the sort which promotes growth, though other administrators would not have this purpose. The interaction between the group therapy leader and his group belongs here. So does the relationship of the community consultant to a community group. Increasingly the interaction between the industrial consultant and a management group is intended as a helping relationship. Perhaps this listing will point up the fact that a great many of the relationships in which we and others are involved fall within this category of interactions in which there is the purpose of promoting development and more mature and adequate functioning.

• • • • •

It seems clear that relationships which are helpful have different characteristics from relationships which are unhelpful. These differential characteristics have to do primarily with the attitudes of the helping person on the one hand and with the perception of the relationship by the "helpee" on the other. It is equally clear that the studies thus far made do not give us any final answers as to what is a helping relationship, nor how it is to be formed.

HOW CAN I CREATE A HELPING RELATIONSHIP?

I believe each of us working in the field of human relationships has a similar problem in knowing how to use research knowledge. We cannot slavishly follow such findings in a mechanical way or we destroy the personal qualities which these very studies show to be valuable. It seems to me that we have to use these studies, testing them against our own experience and forming new and further personal hypotheses to use and test in our own further personal relationships.

So rather than try to outline how the findings I have presented should be used, I should like to indicate the kind of questions which these studies and my own clinical experience raise for me, and some of the tentative and changing hypotheses which guide my behavior as I enter into what I hope may be helping relationships, whether with students, staff, family, or clients. Let me list a number of these questions and considerations.

1. Can I *be* in some way which will be perceived by the other person as trustworthy, as dependable or consistent in some deep sense? Both research and experience indicate that this is very important, and over the years I have found what I believe are deeper and better ways of answering this question. I used to feel that if I fulfilled all the outer conditions of trustworthiness—keeping appointments, respecting the confidential nature of the interviews, etc.—and if I acted consistently during the interviews, then this condition would be fulfilled. But experience drove home the fact that to act consistently acceptant, for example, if in fact I was feeling annoyed or skeptical or some other non-acceptant feeling, was certain in the long run to be perceived as inconsistent or untrustworthy. I have come to recognize that being trustworthy does not demand that I be rigidly consistent but that I be dependably real. The term congruent is one I have used to describe the way I would like to be. By this I mean that whatever feeling or attitude I am experiencing would be matched by my awareness of that attitude. When this is true, then I am a unified or integrated person in that moment, and

hence I can *be* whatever I deeply *am*. This is a reality which I find others experience as dependable.

2. A very closely related question is this: Can I be expressive enough as a person that what I am will be communicated unambiguously? I believe that most of my failures to achieve a helping relationship can be traced to unsatisfactory answers to these two questions. When I am experiencing an attitude of annoyance toward another person but am unaware of it, then my communication contains contradictory messages. My words are giving one message, but I am also in subtle ways communicating the annoyance I feel and this confuses the other person and makes him distrustful, though he too may be unaware of what is causing the difficulty. When, as a parent or a therapist or a teacher or an administrator, I fail to listen to what is going on in me, fail because of my own defensiveness to sense my own feelings, then this kind of failure seems to result. It has been made evident, it seems to me, that the most basic learning for anyone who hopes to establish any kind of helping relationship is that it is safe to be transparently real. If in a given relationship I am reasonably congruent, if no feelings relevant to the relationship are hidden either to me or the other person, then I can be almost sure that the relationship will be a helpful one.

One way of putting this may seem strange, but if I can form a helping relationship to myself—if I can be sensitively aware of and acceptant toward my own feelings—then the likelihood is great that I can form a helping relationship toward another. Now, to accept what I am, in this sense, and to permit this to show through to the other person, is the most difficult task I know and one I never fully achieve. But to realize that this *is* my task has been most rewarding because it has helped me to find what has gone wrong with interpersonal relationships which have become snarled and to put them on a constructive track again. It has meant that if I am to facilitate the personal growth of others in relation to me, then I must grow, and while this is often painful, it is also enriching.

It does reluctantly seem to me that the degree of help one can give is probably a measure of one's own personal growth. I feel reluctant to come to this conclusion because it puts so much on the basis of personal development and, in a sense, takes it out of the realm of professional training. But it does seem that the individual who has profited most from growth-promoting experiences—whether formal therapy, or fortunate

life experience, or good relationships with others—is probably
most able to offer helping relationships.

3. A third question is: Can I let myself experience positive
attitudes toward this other person—attitudes of warmth, caring, liking, interest, respect? It is not easy. I find in myself,
and feel that I often see in others, a certain amount of fear
of these feelings. We are afraid that if we let ourselves freely
experience these positive feelings toward another that we may
be trapped by them. They may lead to demands on us or we
may be disappointed in our trust, and these outcomes we
fear. As a reaction we tend to build up distance between ourselves and others—aloofness, a "professional" attitude, an impersonal relationship.

I feel quite strongly that one of the important reasons for
the professionalization of every field is that it helps to keep
this distance. In the clinical areas we develop elaborate diagnostic formulations, seeing the person as an object. In
teaching and in administration we develop all kinds of evalu-
ative procedures, so that again the person is perceived as an
object. In these ways, I believe, we can keep ourselves from
experiencing the caring which would exist if we recognized
the relationship as one between two persons. It is a real
achievement when we can learn, even in certain relationships
or at certain times in those relationships, that it is safe to
care, that it is safe to relate to the other as a person for
whom we have positive feelings.

4. Another question the importance of which I have
learned in my own experience is: Can I be strong enough as
a person to be separate from the other? Can I be a sturdy
respecter of my own feelings, my own needs, as well as his?
Can I own and, if need be, express my own feelings as something belonging to me and separate from his feelings? Am I
strong enough in my own separateness that I will not be
downcast by his depression, frightened by his fear, nor en-
gulfed by his dependency? Is my inner self hardy enough to
realize that I am not destroyed by his anger, taken over by
his need for dependence, nor enslaved by his love, but that I
exist separate from him with feelings and rights of my own?
When I can freely feel this strength of being a separate person, then I find that I can let myself go much more deeply in
understanding and accepting him because I am not fearful of
losing myself.

5. The next question is closely related. Am I secure enough
within myself to permit him his separateness? Can I permit

him to be what he is—honest or deceitful, infantile or adult, despairing or over-confident? Can I give him the freedom to be? Or do I feel that he should follow my advice, or remain somewhat dependent on me, or mold himself after me? In this connection, I think of the interesting small study of Farson, which found that the less well adjusted or less competent counselor tends to induce conformity to himself, to have clients who model themselves after him. On the other hand, the better adjusted and more competent counselor can interact with a client through many interviews without interfering with the freedom of the client to develop a personality quite separate from that of his therapist. I should prefer to be in this latter class, whether as parent or supervisor or counselor.

6. Another question I ask myself is: Can I let myself enter fully into the world of his feelings and personal meaning and see these as he does? Can I step into his private world so completely that I lose all desire to evaluate or judge it? Can I enter it so sensitively that I can move about in it freely, without tramping on meanings which are only implicit, which he sees only dimly or as confusion? Can I extend this understanding without limit? I think of the client who said, "Whenever I find someone who understands a *part* of me at the time, then it never fails that a point is reached where I know they're *not* understanding me again. . . . What I've looked for so hard is for someone to understand."

If a therapist really enters fully into his client's frame of reference, then he is not only aware of what the client might say at any particular moment, but he is also aware of the context of feeling in which the statement exists. He doesn't have to stop and think, "Ah, this fear is due to such and such." He senses the feeling empathically (I can't get away from the word) as it exists in context. If he can respond to it in the context it has for the client, he may go beyond what the client has said in words; he may also do a number of things which might seem odd in a recording of the session, so that one would ask, "Where did that therapist's response come from?" But if he is really "in there" as therapists say, then it comes naturally because he does sense the context. I don't believe he has to go through any considerable amount of intellectual manipulation to decide how to respond at more than just the surface level.

A very common reaction among beginning therapists is that they can accept warmth, but sometimes fear that empathy would be dangerous and unhelpful. They think, "Well, all right, I can empathize with a lot that this person is saying or expressing, but now he is talking about something too awful to empathize with, or something that it might be really dangerous to go along with, in his feelings. Here he talks about the fact that he feels he is teetering on the edge of a psychotic break. You mean I should really empathize with all that? Might it not be too much for him?"

I think that my own clinical experience and that of a good many others is that it is precisely at that point that the individual feels most deeply alone. To find that one other human being is not afraid of going with him into that very shadowy and fearful and threatening realm is the very thing that preserves his sanity and permits growth. When we think about the ultimates that are always brought into such a discussion—psychotic breaks, suicides, murder, and so forth—the experience which can be most helpful in preventing such extremes is for the individual to realize that he is *not* isolated, that he is not completely different. He is not, as he feels at that moment, the only individual who has had such feelings and who is, therefore, completely abnormal and hopeless. If he finds that another human being can relate to him in these very areas which are most terrifying—that enables him to begin to realize that he can be human and still have these feelings. It also helps gradually to place them in perspective so that they are not all-encompassing. Empathy accurately defined as the ability to accompany a person wherever his feelings lead him—no matter how strong, deep, destructive, or abnormal they seem—is, in my estimation, helpful, and not harmful.

For myself, I find it easier to feel this kind of understanding, and to communicate it, to individual clients than to students in a class or staff members in a group in which I am involved. There is a strong temptation to set students "straight," or to point out to a staff member the errors in his thinking. Yet when I can permit myself to understand these situations, it is mutually rewarding. And with clients in therapy, I am often impressed with the fact that even a minimal amount of empathic understanding—a bumbling and faulty attempt to catch the confused complexity of the client's meaning—is helpful, though there is no doubt that it is most helpful when I can see and formulate clearly the meanings in his experiencing which for him have been unclear and tangled.

7. Still another issue is whether I can be acceptant of each facet of a client which he presents to me. Can I receive him as he is? Can I communicate this attitude? Or can I only receive him conditionally, acceptant of some aspects of his feelings and silently or openly disapproving of others? It has been my experience that when my attitude is conditional then he cannot change or grow in those respects in which I cannot fully receive him. And when—afterwards and sometimes too late—I try to discover why I have been unable to accept him in every respect, I usually discover that it is because I have been frightened or threatened in myself by some aspect of his feelings. If I am to be more helpful, then I must myself grow and accept myself in these respects.

In regard to what I would want to accept in the other person, I think it is more important that I accept the negative and ungrowing and inhibited feelings in him. If anything, that is more important than for me to accept the positive aspects because he is likely to find a number of people in his environment who accept his positive feelings, but it is rather rare that he finds someone who can really accept his negative feelings. Now, if negative feelings are accepted, where does progress come from? My opinion about motivation in such circumstances is that, given an opportunity, the individual inherently, as does every organism that grows, moves toward self-fulfillment and self-actualization. That I feel very deeply.

8. A very practical issue is raised by the question: Can I act with sufficient sensitivity in the relationship that my behavior will not be perceived as a threat? The work we are beginning to do in studying the physiological concomitants of psychotherapy confirms the research by Dittes in indicating how easily people are threatened at a physiological level. The psychogalvanic reflex—the measure of skin conductance—takes a sharp dip when the therapist responds with some word which is just a little stronger than the client's feelings. And to a phrase such as, "My, you *do* look upset," the needle swings almost off the paper. My desire to avoid even such minor threats is not due to a hypersensitivity about my client. It is simply due to the conviction based on experience that if I can free him as completely as possible from external threat, then he can begin to experience and begin to deal with the internal feelings and conflicts which he finds threatening.

9. A specific aspect of the preceding question, but an important one is: Can I free him from the threat of external evaluation? In almost every phase of our lives—at home, at

school, at work—we find ourselves under the rewards and
punishments of external judgments. "That's good." "That's
naughty." "That's worth an A." "That's a failure." "That's
good counseling." "That's poor counseling." Such judgments
are a part of our lives from infancy to old age. I believe they
have a certain social usefulness to institutions and organizations such as schools and professions. Like everyone else, I
find myself all too often making such evaluations. But, in my
experience, they do not make for personal growth and, hence,
I do not believe that they are a part of a helping relationship.
Curiously enough, a positive evaluation is as threatening in
the long run as a negative one, since to inform someone that
he is good implies that one also has the right to tell him he is
bad. So I have come to feel that the more I can keep a relationship free of judgment and evaluation, the more this will
permit the other person to reach the point where he recognizes that the locus of evaluation, the center of responsibility,
lies within himself. The meaning and value of his experience
is in the last analysis something which is up to him, and no
amount of external judgment can alter this. So I should like
to work toward a relationship in which I am not, even in my
own feelings, evaluating him. This, I believe, can set him free
to be a self-responsible person.

I am not saying that there is to be no evaluation and hence
no control. Within the family setting, for example, I think
that if instead of rather rigid evaluational control—"that's
bad, naughty," etc.—we could substitute much more the interaction of the child's feeling with the parents' feeling, there
would be limitations. The sky would not be the limit. There
are things that parents don't like and things they do like.
There are times when they are tired, too tired to be nice,
times when they have had enough, and times when they
won't stand it to have something damaged. But if those
feelings could be stated as the parents' own feelings, permitting the child to have his feelings in counteraction to those,
then it seems to me it would tend to do away with what I regard as the value standards that get introjected into individuals. If we had a situation in which the child's real feeling of
"I want to do this," and "I like that," were continually met
by the real feelings of the parent, whatever those might be,
then I think the child involved would gradually develop real
and growing skills in interpersonal relationships. He would
not be a little monster but would be *self*-limiting in his behav-

ior, in terms of the reactions he would like to get from others. This would be quite different from the feeling we tend to induce in children that "No matter how it seems to me, it's awful." "No matter what I think about, it's bad."

There would instead be a relationship between real feelings on both sides. I think this is the kind of thing we develop in our best relationships as adults. This is the way we deal with our friends. We want certain things. They want something else. Then, we decide on some mutually reasonable course of action. There do seem to be within the biological organism feedback mechanisms, evaluational systems—whatever one might call them—which enable the organism to discriminate, although not always with immediate accuracy, between experiences which are favorable to its own growth and development and those which are unfavorable. Although such natural tendencies can certainly be deceived and thrown out of kilter by various distorting experiences, nevertheless, the fundamental ability of the organism to distinguish between experiences which favor its own development and those which do not seems to be the capacity on which not only therapy but a great many other processes depend. It crosses my mind that the organism shows much of this kind of ability with regard to physical illness. The feedback mechanisms often keep the organism reacting reasonably adequately in ways that will promote its return to good health.

10. One last question: Can I meet this other individual as a person who is in the process of *becoming,* or will I be bound by his past and by my past? If, in my encounter with him, I deal with him as an immature child, an ignorant student, a neurotic personality, or a psychopath, each of these concepts limits what he can be in the relationship. Martin Buber, the existentialist philosopher of the University of Jerusalem, has a phrase, "confirming the other," which has had meaning for me. He says, "Confirming means . . . accepting the whole potentiality of the other. . . . I can recognize in him, know in him, the person he has been . . . *created* to become. . . . I confirm him in myself, and then in him, in relation to this potentiality that . . . can now be developed, can evolve." If I accept the other person as something fixed, already diagnosed and classified, already shaped by his past, then I am doing my part to confirm this limited hypothesis. If I accept him as a process of becoming, then I am doing what I can to confirm or make real his potentialities.

It is at this point that I see Verplanck, Lindsley, and Skinner, working in operant conditioning, coming together with Buber, the philosopher or mystic. At least they come together in principle. If I see a relationship as only an opportunity to reinforce certain types of words or opinions in the other, then I tend to confirm him as an object—a basically mechanical, manipulable object. And if I see only this as his potentiality, he tends to act in ways which support this hypothesis. If, on the other hand, I see a relationship as an opportunity to "reinforce" *all* that he is, the person that he is with all his existent potentialities, then he tends to act in ways which support *this* hypothesis. I have then—to use Buber's term—confirmed him as a living person, capable of creative inner development. Personally, I prefer this second type of hypothesis. . . .

Rollo May

Rollo May, who was a prime developer of the existential approach to therapy, was a minister before he became a psychologist. While a student at the Union Theological Seminary he studied with theologian Paul Tillich, who remained a friend and colleague for the next thirty years. Dissatisfied in the ministry, May turned to a career as a clinical psychologist; his doctoral dissertation formulated what have become basic premises of May's existential therapy.

A unique aspect of May's theory is his stress on confronting the tragic aspects of life, an outlook that makes existential therapy place a positive emphasis on the experience of anxiety as a chance for positive growth. In this regard, May is in accord with existential philosophers and European therapists such as Otto Binswanger and Victor Frankl, who have also translated these philosophical insights into a therapy.

For May, the fundamental psychological malady is the fear of "living fully." By repressing feelings, people cut themselves off from awareness of their own existence; people live in a partial reality, falling prey to a deadening apathy and sense of meaninglessness. But if people will consciously face and assimilate the full spectrum of awareness and feeling—no matter how unpleasant—they can become more fully human, or "self-actualized."

May argues that, for this reason, anxiety is not necessarily negative. The attitude that anxiety is to be avoided, he says, is itself pathological. In his view, growth and creativity require that a person at least temporarily endure the distress of being without their habitual protective structures. He encourages people to be receptive to the widest range of their experience, including the "daimonic" within themselves—those aspects of the self that seem dangerous, repugnant, and shameful. One does not, says May, become fully human pain-lessly.

In this selection, May illustrates the working of existential therapy in describing the treatment of a patient, Mrs. Hutchens, who is neurotically rigid and overcontrolled to the point where she has trouble talking. At the outset he recognizes that a patient's symptoms are natural outgrowths of human tendencies. "Is not neurosis . . . precisely the method the individual uses to preserve his own center, his own existence?" Neurotic symptoms, says May, are ways of shrinking the range of one's world to protect oneself from a sense of threat; "a way of blocking off aspects of the environment so that he may then be adequate to the remainder."

The therapist, by encouraging the patient to be courageous and venture into their relationship openly, coaxes the patient beyond the safe perimeter of his defenses. At the same time, the therapist helps the patient become aware of this experience, so that he can more fully perceive his actual place in the world.

Becoming "self-conscious" in this sense is, in May's view, an act of bravery: ". . . consciousness of one's own desires and affirming them involves accepting one's originality and uniqueness, and it implies that one must be prepared not only to be isolated from those parental figures upon whom one has been dependent, but at that instant to stand alone in the entire psychic universe as well."

EXISTENTIAL BASES OF PSYCHOTHERAPY

by Rollo May

There are several endeavors in this country to systematize psychoanalytic and psychotherapeutic theory in terms of forces, dynamisms, and energies. The existential approach is the exact opposite of these attempts. It holds . . . that our science must be relevant to the distinctive characteristics of what we seek to study, in this case the human being. We do not deny dynamisms and forces; that would be nonsense. But we hold that they have meaning only in the context of the existing, living being—if you will permit a technical word, only in the *ontological* context.

I propose, then, that we take the one real datum that we

have in the therapeutic situation, namely, the existing person sitting in the consulting room with a therapist. Let us ask: What are the essential characteristics which constitute this patient as an existing person, which constitute this self as a self? I wish to propose six characteristics, which I shall call principles, that I find in my work as a psychotherapist. They can as well be called *ontological characteristics*. Though these are the product of a good deal of thought and experience with many cases, I shall illustrate them with episodes from the case of Mrs. Hutchens.

First, Mrs. Hutchens, like every existing person, is centered in herself, and an attack on this center is an attack on her existence itself. This is a characteristic that we human beings share with all living beings; it is self-evident in animals and plants. I never cease to marvel how, whenever we cut the top off a pine tree on our farm in New Hampshire, the tree sends up a new branch from heaven knows where to become a new center. But our principle has a particular relevance to human beings and gives a basis for the understanding of sickness and health, neurosis and mental health. Neurosis is not to be seen as a deviation from our particular theories of what a person should be. *Is not neurosis, rather, precisely the method the individual uses to preserve his own center, his own existence?* His symptoms are ways of shrinking the range of his world (so graphically shown in Mrs. Hutchens' inability to let herself talk) in order that the centeredness of his existence may be protected from threat, a way of blocking off aspects of the environment so that he may then be adequate to the remainder.

Mrs. Hutchens had gone to another therapist for half a dozen sessions a month before she came to me. He told her, in an apparently ill-advised effort to reassure her, that she was too proper, too controlled. She reacted with great upset and immediately broke off the treatment. Now, technically he was entirely correct; existentially he was entirely wrong. What he did not see, in my judgment, was this very properness, this overcontrol, far from being things that Mrs. Hutchens wanted to get over, were part of her desperate attempt to preserve what precarious center she had. As though she were saying, "If I opened up, if I communicated, I would lose what little space in life I have." We see here, incidentally, how inadequate is the definition of neurosis as a failure of adjustment. *An adjustment is exactly what neurosis is; and that is just its trouble.* It is a necessary adjustment by which centeredness can be preserved; a way of accepting *non-being*, if I may use this term, in order that some little *being* may be preserved. And in most cases it is a boon when this adjustment breaks down.

This is the only thing we can assume about Mrs. Hutchens, or about any patient, when she comes in: she, like all living beings, requires centeredness, and this has broken down. At a cost of considerable turmoil she has taken steps, that is, come for help. Our second principle, thus, is: *every existing person has the character of self-affirmation, the need to preserve its centeredness*. The particular name we give this self-affirmation in human beings is "courage." Paul Tillich's emphasis on the "courage to be" is very important, cogent, and fertile for psychotherapy at this point. He insists that in man, being is never given automatically, as it is in plants and animals, but depends upon the individual's courage, and without courage one loses being. This makes courage itself a necessary ontological corollary. By this token, I as a therapist place great importance upon expressions of the patients which have to do with willing decisions, choice. I never let such little remarks the patient may make as "maybe I can," "perhaps I can try" slip by without my making sure he knows I have heard him. It is only a half truth to say that the will is the product of the wish; I emphasize rather the truth that the wish can never come out in its real power except with will.

Now as Mrs. Hutchens talks hoarsely, she looks at me with an expression of mingled fear and hope. Obviously a relation not only exists between us here, but has already existed in anticipation in the waiting room and ever since she thought of coming. She is struggling with the possibility of participating with me. Our third principle is, thus: *all existing persons have the need and possibility of going out from their centeredness to participate in other beings*. This always involves risk; if the organism goes out too far, it loses its own centeredness, its identity—a phenomenon which can easily be seen in the biological world. If the neurotic is so afraid of loss of his own conflicted center that he refuses to go out and holds back in rigidity and lives in narrowed reactions and shrunken world space, his growth and development are blocked. This is the pattern in neurotic repressions and inhibitions, the common neurotic forms in Freud's day. But it may well be in our day of conformity and the outerdirected man, that the most common neurotic pattern takes the opposite form, namely, the dispersing of one's self in participation and identification with others until one's own being is emptied.

At this point we see the rightful emphasis of Martin Buber in one sense and Harry Stack Sullivan in another, that the human being cannot be understood as a self if participation is omitted. Indeed, if we are successful in our search for these ontological principles of the existing person, it should be true that the omission of any one of the six would mean that we do not then have a human being.

Our fourth principle is: *the subjective side of centeredness is awareness*. Such awareness is present in forms of life other than human; it is certainly observable in animals. Howard Liddell has pointed out how the seal in its natural habitat lifts its head every ten seconds even during sleep to survey the horizon lest an Eskimo hunter with poised bow and arrow sneak up on it. This awareness of threats to being in animals, Liddell calls *vigilance,* and he identifies it as the primitive, simple counterpart in animals of what in human beings becomes anxiety.

Our first four characteristic principles are shared by our existing person with all living beings; they are biological levels in which human beings participate. The fifth principle refers now to a distinctively human characteristic: self-consciousness. *The uniquely human form of awareness is self-consciousness*. Awareness and consciousness should not be identified. We associate awareness, as Liddell indicates, with vigilance. This is supported by the derivation of the term "aware." It comes from the Anglo-Saxon *gewaer, waer,* meaning knowledge of external dangers and threats. Its cognates are *beware* and *wary*. Awareness certainly is what is going on in an individual's neurotic reaction to threat, in, for example, Mrs. Hutchens' experience in the first hours that I am also a threat to her.

Consciousness, however, is not simply my awareness of threat from the world but *my capacity to know myself as the one being threatened, my experience of myself as the subject who has a world*. Consciousness, to use Kurt Goldstein's terms, is man's capacity to transcend the immediate concrete situation, to live in terms of the possible; and it underlies the human capacity to use abstractions and universals, to have language and symbols. This capacity for consciousness underlies the wide range of possibility which man has in relating to his world, and it constitutes the foundation of psychological freedom. Thus, human freedom has its ontological base and I believe must be assumed in all psychotherapy.

In his book *The Phenomenon of Man*, the paleontologist Pierre Teilhard de Chardin brilliantly describes how awareness is present, including the form of tropism, in all forms of evolutionary life from amoeba to man. But in man a new function arises, namely this self-consciousness. Teilhard de Chardin undertakes to demonstrate something that I have always believed, that when a new function emerges, the whole previous pattern of the organism changes. The total gestalt shifts; thereafter the organism can be understood only in terms of the new function. That is to say, it is only a half truth to hold that the organism is to be understood in terms of the simpler elements below it on the evolutionary scale; it is just as true that every new function forms a new complexity which conditions all the simpler elements in this organism. Thus, *the simple can be understood only in terms of the more complex.*

This is what self-consciousness does in man. All the simpler biological functions must now be understood in terms of this new function. No one would, of course, deny for a moment the old functions, or anything in biology which man shares with less complex organisms. Take sexuality, for example, which we obviously share with all mammals. But given self-consciousness, sex becomes a new gestalt, as is demonstrated in therapy all the time. Sexual impulses are always, then, conditioned by the *person* of the partner; what we think of the other male or female, in reality or fantasy or even repressed fantasy, can never be ruled out. The fact that the subjective person of the other to whom we relate sexually makes least difference in *neurotic* sexuality, say in patterns of compulsive sex or prostitution, only proves our point the more firmly, for such requires precisely the blocking off, the checking out, the distorting of self-consciousness. Thus, when we talk of sexuality in terms of sexual objects, as Kinsey does, we may garner interesting and useful statistics; but we simply are not talking about human sexuality.

Nothing in what I am saying here should be taken as antibiological in the slightest; on the contrary, I think it is only from this approach that we *can* understand human biology without distorting it. As Kierkegaard aptly put it, "The natural law is as valid as ever." I argue only against the uncritical acceptance of the assumption that the organism is to be understood only in terms of those elements below it on the evolutionary scale, an acceptance which has led us to overlook the self-evident truth that what makes a horse a horse are not the elements it shares with the dog but what constitutes distinctively, "horse." Now, *what we are dealing with in neurosis are those characteristics and functions that are distinctively human.* It is these that have gone awry in disturbed patients. The condition for these functions is self-consciousness—which accounts for what Freud rightly discovered, that the neurotic pattern is characterized by repression and blocking off of consciousness.

It is the task of the therapist, therefore, not only to help the patient become aware, but even more significantly, to help him *transmute this awareness into consciousness.* Awareness is his knowing that something is threatening from outside in his world—a condition that may, as in paranoids and their neurotic equivalents, be correlated with a good deal of acting-out behavior. But self-consciousness puts this awareness on a quite different level; it is the patient's seeing that *he is the one who is threatened,* that he is the being who stands in this world which threatens, that he is the subject who *has* a world. And this gives him the possibility of *insight,* of "inward sight," of seeing the world and his problems in relation to himself. And thus it gives him the possibility of doing something about them.

To come back to our too-long silent patient: After about twenty-five hours of therapy Mrs. Hutchens had the following dream. She was searching room by room for a baby in an unfinished house at an airport. She thought the baby belonged to someone else, but the other person might let her take it. Now it seemed that she had put the baby in a pocket of her robe (or her mother's robe), and she was seized with anxiety that it would be smothered. Much to her joy, she found that the baby was still alive. Then she had a strange thought, "Shall I kill it?"

The house was at the airport where she, at about the age of twenty, had learned to fly solo, a very important act of self-affirmation and independence from her parents. The baby was associated with her youngest son, whom she regularly identified with herself. Permit me to omit the ample associative evidence that convinced both her and me that the baby stood for herself, and specifically for consciousness of herself. The dream is an expression of the emergence and growth of self-consciousness, a consciousness that she is not yet sure is hers, and a consciousness that she considers killing in the dream.

About six years before her therapy, Mrs. Hutchens had left the religious faith of her parents, to which, by way of them, she had had a very authoritarian relation. She had then joined a church of her own belief. But she had never dared tell her parents of this. Instead, when they came to visit, she attended their church in great tension lest one of her children let the secret out. After about thirty-five sessions, when she was considering writing her parents to tell them of this change of faith, she had, over a period of two weeks, spells of partially fainting in my office. She would become suddenly weak, her face would go white, she would feel empty and "like water inside" and would have to lie down for a few moments on the couch. In retrospect, she called these spells "grasping for oblivion."

She then wrote her parents informing them once and for all of her change in faith and assuring them it would do no good to try to dominate her. The following session, she asked in considerable anxiety whether I thought she would go psychotic. I responded that whereas anyone of us might at some time have such an episode, I saw no more reason why she should than any of the rest of us; and I asked whether her fear of going psychotic was not rather anxiety arising out of her standing against her parents, as though genuinely being herself, she felt to be tantamount to going crazy. I have noted several times, it may be remarked, that patients experience this anxiety at being one's self as tantamount to psychosis. This is not surprising, for consciousness of one's own desires and affirming them involves accepting one's originality and uniqueness, and it implies that one must be prepared not only to be isolated from those parental figures upon whom one has been dependent, but at that instant to stand alone in the entire psychic universe as well.

We see the profound conflicts of the emergence of self-consciousness in three vivid ways in Mrs. Hutchens, whose chief symptom, interestingly enough, was the denial of that uniquely human capacity based on consciousness, talking. These conflicts are shown in : (1) the temptation to kill the baby; (2) the grasping at oblivion by fainting, as though she were saying, "If only I did not have to be conscious, I would escape this terrible problem of telling my parents"; and (3) the psychosis anxiety.

We now come to the sixth and last characteristic of the existing person: *anxiety*. Anxiety is the state of the human being in the struggle against that which would destroy his being. It is, in Tillich's phrase, the state of a being in conflict with nonbeing, a conflict which Freud mythologically pictured in his powerful and important symbol of the death instinct. One wing of this struggle will always be against something outside one's self; but even more portentous and significant for psychotherapy is the inner side of the battle, which we saw in Mrs. Hutchens, namely, the conflict within the person as he confronts the choice of whether and how far he will stand against his own being, his own potentialities.

Thus, we take very seriously this temptation to kill the baby, or kill her own consciousness, as expressed in these forms by Mrs. Hutchens. We neither water it down by calling it "neurotic" and the product merely of sickness, nor do we slough over it by reassuring her, "Okay, but you don't need to do it." If we did these, we would be helping her adjust at the price of surrendering a portion of her existence, that is, her opportunity for fuller independence. The self-confrontation which is involved in the acceptance of self-consciousness is anything but simple: it involves, to identify some of the elements, accepting of the hatred of the past, her mother's against her and hers of her mother; accepting her present motives of hatred and destruction; cutting through rationalizations and illusions about her behavior and motives, and the acceptance of the responsibility and aloneness which this implies; the giving up of childhood omnipotence, and acceptance of the fact that although she can never have absolute certainty about her choices, she must choose anyway.

But all these specific points, easy enough to understand in themselves, must be seen in the light of the fact that *consciousness itself implies always the possibility of turning against one's self, denying one's self*. The tragic nature of human existence inheres in the fact that consciousness itself involves the possibility and temptation at every instant to kill itself. Dostoevski and our other existential forebears were not indulging in poetic hyperbole or expressing the aftereffects of too much vodka the night before when they wrote of the agonizing burden of freedom.

I trust that the fact that existential psychotherapy places emphasis on these tragic aspects of life does not at all give the impression that it is pessimistic. Quite the contrary. The confronting of genuine tragedy is a highly cathartic experience psychically, as Aristotle and others through history have reminded us. Tragedy is inseparably connected with man's dignity and grandeur and is the accompaniment, as illustrated in the dramas of Oedipus and Orestes, ad infinitum, of the human being's moment of great insight.

In my judgment, the analysis of characteristics of the existing being, these ontological characteristics that I have tried to point toward, can give us a structural base for our psychotherapy. It can also give us a base for a science of man that will not fragmentize and destroy man's humanity as it studies him.

Sidney Jourard

Sidney Jourard (1927–1975), a clinical psychologist, was a spokesman for the humanistic orientation in therapy. Like many in the humanistic movement, Jourard's outlook was shaped by the writings of philosophers like Martin Buber, theologians like Paul Tillich, as well as the existentialists. His most direct lineage as a therapist, though, descends through Eric Fromm and Carl Rogers.

Jourard was an active advocate of openness and self-disclosure as healing in and of themselves. He saw the distance and aloofness of the therapist's role as it has been traditionally fulfilled as an impediment to authenticity. To help the patient be comfortable with his private feelings and thoughts, the therapist must unveil his own.

In the following article, Jourard traces the therapist's role in our culture, finding too often an agent of social repression, where normative values are equated with "health." Jourard proposes an alternate role for the therapist: "an explorer assigned to discover and test ways to relate to others and to the social order that keep one fit, loving, growing, and inventive in the world. . . ." The therapist, Jourard urges, should not be so preoccupied with whether a patient is normal, but with the quality of his experience.

Toward that end, Jourard sees a new kind of therapist who is more a guru; he himself should be "an *examplar* of a turned-on life, a revealer and sharer of how *he* has found his way." For Jourard, therapy should be a Buber-style dialogue, in which both therapist and client (whom he would rather call a "seeker") engage each other openly, with no set course of therapy. Within the therapy session the therapist uses any method, ranging from Freudian interpretations to teaching Yoga or arm-wrestling. The net effect is for the therapist to become a model for encouraging the patient to take risks in his own life.

In sum, Jourard's position represents a reaction against therapists who would hide in the comfort of their prescribed roles and the rituals and routines of whatever school of therapy they practice. Jourard sees these comfortable therapists' habits as "hang-ups engendered in the academy," just as unhealthy as the hang-ups patients come to therapy for.

From THE PSYCHOTHERAPIST AS EXEMPLAR

by Sidney Jourard

Analogies reveal similarities between things, and conceal differences. Psychotherapists have been likened to physicians, repairmen, thought reformers, animal trainers, and "persuasion" experts concerned with influencing behavior and experience. There is a sense in which the psychotherapeutic task resembles that of guide and mentor, of guru, exemplar, priest or rabbi. This is the perspective from which I want to look at this calling.

I

Psychology and psychotherapy have existed for eighty years as self-conscious professions. The world has changed radically since the 1880s—the Victorian age collapsed and ushered in World Wars I, II, and the imminence of III. Revolutions have occurred in several major nations and dozens of minor ones. Man invaded outer space and rediscovered "inner space." Each of these events has affected man's awareness of his own being, of other men's perspectives, and of the possibilities of the world. Each expansion of man's consciousness has reopened the questions: how to live, how to be, how to pass the time?

Up to the present, psychotherapists have functioned as emergency socialization agents; their job has been to correct the failures of family, school, and other socialization agencies to "shape up" a citizen whose behavior would not be a problem to everyone else. People who didn't "fit" were designated mentally ill. An entire mythology of illness and its cure was gradually evolved by the medical profession, and no psychotherapist was unaffected by this ideology. Psychologists, clergymen, social workers, and counselors of all kinds were trained to view misfitting people as sufferers from "mental disease," and they were led to believe that if they mastered certain theories and techniques for transacting with *Them*, the patients, they would effect a cure. In this way, *We*, the psychotherapists—solid, conforming professional men with a stake in the status quo—served society, and we could take pride in the fact that we did it well, earning our money with hard, scientifically informed work. We always were pledged to foster and protect our patients' well-being but, curiously enough, our concepts of wellness were well-nigh identical with those versions of personality that fit the social system that subsidized us, with its established class structure and its resistance to change. Revolutionaries, anarchists and rebels against the status quo (including hippies, poets, painters, and writers) could conveniently be seen as sufferers from unresolved Oedipus conflicts. We psychotherapists and investigators did not seriously view each man as a unique source of authentic experience, a perspective that in a more pluralistic, enlightened society might be *confirmed* rather than invalidated. We shared the short-sightedness of our established society, and called the officially sanctioned view of the world "reality-contact" and everything else madness or autism. From this view, people who want to make love, not war, are seen as impractical, schizoid, or seditious. No matter what our private sentiments may have been, we were unwittingly pledged to protect the status quo by invalidating the experience of those who found it unlivable. We called this invalidation "treatment." In effect, we were a peculiar breed of commissars, pledged to alter experiencing that was designated "sick" and to replace it with those modes called "normal." Like it or not: there is a politics of psychotherapy just as there is, in Laing's words, a "politics of experience."

II

Man can experience himself and the world in myriad ways. Being can be likened to a projective test. To insist the world has one meaning rather than another is *politics*. To persuade a man that his experience is not real or worthless is to be a propagandist for some vested interest. We have been confirming what Freud, with incredible courage, found for himself—that our possibilities of experiencing are infinite and infinitely beyond that splinter of awareness we acknowledge, call "normal," and disclose to others. In fact, to the extent that we find our own ordinary consciousnesses banal, we have an answer to a riddle: How was it possible for Freud for so many years to spend twelve to fourteen hours daily listening to people disclose their offbeat experiencing to him without swooning from fatigue or boredom? Users of LSD and marijuana offer the hint of an answer. Frued encouraged people to disclose their unselected experience and I have little doubt that it "turned him on." His psychoanalytic practice must have felt like a forty-year psychedelic trip, or forty years in a gallery of surrealistic art. Hour after hour, day after day, exposed to dreams, fantasies and memories that shattered his conventional rubrics and expectations about the human experience—it couldn't help but expand his awareness of his own being and of the possibilities for experiencing the world. That highly prized state, "being normal," must have looked like banality incarnate to a man who had dauntlessly opened Pandora's box and become privy to the secrets of expanded experiencing, which he found in himself and in those who consulted with him. Each disclosure from a patient must have exploded his concepts and expectations of what is possible.

I think that, in keeping Pandora's box open, we have been infected, or perhaps it is better to say disaffected. We have been infected with the truth that we *can* experience much more than we permit ourselves, and more than the guardians of the status quo would like us to. And we may have been disaffected from unthinking complicance to the established ways of living our lives, ways of relating to our fellows, ways of experiencing and living in our bodies. We are starting to study man-for-himself—for his possibilities of development and fulfillment that go beyond mere conformity with prevailing norms. And, properly enough, we are starting by studying ourselves.

III

There is no more THEM—only us, seekers after meaning in a social structure that aims to shrink our being, but in a world that requires us to grow. If we insist that patients and subjects belong in the category of THEM, then I, for one, have become one of THEM. I have come to believe that my task, as a psychotherapist, is no longer a specialized paramedical praxis. Rather it is more akin to the mission of an explorer assigned to discover and test ways to relate to others and to the social order that keep one fit, loving, growing, and inventive in the world, ways that evoke new possibilities for achievement, contributions, and enjoyment. My criterion of success in this quest is not solely whether my behavior appears "normal" to others; but, rather my *experience* of feeling free, responsible, potent, and alive. The criterion of "success" has shifted from exclusive attention to behavior to concern for the quality of experience.

I have been for too long aware that, in appearing normal to others, I felt benumbed and dead within, a habit-ridden plaything of social pressures and expectation. And I have known too many people—fellow seekers (I used to call them patients)—who were exemplary in their conduct, but dead or desperate inside, and who could tolerate their "normal" existence only with the aid of booze or tranquilizers, or periodic hospitalization for an ulcer.

A new specialist is called for in our time, and I believe those of us who presently are psychotherapists may be in the best position to grow beyond our training into the new role. I haven't an acceptable name for this specialist, but I see him as a Westernized version of his Eastern counterpart, the *guru* or teacher. We might call him an existential guide, a "psychedelic man," a consciousness-expanding expert, a growth counselor, or a self-actualization agent. He is a guide to more expanding, fulfilled and fulfilling ways to experience life as a person. He is a "world"* shatterer and rebuilder. As such, he has a robust interest in his own fulfillment, and he pursues this, in part, by helping others to fulfill themselves. But part of his function is as an *examplar* of a turned-on life, a revealer and sharer of how *he* has found his way. He is himself "reborn," in the Sufi sense, or awakened and liberated in the sense of the Zen masters or Taoist teachers. He is a Bodhisattva rather than the Buddha himself—awakened, but not out of this world. He remains in dialogue with those of his fellow seekers who are themselves seeking to become men rather than mystified social functionaries. He shows and tells how he has been awakened, and serves as a guide to others, to help them find their way in their world. He is an experimental existentialist, literally. He experiments with *his* exis-

---

*The word "world" is used here to refer to the way in which a person experiences the existence of the world: what he perceives and ignores, how he attaches meaning and value to the world as he experiences it.

tence, seeking ways that generate maximum enlightenment,
freedom, and love.

This view of a psychotherapist as a guru, teacher, or psychedelic man has implicit in it an entire new theory of suffering, growth, practice, settings for practice, schools for
training—the total paraphernalia of a profession. But first, it
calls for an enlightened perspective on society and for expanded views of human possibility that are authenticated by
having discovered new possibilities within oneself. It calls for
a "going away" and then for a return, renewed. It calls for a
kind of death and a kind of rebirth. One can easily see adum-
brations with Eastern philosophies, Jewish mysticism, early
Christian existential (lived) theology, Marxist social criticism
and utopianism, current existential phenomenology, and
Freud's work, in this perspective. Ancient myths about leaving home to live and learn, then coming back to establish do-
minion over one's kingdom are also relevant. From this
standpoint, hippies and "drop-outs" have taken just the first
step, the leaving. If they are men (and women), they will return to renew and humanize the society they left.

IV

I took part in a symposium at the Southeastern Psychological Association on "Innovations in Psychotherapy." I spoke
of innovations in a *psychotherapist*—myself. I spoke of what
I have done with and beyond the training I received to become a psychotherapist. I spoke of the books I had read; of
impasses in my therapeutic work and personal growth, and
how I transcended them or failed to. I spoke of the impact on
my work as a therapist produced by my experience as husband and father, colleague of others, teacher of students; of
the influence of my research in self-disclosure and body-ex-
perience, and my experience as one of THEM (the patients)
on my work as psychotherapist. I noted that we tend to limit
our dialogue at professional meetings to ways in which we
have succeeded in helping Them by trying out psychoanalytic techniques, Rogerian techniques, Perls techniques—but
we have not deliberately acknowledged one another as *persons,* nor have we shared our problems and solutions in staying alive and growing. We have not deliberately explored or
reflected upon the ways in which we behaved ourselves into
sickness and out of it. Our "technologies" remain authorized

ways to practice upon THEM that, in principle, anyone can learn.

As for myself, I have found in my meetings with people who consult me that WE enter into dialogue, and my commitment is to help the other become more enlightened, more liberated from the bondage of habit, social pressure, the past, of some one mode of experiencing. I try to awaken the seeker to the plastic possibilities that inhere in *his* "facticity." I try to help him reinvent himself and his situation, and then help him try to fulfill the invention. To implement this project, *I respond in any way and every way that is available to me in the context of dialogue*. My commitment in the dialogue is not to a theory, technique, or setting, but to the *project* of abetting another person's wholeness and growth. Of necessity, there are technical ways of embodying this project, but these always reach an impasse, and at the impasse, the seriousness of my commitment receives its test: Am I committed to my theory and techniques or to the project? In the context of dialogue I don't hesitate to share any of my experience with existential binds roughly comparable to those in which the seeker finds himself (this is now called "modelling"); nor do I hesitate to disclose my experience of him, myself, and our relationship as it unfolds from moment to moment. Nor do I hesitate, when it becomes relevant, to tell a joke, give a lecture for a few minutes on my view of how he is being mystified by others in his life and how he is mystifying others. I might give Freudian or other types of interpretations. I might teach him such Yoga know-how or tricks for expanding body-awareness as I have mastered or engage in arm wrestling or hold hands or hug him, *if that is the response that emerges in the dialogue*. I encourage him to try experiments with his own existence, like trying the risky business of authenticity, or changing living arrangements.

Our relationship begins almost always with the seeker expecting it to unfold in a technically predictable and prescribed way (as outlined in popular books, TV, and movies). In fact, I feel pressure from him to stay in an impersonal and technical role. I respect this, but respond with the invitation to dialogue. If he accepts the invitation—and gradually he does—the relationship becomes a shared quest for authentic ways he might live that generate wholeness and growth. I do not hesitate to play a game of handball with a seeker or visit him in his home—if this unfolds in the dialogue. The technical ways of behaving we have called "psychotherapeutic intervention" may have functioned as authentic paths to enlightenment and liberation for someone, at some time. But to congeal them as orthodoxies is to meet a seeker's "hang-ups" with "hang-ups" engendered in an academy. Technical approaches limit the therapist's capacity for relevant response in dialogue and they confuse commitments. *A therapist is defined by his project, not his means.*

The paradox I am discovering is that the most efficient means of fostering therapeutic aims is by sharing the fruits of *my* quest for fuller life (about which I am ultimately serious) with the seeker. This liberates me from technical rigidities. I experience myself as an explorer of ways I invent, or that others invent and I learn about and try, to make life more meaningful for me, and I then share, show, and co-experience these ways with the seeker.

I don't think one can be trained to become this kind of psychotherapist-cum-guru-cum-teacher. It is rather a case of allowing oneself, first, to be trained into one ideology and praxis, then to allow growing experience to shatter or challenge it in a dialectical moment of antithesis—and then to transcend the contradictions in a synthesis that becomes possible through a new commitment to more comprehensive goals. This is what Yoga and Zen are about—they are ways of shattering training, of bringing a person back to center, before commitments, so that he can draw upon more of his possibilities in new commitments. Dialogue is a Yoga of interpersonal relationships.

I think that it is time now for a therapist to tell those who consult with him whether he is a commissar, a trainer to the status quo, or a responsible liberator from congealed experience and the rigid, sickening behavior it mediates. Perhaps there will be joint practices, where Dr. John specializes in helping socially inept, neurotic, and psychotic people (if we still use such dehumanizing jargon) manage acceptable social behavior. He will help the Incomplete Square to become boxed in or bagged. Then Dr. Bill may take over, to liberate and awaken the seeker to more of his possibilities beyond those he has attained. . . .